D0371423

ENDORSEMENTS

"Timeless tips on business success. A must-read for entrepreneurial-minded executives."

—Howard Behar, President, Starbucks (former)

"This book is thought-provoking and insightful; full of engaging stories and real-world examples. It contains intuitive practical value and should be mandatory reading for entrepreneurs and mid-level managers desiring to innovate, not to mention anyone looking to improve their personal lives."

—Doug Lindal, President, Lindal Cedar Homes (former)

"One of my former bosses used to say, 'Good ideas are a dime a dozen. But give me the person who can take a good idea and make it a reality and we can change the world.' Almost everyone has good ideas that they never act upon. Kim Lorenz's book, *Tireless*, will help you become one of those people who change the world—because Kim is one of those people."

—Rich Stearns, President, World Vision US

"During my life I have met a lot of people who were very talented and also very smart who did not take advantage of the talents God had given them. I have also met a lot of ordinary people who showed up every day and let God use them in extra ordinary ways. My friend, Kim, was blessed with lots of talent but also was tireless in his effort to make himself and those around him better every day. That combination is very rare. He was and continues to be an inspiration for me. His life stories are an example of God's faithfulness and a man who never gave up even during some very difficult times."

—Edward Vander, Pol. Chairman, Oak Harbor Freight Lines

"Great book for anyone in management of a business or thinking of starting a business. The real life stories illustrate ways to manage the obstacles you are sure to encounter. A great guide for business and life."

—George Bagley, President and CEO, Alaska Airlines (former)

"*Tireless* embodies two very important truths in business; 'good enough is never good enough' and 'luck is when preparation meets opportunity.' *Tireless* is a testimony to those who strive to seek opportunity."

—James Flaherty, Chairman of the Board, Deloitte LLP (former)

"I have good news and bad news about this inspiring and compelling book. The bad news is that early in the book, you will want to quit your job and start a business like Kim Lorenz did. The good news is that by the time you finish, you'll have found much of the wisdom you'll need to give it a try. What a pleasure to read!"

—Joseph Castleberry, Ed.D., President, Northwest University

"Anyone can succeed if they try hard enough; easier said than done. *Tireless* gives some very practical and common-sense advice about how to drive towards your goals with vision, focus and unwavering commitment. A good read for anyone that has goals in life."

—Tom Captain, Vice Chairman, Deloitte LLP (former)

TIRELESS

KEY PRINCIPLES THAT DRIVE SUCCESS BEYOND BUSINESS SCHOOL

KIM LORENZ

Made for Success
PUBLISHING

Made for Success Publishing
P.O. Box 1775 Issaquah, WA 98027
www.MadeForSuccessPublishing.com

Distributed by Made for Success Publishing

First Printing

Library of Congress Cataloging-in-Publication data
Lorenz, Kim
TIRELESS: Key Principles that Drive Success Beyond Business School

p. cm.

ISBN: 978-1-64146-341-6 (HDBK)
ISBN: 978-1-64146-431-4 (eBOOK)
ISBN: 978-1-64146-458-1 (AUDIO)
LCCN: 2019939284

Printed in the United States of America

For further information contact Made for Success Publishing
+14255266480 or email service@madeforsuccess.net

CONTENTS

PREFACE

FROM A YOUNG age, most of us can remember several individuals who played a role in how we eventually live our lives. In my case, as with millions of others, there were many people at different stages of growth that shaped what turned out to be a very successful career.

Growing up, a neighbor of my parents was an executive I admired. He spent time with me even after I started my professional career, and shared so many examples and experiences with me. During my school years, several teachers stood out who pulled me aside, giving words of wisdom and encouragement. One of them, James Shuman, visited me at my corporate offices 20 years after we launched that company. As a result of his continued encouragement, I went on to complete my MBA.

The person who first hired me for what turned out to be my career path also saw something I was not aware of—a quality I wasn't aware yet that I had—but at a young age, how could we have known? Just starting our 'blunder' stage of life. Thousands of people help others every day, invest time in us as we grow, they are integral to who we become. Hopefully, you also pay this forward as you grow and mature in any vocation.

I found as I grew, I spent enormous energy helping others learn, opening their eyes, gaining knowledge to better themselves. Aside from running the corporations we founded and successfully operated, I have lectured at universities in how to better find opportunity. The most gratifying moments in my life is helping people help themselves. It is never a handout, but a hand-up as those who improve their lives are far better off when they invest in themselves; as they realize that there is opportunity they themselves can benefit from.

For over 35 years a file has been kept with stories, quotes and lessons. The goal of this book is to broaden the reach of these resources and help you improve your work-life and speed-up your success.

INTRODUCTION

OPPORTUNITIES ARE IN FRONT OF YOU EVERY DAY

EVERY DAY, ALL over the world, people like you and I see opportunities and start their own businesses. They come from all walks of life, and they live in all types of places. Today, there are more opportunities to own your own business than any other time in history. Advancing technology adds even more opportunity, and businesses can be started with low capital, even from the comfort of your own home.

The world's largest retailer, Amazon, was started in a garage. You can start your own business in your spare time, or work at it part-time while you are still at another job. The market and ideas you have can be tested before you invest too much money or time.

Millions of people around the world have taken the plunge, so why not you? Is it easy? Absolutely not! Is there risk involved? You better believe it. Will every business launched succeed? No. Most new business ventures fail. But is it worth it?

Without a shadow of a doubt.

As you read on, keep in mind that there are millions of very successful people, just like you and I, who did not start their own businesses and were very successful working for someone else. They saw opportunities to enhance their careers right where they were. Consider where you are working now. Many opportunities are being missed that can lead to greater success where you work now. By reading this book, you will, hopefully, start to see and act upon previously unseen opportunities that are all around you. It does not matter if the opportunities are where you work now, or if you start a business around your ideas. This book will share many examples of what people recognized as an opportunity, and why (and how) they acted on it.

Most new businesses that fail do so in the first few years, for many reasons. Why a business either succeeds or fails is often a result of a person's individual vision, skills, self-discipline, motivation, knowledge, and tireless efforts. Success is not easy. It makes no difference if you own the business or are working for someone else; you alone can make the choice to succeed and make it happen.

All throughout this book, you will read stories of success. There are some told of very famous people, and other stories of people you have probably never heard of. However, all the examples have a common thread: people just like you and I visualized an opportunity and then acted on it.

Success is not dependent upon your level of education. I had started our first corporation at the age of 26, and was a multi-millionaire well before age 30. I went back to school and completed my Master's of Business Administration at the University of Washington's Foster School of Business many years after starting more than one business from scratch. I did learn I would have been more successful had I obtained the MBA prior to starting the businesses, but fortunately, the businesses were still a success. I was also very pleased to learn we had been doing many things exceedingly well.

So, why do I share this? Well, thousands of successful companies have been founded by people without a college education, advanced degrees, or a large amount of money. Our success, in large measure, and that of thousands of others, was in our ability to visualize what a customer really needed and training our employees to do the same. We developed the habits to see opportunity when it presented itself, while others missed it. Opportunity can come in thousands of different ways, but if you are not looking for it, it will be missed. Opportunity can be disguised as an obstacle, but when you face it head-on, in most cases, you will discover new paths to success. But, again, this is only true if you are looking for it.

Our minds are such powerful tools. There are millions of things we might be looking at, but not really seeing what they are or what they could be. What is important is asking *why* what you see is the way it is.

Highly-educated executives in Fortune 500 firms (or any business for that matter) such as Boeing, United Parcel Service, and PACCAR missed or failed to recognize what could be because they were focused on what they thought they knew. Because I asked *why*, I was able to create tremendous new opportunities for success in business. You will read these win-win stories and learn how you can apply this strategy to your own life.

Many times, totally by chance, you will see opportunity and simply fail to follow up. Then the opportunity is wasted. Once you start to see any situation differently, with eyes open to change, you can make a significant difference in your life and the lives of others. If you fail, you can use that failure to power yourself ahead. Use failure as a lesson to build on. I failed many times in the companies I worked for or owned, but in the end, I founded and successfully ran large corporations that were eventually sold to Fortune 500 firms.

We are all familiar with companies like Microsoft, Starbucks, and Amazon. While these are now giant companies that are known all over the world, creating some of the world's wealthiest individuals (as well as millions of wealthy stockholders), they each share similar traits. The founders were able to visualize an opportunity—to see and understand something that could be—when others did not see it at all. While there are many books about the famous, wealthy people who started these companies, remember, there have been millions of other companies started that succeeded for their founders, families, and workers. Some share very similar paths to success of the well-known companies, but many took non-traditional paths to get to the place they are today.

My first business was started with borrowed money in a legacy industry crowded with similar companies. Yet, we succeeded in our markets far beyond any of the competition, including many international firms. One of the companies we started and sold now has thousands of employees. While there were many barriers to starting the businesses, we overcame them. There were obstacles to success that became valuable lessons to learn. When we all learn from mistakes, we become better decision-makers.

As I mentioned previously, a common thread that holds Microsoft, Starbucks, and Amazon together is that the opportunities envisioned by their founders were right in front of them. However, those opportunities were also right in front of millions of other people. Why did these founders see something others did not see? What was it that they saw? And why didn't anyone else jump on those opportunities first? What did these individuals do that set them apart at the time they started and beyond? We can learn so much from their examples.

We can teach ourselves to look past the obvious and open our eyes to see opportunity, examples of which are seen throughout this book. You can train yourself to visualize, learn, and gain a better understanding of what can be ignored and what should be pursued. Always ask yourself *why* things are as they are.

Is there a better way?

What does the customer really need in the future?

Can we do better?

Can we find a more efficient way to do what we do?

My favorite question when I hear, "We always do it that way," is "When did we start *always* doing it that way?" The more you can understand the stories behind many great businesses and their founders, the more you can build the confidence to either start your own business or have greater success in the place you work. I hope that my own success stories add to your knowledge and open your mind to better ways of achieving success.

A close business associate once remarked after a very successful new product launch, "The difference between this success and nothing changing is that the person behind it took the thoughts from the shower, acted on them, and did something great to make them happen." In other words, the difference is in taking the initiative to take a thought a few steps beyond a dream, to investigating what could be and visualizing positive outcomes.

The founders of Microsoft, Starbucks, and Amazon not only saw opportunities, but they took immediate action and made something happen. Microsoft founders Bill Gates and Paul Allen saw an enormous opportunity that opened up with the advent of computerization. Amazon founder Jeff Bezos saw an opportunity to change the way that people buy books (and now *everything*). This was also made possible by advancements in technology. Starbucks founder Howard Schultz, on the other hand, saw the opportunity to avail millions to a café environment with the focus on meeting, sitting, reading, and having a pastry as opposed to just selling a cup of coffee in a restaurant.

Howard Schultz recognized a need for a customer space that was so much more than just a place to get a cup of coffee. He envisioned a place to gather, offer up consistent, quality beverages; a place with a customer-focused culture and experience. I look back at the first trip to Paris my wife and I took, and distinctly remember the desire to visit a café to enjoy an espresso while sitting at a small table on the street. This was well before Starbucks started, but I never gave any thought as to why this same environment could not be replicated in the U.S. (and around the world) in a consistent and more unique way as Howard Schultz, Howard Behar, and Orin Smith (termed the H2O team) did.

The three Starbucks founders created a small coffee shop that went global in a very short time. This team started a few years after some serious coffee aficionados started the first few stores by roasting and selling seriously good coffee. But the H2O team visualized a much bigger opportunity, invested in the company, and the rest of the story is history. As Howard Behar was quoted saying, "I saw it was all about the people. We're not in the coffee business serving people. We're in the people business serving coffee. I knew that intrinsically; that was my personality. Those were my values. That has been constant from the beginning."

While the three companies briefly discussed here are now household names, millions of other businesses small and large share many of the same traits and stories, as well as similar cultures and work habits contributing to their success. When they were just starting out, did any of them know the enormity of the success they would eventually see? Probably not. They could dream, and as their businesses developed, they made thousands of changes, feeding the successful directions and cutting off the ones that were failing. They simply took that leap of faith at first, and the rest is, as they say, history.

The founders of these companies were not all wealthy, highly educated, or from privileged families. They all came from vastly different backgrounds. Bill Gates' family was wealthy, as his father was a successful attorney. His mother, Mary, was a very successful businesswoman who also served for

18 years on the University of Washington's board of regents. She was the first female president of King County's United Way, the first woman to chair the national United Way's executive committee where she served with IBM's CEO, John Opel, and the first woman on the First Interstate Bank of Washington's board of directors.

Bill Gates' founding partner, Paul Allen, grew up in a very modest family. His father worked many years as a librarian in Seattle. They both shared a vision of what could be possible with a computer operating system accessible to anyone. At that time, the giant computer company was IBM, called "Big Blue." It was an enormously successful company with a highly-educated, exceptional global leadership staff. Yet that IBM staff had focused on large, mainframe computers for business and failed to understand; failed to "see" the potential future market for a personal computer.

The rest of Microsoft's story is now history as well. Bill Gates and Paul Allen became two of the world's wealthiest individuals. Some might also know that the connection between Bill Gates' mother and IBM CEO John Opel opened some doors. What's important to note is that few people, when that door is open, take that first step or see what might be inside and act on it. When you learn to recognize the opportunity in front of you, and have the courage to act on it, you will be more successful overall.

Howard Schultz grew Starbucks to global fame but he grew up in a low-cost housing development, creating within him a desire to make a better life for himself. In an interview, he remarked, "I wanted to climb over that fence and achieve something beyond what people were saying was possible." Howard invested in that very small coffee shop in Seattle named Starbucks. Howard Schultz saw the potential. People were buying coffee from various restaurants and coffee shops already. What did he see? There are many, very smart people in the world—why did Howard Schultz see this opportunity that others missed? Even more interesting is how Howard Schultz and his team found the right people to invest in growing a chain of coffee shops. That story alone would fill another book. In the early 1980s, it was inconceivable that anyone would go to an investment banker suggesting an investment in a coffee shop business—inconceivable to anyone except Howard Schultz, that is. Those who shared Howard's vision did invest, and all did very well indeed.

Jeff Bezos, Amazon's CEO and founder, is a very bright, diverse, highly-educated individual who visualized a better way for people to buy books, displacing the centuries-old way people purchased and read books. If this sounds overly simple, that's because it is. There were already several large, successful brick and mortar stores selling millions of books. But the vision Jeff Bezos "saw" led to the creation of the world's largest retailer. Again, more than a book could be (and likely will be) written about this company and its founder.

Today, the same opportunities are in front of us all. There are thousands of new businesses that are waiting for someone like you to start. Keep in mind, there are also millions of new opportunities to succeed in existing businesses where you might work, and you can also lead that charge.

There is information that will be key to your success and future spread throughout this book. Some of it will make you laugh, it's so simple. Other times, it might make you realize your own potential for the first time. Some stories will go over your head. Think about and read that part again! There are stories of a couple of ordinary individuals who took the leap, started their little businesses, and succeeded against some almost insurmountable odds that would have caused others to fail. Thousands have succeeded where others have not. Some of the failures were simply because people just didn't recognize the opportunities that were right in front of them. Every day, everywhere we look, there are opportunities. Seeing them takes an open mind; a realization that these opportunities are there and truly seeing them for what they are, then making the choices that lead to making each opportunity a reality.

Are you ready to start seeing them?

CHAPTER 1

WHY NOT YOU?

WE OFTEN HEAR stories about successful businesses, as well as stories about the successful individuals who earned great fame through these businesses. So often, these people simply saw an opportunity and created a product or a business around that vision. What did these business founders or owners and inventors see that no one else did? What did they do with their vision that others failed to do? How can you do the same thing today?

These individuals saw a need they could fill. They saw an opportunity to start something new, and they figured out the steps to get there and went on to see huge success. However, the question remains: why didn't anyone else do it first? I believe it is because these individuals were *looking* for greater success. If you are not looking for something, you will probably never find it—even if it is right in front of you. Others may have seen the same opportunity differently, but failed to take the next step. Their failure to act contributed to the success of those who did take action, even if it was in a different way.

In the early days of computing, many very smart people were developing code, operating systems, and computer functions. They were focused only on what was in front of them, often not seeing the larger picture. They didn't see those opportunities that people like Bill Gates saw, or even consider moving in different directions.

So, why don't more people act? There are many possible reasons. For starters, there is fear of failure, lack of vision, not understanding or seeing the need, and/or not having enough funds. Some lack the self-discipline to keep moving forward, to keep learning and striving to be better. If you enjoy your work and where you are in life, you are in an enviable position. If you have a desire to do something bigger, make a difference, and be more successful, you have a choice to make. It is up to you whether you want to take action or be content where you are. How you look at everything can make a significant difference in the remainder of your life.

If there is so much opportunity out there, why then do 95% of young companies fail in the first five years? There are many factors, including lack of initiative, poor self-discipline, poor cash flow management, having a wrong vision, and poor execution. However, when asking a person why their business failed, the answers given often do not match the true root cause of the failure. Not many who fail will tell you they failed because they lacked self-discipline, right. What they might tell you or what they might believe is the true cause could very well be clouded by pride.

The same can be said when asking a successful business owner why they succeeded. Often, we find that the core reason for success is individual effort and self-discipline, combined with an enormous will to succeed. This effort may be referred to as inspiration and perspiration, something many people lack in addition to a lack of vision. Yes, I said *perspiration*: the hard work it often takes to succeed. Too many fear perspiration, or, ironically, "work hard" to avoid it.

There are several other traits we see in successful people. These include dedication, perseverance, continued learning, and listening to others. Building a culture of success within an organization is another key ingredient. And remember, age, race, and gender have nothing to do with any of the above. When applied, the aforementioned traits provide the same outcome for all—success.

If you might be tempted to think that age is a limiting factor, let's take a look at the Kentucky Fried Chicken founder, Colonel Sanders. He had already retired from several different jobs when he stumbled upon an idea. Wikipedia reads, "Sanders held a number of jobs in his early life, such as steam engine stoker, insurance salesman and filling station operator. He began selling fried chicken from his roadside restaurant in North Corbin, Kentucky, during the Great Depression. During that time Sanders developed his 'secret recipe' and his patented method of cooking chicken in a pressure fryer. Sanders recognized the potential of the restaurant franchising concept, and the first KFC franchise opened in South Salt Lake, Utah in 1952. When his original restaurant closed, he devoted himself full-time to franchising his fried chicken throughout the country."[1]

---

1 "Colonel Sanders." *Wikipedia, The Free Encyclopedia.*

This story only tells the reader a small portion of what this remarkable person did! He saw an opportunity, developed a vision of what could be, and decided to go for it. The idea was simple: a way to make chicken in a pressurized pot with a blend of secret spices. His first restaurant franchise opened when he was 62 years old, and grew to over 18,000 restaurants. This just goes to show you that anybody, at any age, with any level of education and financial means or experience, can start a successful business.

Businesses come in all shapes and sizes, each meeting a specific need for specific people. Retail stores such as Costco and Target are satisfying the needs of the public. Others, like accountants, small manufacturing entities or consultants serve the needs of other businesses. Often, those needs were not even known to the businesses buying the product or service until that business launched. I compare this to walking into a Costco and finding dozens of items you didn't even know you needed!

Now that I mention it, Costco is another perfect example of a wildly-successful global company that started with an idea and a single store. These days, you can find a Costco in almost every corner of the world. There were hundreds of other entrepreneurs attempting to open large, bulk wholesale stores that were not nearly as successful as Costco. What was that magic formula? What did the Costco founders see that others did not? Much like our other stories, the founders were two ordinary people like you and I. Jeff Brotman and Jim Sinegal founded Costco. Brotman's family operated a small business, as his grandparents migrated to the U.S. from Romania (via Canada). Sinegal was born to a working-class family. Both men had worked in various retail-focused companies and shared a vision of a better way to fill the needs of consumers. One key ingredient in their success, among many, was quality. Regular customers know Costco sells only quality products and backs them all with an ironclad return policy.

All of these individuals share the same starting point. They visualized an opportunity so powerful that they just had to do it. They jumped ship from solid, safe jobs to take the risk and start their own companies. These individuals took the vision and opportunity they imagined and did something to make it happen. Again, they practiced perseverance, took the risk, left their careers behind, and made the leap. Every story is different; every person comes from a different background and environment, yet they each carry the same basic success principles. These stories are of ordinary people taking extraordinary risks. Just think, there are thousands more stories to be written about people just like you and the future companies simply waiting to be founded.

The next story could be *yours*.

I do not know where you are in life right now. You might still be in school, investing in yourself in hopes of landing a career that could provide for you or your family. You might be sitting at a desk, serving someone else's vision and feeling dissatisfied every time you leave for the day. You might be doing exactly what you always said you wanted to, yet you are realizing that you actually have bigger and brighter dreams. Wherever you find yourself, you have the same chance to take a risk as Bill Gates and thousands of others.

So, how do you know it's time to take a leap? The exact reason that people leave a job to start a business varies in every case, but it happens every day. I started my first business when realizing the 65-year-old company I had devoted my early work life towards might fail. I did see an opportunity of what the customer really needed from that company, and was developing a great career around such. So, when the company started to fail, instead of doing my work for another company, I started my own.

When you hear the stories years later from people who left a job or career and started a business that succeeded, rarely do you hear regret, even if they've failed. They take pride in what they've founded, seeing that they have met needs in a unique way, enabled others to succeed, and built a platform. While new businesses often fail, that is rarely the end of the story. Many successful people pick themselves back up, learn from failure, and start over again—this time, with more experience.

Successful companies all began in different ways. Some began with one employee—the founder. Others started with a few employees; others with many. Some started in homes or garages, like Jeff Bezos and Amazon. Regardless of size, their success, for the most part, is a result of the same characteristics, which we will explore as we continue through this book.

Bill Gates and Paul Allen both worked at starting their business while in school and while working other jobs for income before it all came together. They never gave up. They shared a vision of what could be and artfully made it happen through a series of events.

Those who have incredibly successful businesses are always asked the same questions, "How did you do it?" and "What did you do that made it work?"

I will address these questions by sharing stories from several business entities and different industries, as well as my own life as a business founder/owner and the lives of those around me that have modeled success in different ways. People tried to convince me not to start my own business—that it would put my family in jeopardy and that we could lose the new home we had built, as well as the new car my wife drove. But I did it, and against all odds, I did it successfully.

Starting a business is not for everyone, but it could be for you. The same opportunity is in front of every single one of us, and it is up for grabs every day. Will you be the one to take it? Or will you take advantage of opportunities right where you are now? I cannot emphasize enough that opportunities also exist in the company where you work. Open your mind and again, ask what could be, what can be done better.

Why not you? Why not now? What can you do starting today to make tomorrow better, both for yourself and for others? So often we hear excuses about why something can't be done, while at the same time, others are not only getting it done, but exceeding expectations. I beg you, do not think about the reasons not to do it. Simply ask yourself, who do you want to be, and when do you plan to start? Only you can answer these questions.

The best time to start is now.

CHAPTER 2

WHEN OPPORTUNITY KNOCKS

I COULD SPEND the entirety of this book relating the stories of famous people like Jeff Bezos with huge companies and the lessons we can learn from them. I wanted to share a different kind of story—one that you won't find in a magazine or read about online. This one is more representative of the millions of small businesses started across the world. This is the type of story that should be shared at every business school; a real-world story illustrating the risks, pitfalls, and success generated by acting on opportunity.

This story is mine.

This is a story about two normal people who were working great jobs in different, large companies near Seattle. We left our comfortable, successful careers to do what many simply think about, yet never actually act upon. These are two people who took a risk to start their own business with no guarantee for the future. These two risked everything, knowing they might fail and lose their homes, cars—everything. But they believed in what they could do and were willing to take the steps to do it. All the funding to start the business was borrowed from a bank at rates of 15% and up. This is a story about a simple, small company growing over $50 million in revenue, as well as commanding a 61% market share in a crowded, established market, then selling the company to a Fortune 500 firm. Today, that company employs thousands of people, has grown substantially, and is still growing.

My partner and I both shared a common vision of what could be done to better serve businesses and saw an opportunity others were not seeing. We felt we could profit from it. The story is far more than just a success story. It touches many points not covered in business school, including partnership relations, dealing with the challenges of meeting our families' needs while starting and growing a business, and significantly reducing our wages by 75% to start. Then there were the banking relationship issues, intense struggles with a federal lawsuit, and other trying circumstances one might not anticipate when starting from nothing. There was also stiff competition already in place in the form of large, international firms. Anyone could have started this company, really. However, it just so happened to be the two of us starting a low-barrier-to-entry, almost commodity-type of business. We knew our business from working for others. Now, we had to prove we could do it better ourselves.

The marketplace we targeted consisted of trucking companies, construction companies, logging companies, core legacy-type industrial industries that operated trucks, large earthmoving equipment, industrial equipment and such—all running on the same thing: *tires*. The company today is owned and operated by a Fortune 500 firm and boasts the title of largest commercial tire operation in both Alaska and the Northwestern United States.

So, how did we start from nothing, against almost insurmountable odds of new business failures, and in such a competitive environment while leveraging the whole by financing at high-interest rates and exceed beyond our dreams? How did we gain 61% of the market share ahead of the remaining 15 companies, with the largest of them at less than a 20% share? How was this done, and can it be done again? I believe the answer is yes. With the same vision and tireless effort, this level of achievement is possible.

The threat of failure didn't stop us from seeing this idea come to fruition. We saw something that our current employers could not change or adapt to and address. We did the only logical thing we could think of at the time: we acted on the opportunity we saw and believed it would lead to greater success.

I still laugh when I am asked how I ended up in the tire business. It was certainly nowhere on my radar when in school. In fact, I really thought the whole industry was low level, and of no interest to me. Tires were just something consumers had to have, a simple commodity. I worked my way through college at a service station, the same place I had worked throughout high school. My parents always taught us kids to work, make our own spending money, and pay for our own cars. I was also paying for my own education.

One of the regular service station customers managed a large tire store for a regional, long-standing company in town. I remember getting a phone call from him one day as clear as if it were yesterday. His name was Bill, and he asked if I would consider talking to him about working for the tire company. I had been interviewing with some Fortune 500 firms, and, as many in college do, I was always thinking about where I could end up in a career. Like Howard Schultz, I was always attuned to how I could make my first million—what I considered to be successful. I'm almost embarrassed to say my initial response was not very professional!

"Bill, you must be kidding me, who in the hell would want to work in a tire company?" I blurted out.

Bill said, "Kim, you should look into all opportunities. The company is very large and has a commercial department. That department has professional salespeople who drive company cars…"

I really do not remember anything he said after the "company car" comment. I think I was about 20 years old, and the thought of a company car was an extraordinary perk for a person my age, now living in an apartment, going to school, and working nights to support myself. I wound up doing an interview with them despite my initial negative language. I was hired on by Bill. However, I had to start at the bottom and work my way up. There was no company car just yet. There was the potential to get one within the next couple of years, but I would have to earn the position.

After just a few days, I was impressed by the opportunity at hand that I did not previously know existed. Who knew the depth of the commercial tire industry? More importantly, who knew that there was an industry that was virtually inflation-proof? Trucks are running every day, in every economy. The trucking industry has a saying, "If you got it, a truck brought it." Now *that* is an industry that could last a long time. The company also operated truck tire retread manufacturing plants.[2]

It is not this industry the book is written about, but rather the visualization of opportunity and how we realized huge success. There are several other lessons within these pages, examples of how others turned an opportunity they saw into gold. It happens every day. Knowledge is power, and the more you study and understand how to look for the opportunities in front of you, the odds of seeing them improves.

After about 18 months at that job, I got a company car. I was still going to school in the evenings. As it turned out, I was excelling in the business, and I was promoted to management. Ironically, after I started our business five years later, Bill, who had hired me, ended up managing one of the locations we operated. I guess that's just proof that you often "meet the same people on the way up that you meet on the way down!" The business specialized in commercial applications, not retail—a vast market requiring greater knowledge of the customers and their businesses.

I was scared to death when I got that first company car and was given a territory in the industrial areas of Seattle. As I would drive through Pioneer Square and see the homeless people on benches, I was so afraid I would end up like that. I had to call on big companies like Boeing and UPS, as well as garbage companies. Garbage trucks are a tire salesperson's

---

2 By the way, failed retreaded tires are not the cause of the rubber pieces we all see on freeways, but something about that later.

dream. They grind off tires! I also called on dump truck opera-tors, construction companies, and huge shipping companies around the waterfront. I was just this 22-year-old kid, engaged to be married, still doing night school, and here I was in this big world of industry.

It is what I learned along the way that made more sense after we succeeded in our own business. Time has a way of teaching us if we pay attention. At that time in my life, it was not so clear. What was I seeing, and what was I doing that was so different than others? What did the others fail to see?

I resigned after five years, and that is when my partner and I started our first company. There were some obvious obstacles we encountered while looking to start that first business, one of which was our partnership. We both quickly realized the truth that while most new businesses failed, the rate of partnerships failing was even higher. We had only worked collaboratively between our two previous employers, but we really did not know each other well at all. Our respective families and spouses had never even met the other! All we knew for sure is that we shared a common vision, saw an opportunity, and trusted each other in a working relationship. We both felt comfortable with the way the other conducted business and had similar ethical standards, always following through on what we said we would do. We agreed to each own 50% of the stock issued. I was very fortunate to have a great partner as a shareholder. We are still partners today in several ventures, even after 40 years.

Together, we had completed several large, successful col-laborations for both our respective companies in the years leading up to us starting our own company. John had run the manufacturing operations as company president. He had many skills I did not have. He had also started from the bottom and worked his way to the top in a relatively short time. My background was in marketing, operations, and sales. I was promoted several times up through management positions, becoming a young Vice President by the time we both left our jobs. While I appreciated the promotions, one thing nagged at me. It was simply not clear to me why I had been promoted ahead of so many others who had held similar positions for 20, 35, or even 40 years at the company. Why me? It became very clear as time went on.

As we grew, it was apparent the opportunity we saw proved to be the correct path. Perhaps our greatest partnership asset as we started the new business is that we had such diverse corporate experiences in the same industry. One might also say that our young ages would indicate we did not know yet that failure was a real possibility. I was 26 when we started the new venture, and John was 29. Ignorance was bliss.

Another reason we started our own venture was fear the company we both worked for might fail. The owner had turned the company over to a son after 65 years. The father held the large capital assets, while the son only had the operating company. As can often be the case when family takes over a business, the son did not share the same passion, business acumen, or decision-making abilities as his father, who had worked hard to build the large group of companies. A few years after the son took control, we saw signs of financial concerns that could affect the future of all the family companies, including the ones John and I ran. I was getting more and more concerned, pouring my time and effort—my life, really—into this business, realizing a little at a time that the son might be running it into the ground with poor decisions and management. The companies we both left to start our business did fail just a few years after we resigned. Hundreds were out of work, and a 65-year-old company was history.

Prior to that company failure, John called me out of the blue saying we needed to get together to talk. John told me he had given notice and resigned. We discussed starting our own enterprise, and that short meeting led to an all-night session developing pro-forma income statements and balance sheets. By 4:30 AM, we shook hands and agreed that, "Unless we ran into an insurmountable brick wall," we would start this new company. There was simply no other company in our market I felt could do what our vision was telling us we could do.

At the time, I thought I was already near the top of Maslow's hierarchy pyramid. I was at the top level of management. I had a company car, recent salary increases, a new home we had just built, and kids in a private school. My life was about to take a huge change!

John felt assured that he could run an efficient retread plant operation, building it from scratch. He had planned to buy used equipment as cheaply as he could, possibly at an auction, and have it shipped to Seattle. I, on the other hand, felt strongly that there was still a market for a commercial tire company working with the customers and educating them on how to reduce their operating costs and significantly reduce expenses.

It's important to note that this had nothing to do with selling tires cheaper than the competition. That was already being done. There were several areas we had learned that would save customers a lot more money than simply buying cheaper, but the customers did not understand that yet. Again, this was thinking outside the box, doing something others did not understand. This involved really learning the customer's business, not just our business. The examples later in the book are there so you can think through what we did. There are also examples of what many others did and are doing that might apply to your own business, or any business. We showed Fortune 500 firms how to operate their own businesses better with our knowledge, as well as helping them see what industry trends could benefit them. *That* is the story worth reading. Who cares that two people started a little company that grew very big? What matters is looking at what your company does and asking yourself how it could be done better.

Our vision was not complicated. It seemed like everyone else in the marketplace was simply selling tires and services. There was no one educating the customers on their options and what could happen if they changed the way they did their business. It was a vision that could change the paradigm of the companies we targeted and lead our business to success.

One such area was outsourcing—showing the customer that with changes, they could reduce labor costs and the associated expenses and liability. In the past, the customers were hiring their own staff for the tire programs. We could show them why they did not need to do that. We could be an outsource entity that could significantly reduce their operating costs, and we could prove it. Companies could experience huge savings by looking at operations in a different way. Our new venture would be a company that specialized in outsourcing and educating the customer.

Of course, selling new tires and retreaded tires went along with this, but no other company was in this space doing what we believed the customer really wanted but did not know how to do. Anybody could sell a tire or lower a price, but that was not what the customer really needed. All companies strive to find ways to do business more efficiently. Any business running trucks needed to buy tires, and if somebody could show them a better way to do that, it would result in a win-win situation. To fulfill this vision, we were hiring staff with no experience in our industry and training them how to do it our way. We wanted people with no baggage or bad habits.

The opportunity was right in front of thousands in the industry, but nobody, especially the global companies, could visualize it. Those big companies just wanted to sell more tires, but the customer could realize huge cost savings by changing the way they operated and used tires. Why would a customer hold $100,000 of inventory when we already had a warehouse? This will all make more sense as you read further.

Our largest success story was with Boeing. They operated several thousand trucks and equipment over several cities that all ran on tires. They spent about $500,000 a year buying tires. We saved Boeing over $600,000 in direct costs by changing *how* they bought the tires, managed the tire program, and warehoused the tires. Really, they still spent $500,000 on tires after changing to our company as a supplier, but they also saved $600,000 a year in cash as we assumed the management of the tire assets, warehousing, and maintenance. We won a huge award for this, covered a little later in this book. Trust me, it was not rocket science, and anyone could/should have been able to do this. However, nobody did until we came along with our vision and new company.

After that all-night planning session that led to the founding of our first company, John agreed to research the availability of the plant equipment to fit within our budget, while I would discuss our ideas and plan with the major tire companies we would want to use. We both agreed that the likelihood Michelin would even consider us was low, but we had to shoot for the moon anyway. Even if the chances were small, we both knew that in order to fit this new model, we had to become a Michelin tire dealer. The Michelin products fit our model of business. The Michelin truck tires lasted longer and could be retreaded more successfully than any other tires, and we made more money (and the customer saved more money) using retreads.

From the time the Michelin brothers started the Michelin Tire Company in the late 1800s, almost every advancement in tires, even today, has been first introduced by Michelin. The company saw an opportunity to make a simple bicycle tire that was filled with air in 1889. Up until then, all tires were solid rubber. Ouch. Michelin was (and still is) a global, innovative, industry-leading company. Every car, truck, or vehicle that has tires is benefiting from something invented first by Michelin. Michelin invented the pneumatic tire (tires with air inside), the tubeless tire (and wheel), the radial tire, and so many more products we all use today. But more of that story and the parallel reasons for our success later. Michelin had vision, and for over 130 years, they focused on what the industry needed and invented it. They had a similar focus to our own.

After John and I settled on our marching orders, off we went on our separate ways, planning to stay in touch with any and all updates until we found the manufacturing plant. After we secured the building, I would need to resign from my job.

Just like that, we had decided to start a new business together, leaving the security of our old jobs behind. Would we succeed? Could we make it into the five percent of new businesses that make it longer than five years without failing? We didn't know for sure, but what we did know is that even the best plans have no guarantee of future success. You will never know unless you try, and our company started from nothing just a few months after that meeting.

CHAPTER 3

TAKING THE LEAP

A FEW WEEKS after our all-night session about starting this new business, I found myself in Sitka, Alaska, sitting at the Shee Atika Lodge. I was still working for the tire company who hired me out of college. This Sitka trip was to meet with and present a proposal to Alaska Lumber and Pulp, a very large pulp mill. I had called this company for years, but had not yet done any business with them. They had hundreds of "rolling stock," meaning equipment using large industrial tires. I traveled with Bill VanSomeron, the West Coast Manager for Michelin, along with our Michelin sales representative, Norm Toomey. Both were great people to work with, and fun to be around. We had all been collaborating on a proposal for this pulp mill.

That day, during the meetings, we succeeded in getting all the business. Later that evening, we were celebrating in the bar. The bartender came to the table, asking if there was a Mr. Lorenz there who could take a call at the bar.[3] It took a moment to realize that the Mr. Lorenz she was referring to was me! At the ripe, young age of 26, the only man I'd heard called Mr. Lorenz was my father. Curious, I picked up the phone at the bar, wondering who might be on the other end and hoping my wife and the kids were all okay at home.

"I found a retread plant that will work for us! I just booked a flight to Kansas City to look at the equipment. It leaves tonight at midnight; red eye." John's familiar voice rang out on the other side of the phone. It turns out there was a complete retread manufacturing plant in a bankruptcy sale, and it was well below what we had budgeted. It seemed like the perfect scenario.

"If we buy it, you will need to resign from your job next week. Are we still good on our plans to start the company, Kim?"

Pausing for half a second to get a grip on the fact that this was becoming a reality, I made my reply. "John, we shook hands on a deal—at 4:30 AM, nonetheless. I am committed. Let me know as soon as you find out how this goes with the equipment acquisition."

Needless to say, a lot was going through my mind as I made my way back to the table where the Michelin guys were seated. I had a new company car, a new beautiful office in Seattle, and I had just landed another promotion. Making the choice to walk away from all of that without knowing how the future might unfold would be a very bold move, to say the least. My wife and I had just barely moved into a new home, not

---

3 Note: This was prior to the use of cell phones.

to mention having two children who were only two and four years old. Reality started setting in, and my thoughts raced a million miles an hour as I prepared to break the news to the table. All the initial and very primitive plans we had discussed about starting this new business involved having a Michelin dealership agreement in place. At that time, only the large, well-established companies had dealership agreements with Michelin. Having the Michelin dealership was something I felt had to be in place for John and me to succeed.

I sat down, took a drink from my glass, and looked Bill and Norm straight in the eyes.

"Gentlemen, I am planning on leaving the company and starting my own tire company." I took a deep breath, expecting the worst. After all, what company like Michelin would want to take on some small fledgling new company with no credit, no assets, and no customers? Their reaction nearly made me fall out of my chair. Bill, the head of all the West Coast, slammed his fist on the table and shouted, "Damn, Kim, this is the best news I have heard all year! It's about time you realized it was time to leave this company and start your own tire business!"

Not skipping a beat, I launched into my next order of business.

"Well, Bill, we need to have Michelin to make this work. What are the chances we could have a dealership?"

"I do not care what it takes on our end. You've proven that you're a smart kid and you know what you're doing. Congratulations, you're going to be a Michelin dealer! One way or another, I will make this work!"

Before I could even thank him (or pick my jaw up off the floor), he continued, "Kim, this is fantastic news. Whatever it takes, we are going to make this happen together!"

I didn't sleep much that night, reeling with excitement and anticipation. I had a long trip home the next day, and I had to sit down with my wife as soon as I got home. While the Michelin deal far exceeded my wildest expectations, there was still so much at stake. Since the initial conversation with John, I had talked to my wife often about the possibility of leaving to start a new company. We had spoken candidly about the risks involved, and she was incredibly supportive. I remembered our last conversation, where she encouraged me as only a wife can.

"I trust you, Kim. I think you should do it. How will you ever know if you can succeed if you don't take the risk? Besides, you made a commitment to John, and he has already quit his job. We can't let him down," she had said, instantly putting my fears at ease and reminding me of the truth. I was thankful to have a spouse who was willing to take the plunge and trusted me. When starting up a company, communication is tremendously important, especially with a spouse or significant other.

But now, as I lay wide awake before going home, doubts started to creep back in and threatened to take over. Once again, I was pulled back to reality—you know, the "what if we fail" reality. Anyone starting something with this much risk really needs to think through the alternatives and worst-case scenarios. Jill, my wife, is very sharp. We met at college. She had her own career before we started having children. I was fortunate to have excelled at work so she could stay home and raise the children. Being a mother at home is far more difficult work than having a normal job. We were both glad we could do it, and she had the will. She always gave excellent advice. She also knew of my concerns about the current company I worked for possibly failing.

After I had gotten the final green light from my wife, John and I headed to the bank. We met with a trusted banker that John had worked with named Andy Clark. We laid out what we expected we would need and what we would bring to the table. Our banking plans were to put a second mortgage on each of our homes and borrow additional funds secured by the retread plant equipment as well as other equipment. Then we would ask for receivable financing to cover the lag from collection on sales and due dates from suppliers. Andy listened carefully, asking some valuable questions along the way. I slumped down in my seat a bit, not able to read into how Andy was feeling about the risk involved with the bank taking on a fledgling unproven new startup. Though it was not immediately clear, Andy was sizing us up. He not only cared about the numbers, but he was looking at our character, knowledge, and track records. He wanted to know as much as he could before he made a decision.

Finally, Andy told us he thought he could secure financing for the equipment, as well as a credit line for running the business. He let us know that both John and I would have to take out the second mortgages on our homes as discussed. This might seem like a normal thing to you now, but let me share with you that interest rates were 17% (and still on the rise) at that time as compared to the 3% and 4% rates of more recent times! Those high rates are unheard of today, but that was the reality in the late '70s. It was incredibly expensive to finance any business (or home, car, or anything that required credit), and most people thought it was crazy to start up a business in that sort of credit environment.

Around this time, I remember reading a biography on the founder of the world's largest privately-held commercial tire company, Brad Regan Inc. In the book, Mr. Regan says, "It would be easier to start a new tire business today than when I did it." Though I never forgot that statement, I always had doubts that it was true. Was it possible that, even with interest rates sky-high, it was easier to start our business now than if we had decided to start it ten years before? Brad Regan had started his company 30 years earlier. What could he know about starting again now?

As I would come to find out, it was true, and still is true today. There are still so many opportunities, and as stated so many times already, they are in front of all of us, just often not seen. With today's technological advancements, much of running a business is easier than it was then.

Little did we know this fledgling new enterprise John and I had visualized would one day surpass the market share and sales of what was once the largest privately owned multimillion-dollar tire operation of its time. However, this success did not happen easily. We had our fair share of humongous brick walls ahead to conquer and hardships to prevail through.

When considering any new business, especially one with high cash needs for equipment and labor, it pays to understand what risks can be involved. More importantly, it pays to understand how to deal with those risks. In business school, you read many case studies of mergers and acquisitions; of huge corporate decisions that either worked well or failed. You study accounting, profit, and loss. But rarely could any school touch the reality of those of us who simply started a business from nothing and explain both the good and bad consequences.

Remember when we laid out our original profit and loss pro-forma statements? The ones we completed at 4:00 AM after working through the night? Those statements had forecast first-year sales at $700,000 while showing a small profit. Though many business schools spend time teaching cash flow—the life and death of any business—the schools often fail to show the difference between a profit and positive cash flow. "Cash flow" is simply the amount of money you have coming in compared to the amount needed to pay bills. The majority of business purchases and sales are on credit. The inventory we have to pay for is due to be paid before we have sold it and collected the money, which creates a negative cash flow when growing. While on paper, the new company could predict a profit, the pro-forma numbers can rarely predict cash flow adequately. Cash flow has many determining factors, such as inventory management, financing terms, and so much more. Many profitable companies fail for lack of cash flow, which makes them unable to pay their debts on time. Cash is the lifeblood of growth, and it is of utmost importance to understand.

As it happened, our first-year sales exceeded $1,450,000—over double our plans! The second year we forecast $1.8 million, and sales came in at $2.2 million. With third-year sales exceeding $3.3 million, we were growing at 50% annually, far exceeding what our cash flow generated and causing greater borrowing and dependency on the bank. Though we never had a negative profit year, the profit was still not enough to keep up with cash needs, increased inventories, and increases in account receivables.

We were heading for trouble at this growth rate in such a competitive, commodity-like business.

CHAPTER 4

BUT THAT'S THE WAY WE'VE ALWAYS DONE IT

HENRY FORD ONCE said, "Obstacles are those frightful things you see when you take your eyes off the goal." Everyone faces obstacles at different times in their lives, but it is how they are dealt with that makes the difference between success and failure—both in our personal lives *and* in business.

Thomas Carlyle says, similarly, "Nothing stops the person who desires to achieve. Every obstacle is simply a course to develop their achievement muscle. It's a strengthening of their power of accomplishment." How you handle a crisis or significant setback defines your character and resolve.

In business, we face challenges every day. Our characters develop in how we react and face them. You know that in your lifetime, you will experience difficult times, and most are not predictable. Think through how you might handle the loss of a loved one, or some other possible personal or work-related obstacle. Maybe you lose your job, or a parent or loved one dies. These things happen. We cannot control everything. It is only you who can decide to be strong, accept the current circumstance, and rationally think through what can be changed. No matter how hard we strive to separate our personal and business lives, each has an effect on the other.

The new venture was growing, and growing *fast*. We were always on the go and busy. The business was expanding, requiring more equipment and employees. With an additional location in Alaska and another in Washington, our store count was up to four, with more in planning. A mere two years into this business, our growth was still far exceeding our plans or expectations. Both John and I had had more work than we knew what to do with. Twelve-hour days were short days then. Leaving the house by 5:30 AM, returning home after 8:00 PM was normal.

The manufacturing plant was running smoothly thanks to John, who now had a crew of full-time employees helping him. More service trucks had been purchased, and the drivers were hired and trained to manage customer needs. Commercial tire salespeople had been hired to grow that side of the business, and additional office staff was hired to handle the paperwork, billing, HR, and accounting.

Everything seemed to be running successfully.

One of the key success drivers and part of the original vision shared by both John and I was that our competition was simply selling tires. We were focused on educating our customers on the total cost of their operations and how we could reduce that cost *with* them. We taught our sales and service personnel to understand the customers' business well and act as their consultant, or even an inside employee.

Though it was true that every customer needed tires in their business, that was not all they needed or wanted. In an effort to save money across the board, our customers (much like any customers of any business) wanted to make sure they were getting the best price. We all love a good deal, don't we? So, what if you could educate the customer that proper management of their tires—managing the retreading and inventories better—would save them thousands of dollars a year? We wanted to show the customer how to reduce the needs for different sized tires by standardizing the size used, reduced inventory, spares, and space. We also wanted to show the customer that they did not need to have a tire employee on staff with all the associated wages, insurance, taxes, and liabilities because we could do it for far less overall cost. What if we could educate them about the whole process regarding how a company buys tires and retreading and also save them a huge amount of money every year?

There are a couple of humorous stories that relate to how decision-makers view salespeople, especially when those salespeople can save the company money. Saving money does not involve just buying a product for less. There is much more to be saved through improving efficiency, productivity, and long-term change improvements. It is the salesperson's job to help buyers understand that.

CartoonStock.com

One comic that comes to mind is an infantry field General fighting the enemy with swords and arrows shown above. A salesperson stands before the general with the clear solution to his problem, but the general cannot be bothered with "solutions," as he has a battle to win (he is super busy). The salesperson clearly has not demonstrated his ability to solve the general's problem and create efficiency through improvements!

The other anecdote relates to quality, and goes like this: when a customer buys a low-grade product, they feel pleased when they pay for it because they believe they have saved money. However, they are then displeased every time they use it because it is of a low-grade. But when a customer buys a well-made article, they feel extravagant when they pay for it but well-pleased every time they use it because of its quality.

In the business of selling commercial tires, it is the same. In fact, it is the same in almost any business today, including high tech. Think about this: in past years, companies continually added and upgraded their data and computer servers in order to maintain their systems, accounting software, data storage, and manage growth in their business. Today, it's as easy as opening a cloud drive that exists across platforms, which can be used as needed without the massive investments in space, equipment, and maintenance. "The cloud" represents a way to outsource data storage at significant savings, as well as adding flexibility for growth and needed changes in operations. When we started our company, trucking firms had been employing people to take care of the tires on their trucks. If managed properly, we could reduce their daily needs, and the customer could eliminate the position and its related expenses.

The "old way" of doing business is constantly changing in every industry. In the case of our new venture partnership, at the time we started, many of the tires were about the same and price was the main selling point. Every company sold essentially the same product; the only difference was who made it. Many buying decisions, as today, were based on personal relationships with the salesperson. People deal with people. Often, purchasing decisions were based more on personalities than what made better sense for the customer.

But what if you could shift this paradigm?

We see today that everyone, to some degree, operates in the paradigm they know and understand. If you can introduce a new knowledge base that changes this perception—granted, you are dealing with a reasonable individual or company owner—an opportunity emerges. Put another way, if you can show a company owner or manager a better way to do what they want done, the customer can save money, increasing your sales and customer base.

Many large companies have staff operating in an old paradigm, as change might negatively affect their job stability, such as in IT departments. They are reluctant to support a change. Change is often not easy for most people, and unless you can clearly present a better way to do what needs to be done, it tends to be a very slow process.

As mentioned with Boeing and elaborated on later in this book, they spent $500,000 a year on tires for their fleet of vehicles (not airplane tires). In addition to that expense, they had a warehouse and several staff members managing it. They also had drivers delivering the tires from their warehouse to the various plants around the Seattle area. This is how they "always did it." Boeing really did not need a warehouse. Our company had a warehouse full of tires already. We could supply them as needed, and we could just as easily deliver to their various locations at about the same cost as delivering to their warehouse. So, by eliminating their warehouse and all the related rent and labor expenses, they could save $600,000 in additional costs annually!

Understanding this, in order for our new venture to succeed, we would need well-trained service people and sales professionals who were not afraid to do things differently, having the ability to consult, educate, and be a true *partner* to a customer, not just a salesperson.

As you may or may not be aware, salespeople generally do not garner a lot of respect, and for good reasons. I remember a paper I read when first starting in this industry that stated 95% of salespeople do not know their product well enough to defend or properly respond to a complaint or criticism. The paper also went on to say that it takes an average of five to seven calls to win over a new customer, and the average salesperson makes an average of two calls or less on a lead for a new account. There were several other less-than-flattering statistics in that paper on why salespeople fail. Statistics like those contribute to the less-than-stellar reputation salespeople have earned. Of course, there are great salespeople in every industry, but they are the exception. When a company finds a good one, they do everything they can to keep them.

In our situation, our service people—the truck drivers—were the most critical part of the vision. When properly trained on the management of the customer's fleet, that person could be an extension of the customer's company and act as an employee of that customer. Besides, who does the customer see more often anyway, the salesperson or the service person?

Companies with these larger fleets had hired their own tire people for many years, dating back to a time when tires did not last long, failed often, had dangerous, multiple-piece tube-type rims, and required almost full-time work to keep the fleet rolling. At the time our new business was starting, fleets had the option to change to tubeless rims, just like regular cars. They could also run radial tires that would last twice as long and rarely failed.

Most tire failures are a result of flat tires, and radials reduce the number of flats by 90%! If they were wise enough to understand and make the switch, the fleets could outsource the tire work to a vendor such as our company, who could do all the work for them in a fraction of the time, saving the customer thousands every year. The opportunity here was that most of these customers did not realize this huge step in tire technology and the resulting opportunity to decrease costs. It turns out that the competition did not see this opportunity either. They wanted to keep selling what they were selling and were resistant to change. Unfortunately for them (and fortunately for us), this meant that they were missing out on an opportunity the customer didn't recognize they needed yet.

Customer by customer, big and small, we started gaining market share. The ball was in our court, and the shot was wide open. But we still needed to execute and make the shot.

The same education and training were needed for the sales team as the company expanded. Much like our competitors' way of thinking, most salespeople in the industry were also neglecting to see what the customer actually needed. They were simply trying to sell the customer what they currently had, and price was their only sales tool. The customers also were primarily buying on price because that was all they knew! If we could show the customer a better way to reduce all the costs, not just the price paid, we represented far greater value to that customer, but it required change and a different way to look at the opportunity.

We had come up with a different plan in order to succeed. Though it might seem like a foolish decision, we actually found it best to hire salespeople from outside the industry—the less experience in both sales and tires, the better! I know you might be questioning this strategy but think about this: it is easier to teach a brand-new habit and knowledge base than to change the old. You know the saying, "You can't teach an old dog new tricks." Same example here.

We endeavored to apply the same wisdom to hiring service people. Most of our hires had no experience changing and handling large commercial tires, driving a large service vehicle, or making service calls on customers. It was a slow process to do this training correctly, but it paid off. The company was growing, and more importantly, garnering an exceptional reputation while gaining market share. This caught the attention of some international firms, and the results almost crushed our little enterprise.

We had started with zero market share. Now, after two full years, we had maybe 5% market share. We were competing with big companies like Goodyear, as well as large independent operators—some who had been in business for a few generations.

Though I had experience in my earlier job with many of the world's largest transportation companies such as UPS—who was operating many thousands of trucks—and other large commercial operators, our new company was too small to properly service these larger companies in the beginning. A commercial tire operation had to have 24-hour service, which meant they were able to respond quickly at any time in order to keep the customer moving or repair vehicles on the road, handling truck breakdowns or tire failures. The good news was that we kept in good standing with our contacts at these larger companies. I knew they greatly respected both John and me after having built relationships with us over the years. Someday, we knew our company could grow large enough to be able to handle these customers and markets.

One morning, everything changed for us. The world surrounding our new venture was turned upside down. We had been served a U.S. Federal Court summons. A large international corporation, called Bandag, was suing us for patent infringements and was asking for an immediate injunction to shut down our operations. We were still a small, fledgling operation at the time. We had maybe 40 employees, but the competition was starting to see us as a threat. Bandag was a large Fortune 500 firm, while we were a very small company.

Immediately, our energy and focus shifted to surviving this lawsuit and impending manufacturing shutdown. As you may recall, we started this company with the purchase of a retread manufacturing facility in a bankruptcy auction. We had bid on the equipment, bought said equipment, and shipped it all to Seattle to set up our first manufacturing facility. The equipment had been manufactured by the world's largest retread rubber and equipment supplier, Bandag, from Muscatine, Iowa. Our new venture was not a Bandag franchise, however. We did not use any Bandag rubber, and we had not once said that we were a Bandag dealer. We had no idea how things had escalated to the point of a lawsuit.

Bandag was not only asking for an immediate injunction to shut down our operation, but there was also a monetary component that would follow. If this lawsuit were won, we would lose everything we had put into the company thus far. Our success would be ripped right out from underneath us. We only had a short time before we had to appear in front of a federal judge who could shut us down in a matter of minutes, so we knew we needed to act fast.

The original attorney who helped us set up the new corporation, Pete, agreed to work with us again. He set up a meeting with us to strategize. After our meeting, he agreed that we were not violating Bandag's international patents as the equipment was sold in a public auction, meaning there was no copyright or patent infringement at the time of purchase. Bandag had allowed the equipment to be sold on the open market.

As if the impending court date wasn't threatening enough on its own, it didn't take long for our competition to hear about the ordeal and use it to their advantage. Since the local Bandag dealers were a part of the suit, word traveled fast around the area. One customer called that very morning, catching us off guard, to say the least. This negative information could seriously cut into sales and customer confidence if they feared we were going to be shut down.

"I heard your company has been shut down? What's the deal?"

We knew that we needed to do some damage control—and *fast*. Luckily, we had a top-notch attorney on our side. We had no idea how crucial that would be in the long run.

As we sat in a large federal courthouse with our attorney by our side, I couldn't help but think of everything that could possibly go wrong. I can't say either of us had spent much time in a courtroom before this, especially federal court! I hadn't got much sleep the few nights before, and the stress of it all was wearing heavily as I thought about our employees and how this wasn't just putting our livelihood on the line—it was theirs, too. I had to remind myself to breathe as I listened intently while a well-polished, New York City attorney pleaded the case of how this little start-up company was causing irreparable harm to an international firm. The attorney went on to share how Bandag had visited many of our biggest customers looking for evidence, fishing for any incriminating information that could be used against us. This was also eroding customer confidence in our firm, as those customers were being interrogated by someone from a highfalutin, New York City attorney's firm.

Unfortunately, we had a few customers that expressed concerns regarding the viability of our new business, and one of our larger accounts had already stopped doing business with us as a result of this lawsuit. We also learned that the judge knew of Bandag's founder, who had passed away a few years earlier. Things looked very bleak indeed.

Our attorney made the case for our fledgling company, laying out all the reasons he did not believe Bandag had any right to bring suit for patent infringement. The situation seemed like a re-enactment of David and Goliath as we both sat there, completely helpless. Our whole future, our whole lives, hung there in suspense for what seemed like an eternity that day.

Though the judge ruled against the injunction, it wasn't the end of the road for us. Bandag was not able to shut down our operations yet, but they weren't going to give up without a fight. Even though we were still able to run our business, we had the constant threat of financial ruin looming over our heads. Bandag would file other injunctions, interview other customers, and make our lives very miserable for a long time to come. It was an obstacle we had never expected. Our employees were wondering if we could still pay them and keep them employed. Customers were questioning if we would still be in business.

The following year, Bandag filed an injunction appeal but failed again. Even though we were successful in defending the lawsuit, the financial burden of attorney fees looked like it could be our demise. It was hard to see if there was a light at the end of this tunnel, and if there was, it might be a locomotive ready to crush us.

While all this lawsuit business was going on, at 3:00 AM on a cool, wet, Seattle-type, gray October day, my wife and I welcomed our third child into the world. Feeling both euphoric and exhausted, I remembered I hadn't checked my messages all day since we had been at the hospital. Still, no cell phones or text messages then. I picked up the phone and dialed my voicemail.

"Hey, Kim! It's John. I know you've probably had a long day, but Pete needs us at the office at 8:00 AM sharp tomorrow. It's gotta be important. See you there." Tomorrow was now today, this morning, just a few hours after Jill gave birth to our third boy (Jill needed a girl, but that was never meant to be).

I maybe slept about an hour before it was time to head over to Pete's to see what all the fuss was about. Imagine my surprise when I walked in to see the Bandag attorneys! They made the trip to Seattle as Bandag management had decided they wanted to settle the case that morning, out of court. John and I knew that our key witness had totally refuted what the Bandag attorneys thought was their best opportunity to win. Still, it seemed a bit odd that all of a sudden, they wanted to settle the case. We both knew the basis for the suit was weak by this time, and Bandag had poor odds, but we would not know the real reason for the fast settlement until a few years later.

Regardless of what was to come, the real victory was this: that morning, the attorneys for Bandag dropped the suit for a very small sum, which was to be paid over the next year.

Suddenly, it was as if the anvils we were carrying on our shoulders were gone. We were finally free to grow and build our business further while shedding the awful burden of a federal lawsuit and possible demise. Though we are now thankful for the opportunity to learn and grow through that painstaking process, it was certainly an expensive lesson to learn! We were grateful for the hard-working employees who stayed with us through the whole ordeal, as well as many customers.

On the other hand, we had run up over $100,000 in attorney's fees, and Pete knew we did not have the resources to pay him at that time. He had held most all his fees over that whole year, never billing us. He generously offered that we could have the next couple of years to pay him in installments, with no interest. I still get a little choked up by his generosity. Not only did Pete save our business, but he was a true friend to us. I can't say I know many attorneys who would be so kind.

Thankfully, we eventually gained back the customers we had lost and continued to take larger percentages of the market. We were back in full-charge mode and growing again, gaining back what we lost and more.

During the lawsuit process, the world had seemingly stopped around us. It felt as if there were an eerie, dark cloud that rendered any thought or focus on the future an impossible task. Every day we woke up thinking, "This could be the day we get shut down for good." But the light at the end of the tunnel finally came, and it was not the train! The sun instantly pierced through the clouds, exposing hope for the future once again. Just think, I had gotten the gift of a brand-new baby and a settled lawsuit on the same day! The future was certainly looking bright.

The company that was suing us, Bandag, called ten years later, asking that we start doing business with them. There were some interesting negotiations regarding that step in our business. We eventually became one of their largest dealers in North America, operating four large Bandag manufacturing plants! How that all happened is an example of why it's important to be open-minded, professional, and able to look at mutually beneficial opportunities all the time. This book will focus on decisions and choices, self-discipline, and how we deal with the 35,000 or so choices we are confronted with every day. Some of them carry long-lasting consequences that can affect the rest of our lives, so we always want to choose wisely. In our case, becoming a Franchise Dealer for Bandag was a great decision for both companies.

CHAPTER 5

POTENTIAL PITFALLS OF PARTNERSHIP

A BUSINESS PARTNERSHIP is defined as the following: a closely held corporation with two or more managing shareholders.

Any business with two or more owners can be a Limited Liability Company (LLC), a fully incorporated entity, a simple partnership, or any relationship where two or more share responsibility to manage the entity. As the managing shareholders, each assumes the financial risk, and it is important to ensure they have a way to agree when making decisions. There is much more to this, but these are the key points: keep in mind, if you own anything less than 50% of the entity, you do not have the ability to *make* the decisions. You can add your input, but if there are only two individuals and you own 49.9%, you might as well only have 1%. The controlling shareholder has the final say on all decisions.

If you are considering entering into a partnership, it is very important to keep in mind that many people do not make great business partners, even if you have a great relationship with them. It takes hard work to keep a partnership successful, much like investing in a marriage. Due to possible differences in skill sets, one partner might need to do much more work than the other. The workloads and time spent can be defined by the skills of each partner, as well as what is required to keep the business moving forward.

For some people, the imbalance of workload bothers them. Of course, if one partner is lazy and does not do their share of the work, that is most certainly cause for concern. But, if each person's skill set dictates the amount of time required to do the work, and the work each partner does meets those expectations, then you expect each person will fulfill their respective responsibilities.

Think this through, if the partnership is successful, growing, and making money for both partners, it should not matter that one partner might be required to work longer hours or travel for the company more. That is simply the result of that partner's skills and contribution to the overall success of the entity. Both partners benefit. The main point to understand here is that every person is different. They have different skills and talents, as well as unique strengths and weaknesses. Everyone has a specific way of doing things, and often, these differences are what make up a great partnership—their weakness is your strength, and vice versa. However, sometimes these differences, if not understood or handled properly, can cause dissension and irreparable damage to the relationship.

It has been said that one of the main reasons for a partnership failure, aside from financial reasons, is because of one of the partner's spouses. To be successful, it is important for you to maintain a separation between your business partner and your personal relationships. You will need to have conversations and open discussions with your partner(s) about difficult business decisions, goals, finances, etc. Your spouse could never have the knowledge of all the issues from all the perspectives to make wise decisions. It is simply best to keep business conversations among the partners. Think about this: whenever someone shares a frustration or conflict with another person (such as a spouse), that person only hears one side of the story. It is impossible to understand or make a reasonable suggestion if you do not know all the facts or hear both sides of any issue. The person who hears only one side tends to support and reinforce the person giving them that one-sided story. That's just a natural human tendency. The other party then makes a decision lacking the complete information.

And who do you think hears these stories most often? That's right, our spouses or significant others.

Again, stories like this are not the normal case studies one will encounter in business school, nor read in a textbook. Most professors and business book authors do not have the real world, hands-on experience of starting or running a business, especially a partnership. They may have book smarts, and the statistics but often do not have the practical hands-on experience, or what might be called street smarts. Street smarts come from life experience. That is why you won't be able to learn everything you need to know about running a successful business—or be successful at anything you do, for that matter—by *only* reading a book, watching a video, or searching the internet.

However, you can learn some important lessons from our real-life experiences (and hopefully learn even more from our mistakes).

John and I both agreed during that first all-nighter planning session when we decided to launch this business that we should never bring work home. What we meant by this is that we would leave our business between us. Even when it was difficult to not say anything, we both knew it could make matters worse to come home and vent to our spouses. Looking back, there was a situation that turned out to be the perfect example of why this agreement was important for the health of both our business and our marriages. We might be laughing now, but it wasn't so funny when it happened!

One night, my wife was livid as I drove into the driveway at 2:00 AM in a company truck. I'll never forget her words piercing through the cold, winter night, "What is *John* doing?!"

Let me paint a backstory for you before we get there.

As you may remember, John was the one with the manufacturing skills. He purchased the retread plant equipment and was responsible for the construction and buildout of the plant as well as the ongoing retread operations. He was a generally quiet person and spoke very little. I, on the other hand, had the interpersonal skills. I was responsible for bringing in the customers—the "rainmaker" if you will. I was definitely the more outgoing of the two of us, but this was not the only difference in our skillsets, thankfully. Both of us were well-versed in operational management, we both had experience with budgeting and planning, and we were both early risers who did what it took to get the job done. My skills required more travel, time away from home, and spending time with customers at events, often in evenings.

From the very first day our business got started, I was the one knocking on doors, making face-to-face calls on customers, trying to get companies to believe in us and use our services. We started from scratch. We didn't have a single customer lined up the day we opened for business. That alone was daunting! That meant that *somebody* was required to work incredibly hard in an attempt to build a customer base. And that someone was me. The business we were able to secure, then provided John with the tires to retread in our new shop.

Thankfully we weren't by ourselves in the very beginning, as is the case with many startup companies. We were lucky enough to have found two great employees who helped us get off the ground. One was an administrative person to answer the phone we hoped would ring, as well as handling the paperwork on those customers we didn't yet have. The other was a service person who would drive a truck to different customer locations, or on the road servicing equipment and mounting the tires we hoped we would sell. The truck had an air compressor and the heavy tools required to change or repair large truck tires.

Though it was in the plan to incorporate retreading from the beginning, we had yet to find a facility for lease to build the retread plant, and we wouldn't have a place for the first few months. The plant could only be constructed in the proper city-zoned industrial areas. Not many people are willing to rent a space to a new business with little credit established and no customers. A landlord wants to be assured the tenant will pay the rent on time. It was hard finding a landlord willing to take that risk. Remember Bill Gates and Paul Allen, who founded Microsoft? They also had real estate problems when they started! There was more than one landlord who has since regretted not taking a risk on Microsoft.

Without a space secured yet, our business was housed in a mobile office ("job shack") behind a warehouse in the south industrial side of Seattle. I found myself on the road early every morning, calling on potential customers in person, knocking on the doors of businesses that could be a great fit. John, on the other hand, could be found in the office at the same time. However, I would not get home until 7:00 PM most days, while John went home in the afternoons as he was out of work. Until we found a building for our retread plant, there really was not a lot for John to do. As is the case with many people, John was not comfortable walking into a company office uninvited and asking for business. So, that ball was mostly in my court.

I could not operate the retread plant. John did not have the knowledge or experience calling on potential customers. We both had excellent skill sets, but very different; a highly-rated reason for a business to succeed.

Having turned in my new company car when leaving my management job to start this new company, I bought a used Volvo to start making sales calls at customer locations. Most tire salespeople drove pickup trucks… not me. John, on the other hand, had purchased the truck of his dreams: a black, fully loaded new Ford F-250 Lariat, complete with fancy wheels and big tires. I wore slacks and a tie every day, while John considered himself dressed up when he had on his jeans and a long-sleeved shirt. We ended up taking John's new dream Ford F250 into the business and adding a big compressor and tools so we could use it to service customer trucks and make deliveries.

Can you see the pattern developing here?

John and I had different skills, different personalities, different lifestyles, and different experiences. Is one more important? Is one better than the other? Or are they complementary, both important parts of the equation? I'd say the latter. That said, when choosing any partner, it is best you both possess valuable skills needed to operate a business.

My day would start at 6 AM every day, and often away from the office or even out of state as we operated in both Washington and Alaska. I worked hard all day, and often would not be home until after 7 PM, or out even later with customers or employees.

One day, I needed the service truck (John's dream truck) to deliver some tires to a customer on my way home. The tires were too large to fit in my car. This truck was our only service vehicle at the time. It was needed 24 hours a day if any customer called with an emergency flat repair. We had to be available to quickly respond to any emergency if we hoped to keep the customer. So, off I went with our only truck, hoping a customer did not call that evening. It was December, so it was cold, and it was starting to snow lightly.

Of course, the inevitable happened. I got home late, well after dinner time, and was in the house a short time when our service person, Dave, called me and said, "The answering service called. Darigold has a milk tanker truck on I-5 with a flat!" Dave was in bed and lived 30 miles south of me, and the truck with the flat was 15 miles north of my home on the side of the freeway. The customer was huge—they ran trucks 24 hours a day. The milk tanker was a 105,500 pound, 9-axle, huge vehicle that was on a tight schedule to make it to the dairy processing plant. We had to perform. This was a new customer to us, and the largest customer for us at that time with hundreds of trucks. We would lose the account if we could not service them properly.

So, off I went. No dinner, tromping in the snow, heading out at 10 PM to fix a flat tire along a busy freeway. The bigger problem was that I had never done this from a truck before! I can change the big tires. I had done it in the shop over the years. I thought I knew what to do, but had never really done it by myself. I had been an executive. I wore a tie every day. Now I found myself on my back with a hydraulic jack, on the side of the freeway under a huge truck changing a tire and wheel that weighs more than 150 pounds. I had a tire gun that also weighed about 80 pounds connected to a huge airline that allowed me to remove the big bolts. The Darigold truck was back on the road in short order, and I packed up the tools and headed back to our home just after midnight.

Jill, my wife, was up, worried and in tears for lots of reasons. It seemed to her that I had to do all the work. This is the point of this little story. As I entered our home through the garage to remove my now wet and filthy clothes, I apologized to Jill, and explained it was all part of building this new business. She understood the hard work, respected that, and knew starting and growing a business would be hard, but she still couldn't help but blurt out, "WHAT IS JOHN DOING?!"

"Jill, for all you know, John is doing everything I am doing and more." I left it at that even though I knew it was not the case, but also knew there was nothing more John could be doing at that time.

A partnership does not have to be fair or equal, or anything else. Both John and I needed to do what we were best at doing at that time to grow our little business venture. I was not proud that a year earlier, I wore a suit, drove a new car, had a great office and expense account with many employees and here I was getting out of wet, dirty clothes doing hard physical work. John would be building our manufacturing plant soon and have his hands full, doing work I was not able to do, as he had a different skill set than me. I was hoping John would be holding up his end when the time came. While we do not know the future, I felt he was a man of his word. He wasn't a slacker; he was a genuinely hard-working person.

Think this through, though: at this early stage of the business, I was putting in many more hours than John. I started earlier, worked later, and was away from home more often. It might be I was doing 70% or more of the work to get the company started, but does that matter? Looking at Jill's point of view, all she knew was that her husband seemed to be doing all the work in this new company. She could only make a judgement based on what she heard and saw, and at the moment she saw her husband having been on a service call in the snow at night. She was rightfully concerned. Not to mention my ruining a nice shirt and shoes. The Darigold driver did mention I was the best-dressed service person he had ever seen!

After a few years, we all laughed at Jill's question, "What is John doing?" and the story behind it. There was no way Jill could know all the details behind the current situation. The lesson here is that it is simply best not to bring work home. At that time, neither partner or spouse had any idea if we would succeed or what the future would hold. So, while I did want to reply to Jill that John was really not doing much at that time, my gut feeling was to simply say what I said, that he was "doing everything and more."

A few weeks prior, John and I had spoken about this at length. John knew I was carrying the lion's share of the workload as we still had not moved into a space for the new plant that was sitting in storage. We were both in the office and he said, "I know you are working a lot more than I am, Kim. When we are able to build the plant, I promise I will more than make up for this." There really was not much I could say; I was pleased he acknowledged my work and really hoping he would contribute his share when he could.

Although I still had some reservations, I was smart enough to keep them to myself. More importantly, I did not share any of my thoughts or reservations with Jill, who could never fully see the other side of this story—at least not yet.

A few months later, we finally secured a lease and moved into our first building. We were still in the industrial area of South Seattle, and thus were close to many trucking companies and industrial firms. As promised, John built the retread manufacturing plant we had purchased to start the business. He was in the plant around 5:00 AM every day, working weekends and late evenings as well. John more than made up for his share of the work, and to this day, we have both kept up our sides of the bargain. Nobody worked any harder than John did, and thankfully, we can look back and laugh at Jill's frustration. After a number of years, Jill and I shared that story with John and his wife, Sharon. While it may be funny now, it is a good lesson on humility, holding back your immediate thoughts, and not bringing home any one-sided stories, especially if the outcomes are still unknown.

Our different skill sets, when combined, added up to a successful partnership. I had knowledge, education, and skills John did not have. John had manufacturing skills, an education, and knowledge I did not have. We combined our strengths and weaknesses, had open communication, pushed through conflict, and watched our company succeed. Of course, as I mentioned in the last chapter, we grew way too fast for a small, privately-funded enterprise. We funded the company 100% on our own, with no outside investors, family funding, or gifts. We didn't have a glamorous startup or enormous profit at the beginning. We were just a legacy-type business with knowledge and insight that our competitors did not have.

The process of starting up our business provided several opportunities to test the mettle of each of us. These hardships are worth reviewing, as these instances are yet another area not covered in depth by schools or books as mentioned already. In school, we aren't taught why partnerships fail, or why partnerships succeed. Perhaps because every story on success or failure has so many variations and twists. What makes a business fail or succeed is a different scenario in every case. Our story is a basic example that can go very deep and needs to be understood. If you only concentrate on how much each person is working, you can fail to see that the success might not be possible unless one person works more. The sum of the inputs can be a great success, while they do not need to be equal inputs. Together, you can accomplish much more than by yourself.

Even though this new company was a corporation, we were still two individuals running it equally. We each owned 50% of the shares of stock issued. We paid ourselves the same amount of money each month, shared equally in any gains or losses, and vowed to always be fair with each other. We shared equally in the risk and invested the same resources, time, money, and talent. But the number of hours needed each day was not equally divided, and could not be. Each partner needed a perspective on this fact in order to succeed. Our skills balanced each other out, but the workload required would never be equal, and it varied at times. One partner always worked more than the other, but the sum of the whole was far greater than it ever could have been individually. I could have never succeeded without John, and vice versa.

One last comment on how decisions can be made when the two owners are equal partners: today, John and I are still partners, now in several LLCs. After 40 years of being partners, we still have never had a serious disagreement between us. That is not saying we always agreed; in fact, that is far from it. But we did develop a process from day one on dealing with situations. This way of working through a decision still works successfully today as it did when we started and can be used in any business.

We agreed on a way to communicate up front, explaining our thoughts and how strongly we felt about any major decision, a process that would serve us well over the years. It was

John's idea that whenever we needed to make any important decision, if either felt strongly against the idea, then we would not do it. Think this through: one partner might not agree but still voice that opinion and let the decision be made to proceed. But unless either partner strongly objected, they could still move forward. An example later in the book relates to a large real estate acquisition I wanted to do. We needed to expand, and I wanted to buy a large piece of land and develop a 60,000 SF building for manufacturing, warehouse, and offices. It would cost millions and consume a lot of time. John felt it too big a risk, but said, "I am not comfortable taking this big a risk, but I trust you and believe you have researched this well. If you feel strongly, that this is a good decision and will work, I will agree to move forward."

Fortunately, that investment did pay off in huge ways, but had John said no, we would have chosen some other alternative. Either way, we would have kept growing and would have continued to work together. All decisions were important, and we agreed upfront on a process, communicated, talked things through, and provided valuable insight to each other in order to make good decisions.

CHAPTER 6

IT'S ALL ABOUT THE CUSTOMER

OVER THE FOLLOWING two years, our company continued to grow rapidly. Sales revenue was still increasing at 50% a year! We knew we could not sustain that kind of growth, yet we were trying to manage it as best we could. Keep in mind, we had no outside investors, no bonds to sell to raise capital to buy equipment, and no stock offerings to maintain adequate cash flows and expansion. All this growth had to be financed by John and me, using our available bank credit lines and debt, which added interest expense. Our valued suppliers also participated by allowing us attractive purchase terms on inventory.

Why were we growing so fast? Why were we able to capture so much market share from large international competitors as well as long-established local competitors? What were we doing differently? Well, for starters, we were not selling our products at reduced prices as so many competitors were doing. We were following the plans that we laid out at the beginning of our business: focusing on what the customer really needed. We were passionate about the business of showing customers how we could save them money in their operations. That passion was a proven belief that all customers wanted to spend less money on tires, and we could show how changes in operations could accomplish the savings. By educating the customer on several aspects of their operations as they relate to tires, we could save the customer money on labor cost and related expenses in addition to having to buy fewer tires by making our recommended changes.

Think about that last sentence. If you or your company can show a customer a better way to operate their business that saves them money, you become a trusted and favored supplier. Even if the customer might have to pay more for your service or product, if you can show them how to operate their business more cost-effectively, it would only be logical to choose you to supply the products they need.

Implementing this sort of model requires knowledge and training that exceeds that of the competition—training in understanding the customer's operations and needs. While John had the knowledge and technical expertise to build and successfully run the retread manufacturing plant, I had the expertise and knowledge of the trucking industry and how we could improve operations for our customers as it pertained to tire applications. It was a perfect example of a great partnership as laid out in the previous chapter, a division of responsibility and complementary skillsets.

We had an employee base of individuals from outside the marketplace with little experience in tires. As I mentioned before, most sales and service people already working in the industry had some less than stellar habits and were not trained the way we desired. The salespeople we were looking for had to be professional, able to learn technical skills we would teach, and keep excellent records. We would train our truck service personnel in customer fleet operations so they understood what the customers needed.

The ideal service person had to be able to work with the customer as if they were running this aspect of their business *for* them, almost as if they were an employee of the customer. That means they would always make decisions that made the most sense *for the customer*, not for our company. Decisions were to be based on the long-term benefits to the customer which, would, in turn, benefit our company.

A humorous example of this strategy involved one of our largest customers. To take it a step further, it was the same customer we lost for a short time during the lawsuit debacle. The customer owned thousands of trailers spread all over the northwest and Alaska, as well as in Texas. They were heavy into the transportation of the oil industry's goods and equipment, and used thousands of tires a year.

In their main yard and maintenance facility, the tire service person was *our* employee. That meant that the customer understood the value of outsourcing, meaning they were not being tied to the expense and liability of additional employees. One of our tire suppliers had a special short-time discount on tires this company used, which meant it was a great time to stock up. I went to the maintenance director, who was not my employee, to share the opportunity. I let him know there was a special discount if they ordered 100 tires or more.

His reply to me was, "Go ask Zane. If we need them, put them into stock."

That should have been an easy sale, as Zane was the service person that worked for our company. It is important to note that Zane, our employee, would also receive a commission on this sale.

However, Zane told me, "We really don't need these tires now, Kim. I am using a lot of tires from trailers they have in excess for a while, as they are not currently being used. When these trailers get back into service, then we will consider buying. Right now, they really do not need any additional inventory."

While I might have been disappointed, it was clear that our training was effective. Zane was acting as if he was an employee of the customer, and made the decision accordingly. This was exactly what made us more successful than the competition, and the customers could see this in action. I went back to the maintenance director and said, "I used to think I was a pretty good salesperson, but I can't even sell to my own employee—I couldn't get him to spend your money!"

His response confirmed we were doing business the right way when he remarked; "Kim, that is precisely why we do business with you."

What he meant by that is we were not simply selling tires; we were partnering with the customer, showing them ways that reduced overall costs and increased productivity. We were building market share by saving the customer both money and time in many ways. This customer didn't need a bulk discount—they needed our expertise and training in how to manage their services more effectively, saving them infinitely more money in the long run. We had a passion and goal that we could become the dominant market leader if customers were willing to listen and learn. Examples such as this were proving we were doing what we said.

In any case, we were well on our way to building a well-oiled machine. It was time-consuming and costly, but it was worth it in the long run. This was because we not only had to train employees from scratch about the products, but more importantly, we had to train them about the customer's operations and why and how our sales and service employees could make this a success for themselves personally. Our competitors often spent their time training people on the product, explaining all the reasons their tires were better than other tires and always giving some incentive to the salespeople or a discount to the customer. What we were able to see is that tactic is not what was best for the customer, though the customer would not know this unless we could teach them our vision of a better way.

As we continued to gain market share, we were able to start doing business with many of the largest transportation and truck-related industries in their respective markets. We had been building up an excellent reputation and building a portfolio of satisfied customers that could be used as examples and references. The way we were marketing, selling, and servicing didn't make much sense to our competition as we continued to rise to the top. They couldn't understand why people would be doing business with our company, even when they offered a lower price for a product. The saying, "You do not know what you do not know," defined our competition, and we hoped it would stay that way. Meanwhile, little by little, their customers started coming over to us.

Our strategy is nothing more than using common sense. Our method of doing business was right in front of our competition, yet unseen or possibly not understood. Our customer-focused strategy could be applied in any business today as it was then. For us, in our industry, the customer had to buy tires in order to operate. They could buy from anyone. They had lots of choices. But our company developed the knowledge of their business and was able to show the customer better ways to operate as it related to tire usage. Simply put, we could show the customer how to spend less, buy fewer tires, and save money in operations. We became the trusted, value-added supplier.

Your business could be an industrial application or even a cloud-based service. People, in any industry and from all walks of life, have the ability to see something right in front of them and wonder why it is that way if only they try. Anyone can think through the problems around them and see solutions. Often, they can visualize a business that can profit from what they see that others do not. Every business needs continuous improvement and to strive to find better ways to operate and be more profitable. No matter if you have that idea to improve something where you work now, or where you can improve the operations of your customers, you have the ability to see things differently and consider the question "Why?"

In our case, we had taken our operations from a fledgling company facing a large Federal lawsuit to an enterprise that grew almost too fast. Smarter, more business-savvy individuals might have taken this company public, expanded the proven concept, gone into franchising or brought in private equity. A Harvard or Stanford MBA case study could be developed around our business, as all those options were a distinct possibility. The study would be on what alternative made the most sense. As we grew, we had discussed some of these ideas early on with our banker, Andy. Unfortunately, Andy was no longer in the banking industry by the time any of these ideas could have become a reality. The bank he worked for had been sold, and he accepted an offer to become the CFO for a large company. Although we had a new banker, the discussion on alternative means of financing the growth just did not happen. And besides, our time was consumed with the growth: training, hiring, buying equipment, and learning what the competition was doing. We were also opening new markets. We now operated six locations, and market share was growing in all of them, and all that new business was at the expense of our competition as we were taking their customers from them.

A few years later, we saw another huge opportunity. From a simple, insignificant transaction in our business with a global Fortune 500 firm, we saw something in that company's operations that could be improved that might lead to a whole new enterprise. This customer was an enormous and successful Fortune 500 firm. I had been studying W. Edward Deming and his "what, why and how" strategies. He had transformed manufacturing processes that resulted in increased profits and sales starting with Toyota after WWII. Both John and I were studying his work as it related to our own manufacturing operations, but the same knowledge could also be applied to how we see other opportunities and improve customer operations through our services. This new opportunity we visualized was with PACCAR, one of the world's largest manufacturers of large trucks. There is a more detailed story about this later, but we did end up starting another business surrounding this vision that ended up going global. This new enterprise created another drain on cash initially, but became an extremely profitable, cash-flow-positive operation in a very short time.

The point here is that the future is anything you want to make of it. It is your choice, and it is a result of the decisions you make today. It is not dependent on your education, although more education is better than less education. You can train yourself to see opportunities all around you. Some of what you "see" might lead you to starting a new company. Others may cause you to join a company already in existence. Some companies have very low barriers to entry, meaning they are easy to start, such as driving for Uber or starting a home-based business. There is very little capital required. Other startups are more complex, like ours. Our barriers were quite high, as we needed a deep understanding of how to both build out and run our manufacturing plant. It also required greater amounts of capital. However, this is just our story. There are many businesses, many not even thought of yet, that will not require a ton of capital, investment, or understanding before getting started.

Think of that: there are thousands of businesses no one has even thought of yet. These businesses are waiting to be discovered, and it can be *you* who makes it all happen!

Most people overlook opportunities, even when they are right in front of them. At one point in the 1900s, it was said, the head of the U.S. Patent Office suggested they shut down that office. Why? Because he was convinced that everything that needed a patent had already been made. This is one of the world's best examples of short-sighted thinking. Today, millions of new patents are applied for every year! If you can believe there are opportunities all around you and start training yourself to be on the lookout, the opportunity you find could wind up to be the next big enterprise. However, you do not have to start a business. Most companies reward those who constantly strive to improve, find better ways to take care of customers, and bring in new business. There's something to be said about taking initiative and going above and beyond your job description. As Steve Jobs is quoted, "You don't even have to come up with something new. Just make something that's already in existence better or more useful to the end user."

Regardless of where you might find yourself now, you can make a conscious choice to change how you view your work and personal life. As Albert Einstein was quoted as saying: "Insanity is doing the same thing over and over again but expecting different results." It is up to you to make a difference. You can choose today to make decisions that improve your company or yourself, or you can do what you always have done and *hope* something might change. What are you going to decide?

You might be reading this as a student. Maybe you are on a business trip, possibly already in sales, or any part of operations. Maybe you dream about owning your own business or growing your income and being more successful. Remember the saying, "The grass is always greener on the other side." Owning a business is not easy, but then again, life is not easy. There are millions of very successful people—way more successful than we are—that never owned their own business.

There are also thousands of people who tried to start their own business and failed. More people have failed at their own business than failed at their jobs.

Think about this: If you stay at your profession and work hard, learn from the examples throughout this book and apply them where you work, your chances of success are far greater than taking the risk of starting your own business. Look carefully where you are first. There may be an excellent career path where you are that you are not seeing yet. While most of new businesses fail within the first five years, employment at your current job does not have a 95% turnover rate. Do the math and choose what is best for you. However, you may need to look outside your current company, if your career path does not look like it leads to more success or opportunity.

Many years after starting the first company, I was completing an MBA at the University of Washington as John and I were looking to launch our new PACCAR entity globally. I was in the two-year EMBA program, which attracted many students who had their tuition paid by the companies they worked for. Every single person who had their tuition paid for was openly looking to leave that current employer in hopes of a better job! Here they were, working for a company that was investing significant funds and time into helping them grow, but instead of taking their new knowledge into that company, they were focusing on something outside the ones who were funding their education.

Yes, you read that right. These students had an employer interested enough in them to invest $50,000 a year for an advanced education, as well as allowing them time away from their jobs to study. Do you think these companies would spend that kind of money on someone they knew was planning to leave? Of course not! They invested in their employees so they could share the benefit of what the students would bring back to their company. These students had an incredible opportunity to better themselves and their companies. But what they lacked was the vision—the thinking outside the box required to see the opportunity of what could be if they applied themselves in a different way at the company where they already worked.

We all fall into this blinded thinking from time to time, and it happens in all workplaces and relationships. It is quite common to see things from a narrow point of view, meaning we are normally focused on ourselves instead of looking at the much bigger opportunities that exist all the time, all around us. We simply are not looking for them. So we do not see them.

As I got to know my fellow students better while we studied together, it was increasingly apparent that any of them could have exceeded well beyond where they were at the time of our MBA program. In fact, I bet they eventually would have been in top management or helping to run one of the larger companies. All that to say, I assure you it is safer, and sometimes much wiser, to stay with a company and help them succeed rather than thinking that starting your own business is the only way to succeed.

I remember talking to a very successful stockbroker about the amount of businesses that fail. At the time of our conversation, he was the second most successful broker at his firm. We were talking about why so many people from large corporations who start their own business fail. There are many examples to choose from, including people from companies like Boeing as well as a growing number from Microsoft.

Why were these people failing when they had such high-level training and expertise? What was the root cause of failure? We could only speculate, and in a broad sense, since failures can be traced to many individual reasons, but there were two main reasons we came up with.

The Boeing employees and executives the stockbroker dealt with did not understand the real-world realities of business acumen and street smarts needed to run a complete business. The Microsoft people, who had accumulated millions of dollars from stocks after skyrocketing growth, felt they were smarter than the average person, emboldened by their wealth as proof. Both the Microsoft and Boeing employees failed due to a lack of understanding the real world of operating their own business and the complications, regulations, competition, and strategy required to exceed. I heard it said once that running a business is easy; you simply buy or make something and sell it for more than it cost you, *plus a million things in-between.*

As we've said before, starting your own business is not an easy road to take. Ask anyone who has made it beyond five years in business! Maybe you are called to start your own business, but I hope you sincerely weigh all the options in front of you before taking the leap. You just might have an incredible opportunity sitting right in front of you at the company you are currently working for and have yet to see it. That was surely the case with my fellow MBA students.

In my case, I not only had passion for the business we were starting, I also had valuable experience before taking the leap. There was knowledge that when I jumped, I could see where I might land. Early on, each of us as partners often wondered if we had made the right decision as we struggled with low pay, long hours, hardships, anxiety, and despair before realizing our passion and knowledge would finally pay off. I left my previous employer because it was apparent that they were struggling financially and there was no opportunity for me to continue to grow. I am glad I did, because they eventually had to close their doors after 65 years of business. If you are currently working for a well-established firm, you can be the one to take it to the next level or raise your department to higher levels of success. Of course, there are also thousands of companies for sale. You could buy a business, but be sure you study and know the industry you are buying into. Often, the previous success was in part due to the relationships and knowledge of the founder or owner that may not be easily transferable. That type of situation could be covered in another whole book. Think through and investigate all the data you can about both your current situation and the vision you have of your future, and make the decision carefully.

CHAPTER 7

SUCCESSFUL DECISION-MAKING

IN OUR FORMAL education growing up, we learn much of what we apply to life as adults: math, science, engineering, business management, accounting, statistics, and so much more. We take classes in history, architecture, trades, and electives that all add to our knowledge base, including an appreciation of the arts. During our years of formal education, we are increasingly adding inputs that shape our social skills, attitudes, beliefs, how we think, react and even our language, other languages, and the way we speak. The simple lessons we learn on our own and from family, friends, neighbors, and the world, expand through our experiences such as touching a hot stove, the taste of different foods, and riding a bike. During all this time, we are creating memories, talking to ourselves, developing deeper thoughts and adding millions of bits of information into our subconscious minds. As I was writing this book, I clicked the search icon in Google® asking how much we can learn in life and received 109 million results!

Scientists are still learning about how we learn. It has been suggested that we will never know all the answers to how we learn. In fact, the brain actually grows as we learn. Depending on what we are learning, differing between motor skills, analytical, and emotional, all are adding connections between neurons in the brain. These repeated lessons get "coded" into our subconscious minds. Our subconscious is part of our automatic responses to our learning.

As the old saying goes, practice makes perfect, as a person does not need to think through an action once the brain has added the "code" into its processes. In most cases, the more we practice, the better we become in everything we do. I happen to be a pilot of some 40 years now, and just like driving a car, so much of what is required has become automatic, requiring very little effort or conscious brain work. That expertise is ingrained already through my time in the cockpit.

You have the ability to expand how you think about everything you do every day, both personally as well as how it relates to your career and work. There are thousands of unknown opportunities surrounding us all, every day that we fail to recognize. You can improve your ability to see these opportunities and learn from them. Simply training yourself to ask why something is done the way it is continues your learning process and can lead to discovery and greater knowledge.

In one of my first jobs, to me, it seemed logical that if you worked hard, you advanced at the job and could make a higher wage. A co-worker of mine seemed very lazy; he was slow to accomplish any tasks. What I could do in 30 minutes, took him over an hour. One day, I said, "Jack, get the lead out" as he very slowly made his way up some stairs to the shop floor.

His reply stuck with me, as he said, "If they paid me more, I would work more!" Some twenty years later, as I was building my own business, I stopped for a visit at that location where I first started. Jack was still there doing the same job, and apparently still slow, waiting to get paid more.

The opportunity for both Jack and I was in front of both of us. I simply worked harder, learned more, and was promoted. Why Jack could not see that opportunity is the subject of many books in psychology. The example here is simply that some of us learn life lessons sooner than others.

What inputs did I have growing up that Jack did not? One might be my insatiable desire to see successful people and consciously think of the why and how they became that way. I have been a long-time believer in the Pygmalion Effect, caused by the expectations of a superior regarding the performance of their subordinates. It has been called a form of self-fulfilling prophecy. It has actually been found to enhance the performance and morale of employees due to the positive expectations of management. As it relates to my co-worker Jack, I simply saw an individual with low ambition who did not care about management's expectations, but only his own. We both had the same managers, and initially did the same work. I believe we both had the same opportunity, but Jack could not see it.

As we grow, every input leads to more knowledgeable decisions. Reading this book or any book on business adds to the valuable lessons that can be applied every day as decisions are made. Keep in mind, it is both the conscious and the subconscious mind that is learning as you grow. Good or bad decisions are made by only you. Your life can depend on them. Your success and future will be the outcome of many thousands of decisions.

Just as the story about Jack early in my career, we can all see the same traits among many people in any situation, business, or position. It was not so clear then why some make poor decisions on how they invest their time or made excuses why some tasks could not be done. Others who appeared more successful seemed to always find a way to get things done.

We all have the same amount of time in any given day; some spend it wisely, others, not so much. In any business, the people you see promoted are those who get it done, find the answers, and tackle the difficult tasks. They are the ones that always seem to complete and exceed in all they attempt to do. I developed the self-discipline to always follow through even though it often meant forgoing something else I would rather be doing.

Later as a business owner, I naturally invested more of my time into those employees who followed through and completed what was asked or showed us why something should be done differently. We all learn quickly who those people around us are who simply get things done. You, my friend, no matter what age or position in life, have thousands of choices to make today, right now, and for the remainder of your life. Balance is important between taking time to relax, vacations, family and work. Make decisions that improve all areas of your life and invest your time wisely to develop that self-discipline that always guides you to make the choices you know inside are best for all concerned.

According to a study cited by Roberts Wesleyan College, the average American adult makes 35,000 decisions every day![4]

---

4 *https://go.roberts.edu/leadingedge/the-great-choices-of-strategic-leaders*

According to another study by Cornell University, on average we make over 226 decisions each day on food alone (Wansink and Sobal 2007). How you make these decisions has a lot to do with the amount of success you will reap in any endeavor, especially your career.

In the post by Dr. Joel Hoomans on the Roberts Wesleyan site, he says, "As your level of responsibility increases, so does the smorgasbord of choices you are faced with."

The post lists a sample of some of the decisions for which we generally have a free will to make and can carry an impact on the balance of our lives:

- what to eat
- what to wear
- what to purchase
- what we believe
- what jobs and career choices we will pursue
- how we vote
- with whom to spend our time
- who we will date and marry
- what we say and how we say it
- whether or not we would like to have children
- what we will name our children
- with whom will our children spend their time
- what our children will eat, etc.

The author goes on to say,

"Each choice carries certain consequences—good and bad. This ability to choose is an incredible and exciting power that we have each been entrusted with by our Creator and for which we have an obligation to be good stewards of."

Nearly all the above examples involve the conscious part of our brains. However, our subconscious plays a big role in how we make these decisions. Just like driving a car, or in my case, flying an airplane, the more we train and practice doing it correctly, the more we make decisions along certain paths with little conscious thought.

We also have the choice to visualize what can be; what our future might be. We choose to work, to support a lifestyle of our choice, own a home, buy a car, and pay everyday expenses. Because we have the choice to work or not, I believe we should never have a negative attitude towards the company providing the jobs we have. It is your choice to continue to work there. You could choose to not work and to live off social welfare or in a homeless camp instead. It is all your choice. The decisions you make today create a very direct consequence regarding the goals you have in mind, such as where you want to be in one, five, twenty-five years. The key point here is that the decisions you make today directly determine where you might be at any future date.

Having an added mental (and possibly subconscious) awareness that there are thousands of opportunities in front of you increases your ability to see those opportunities. They could be simple ones, or they could be life-changing. Examples of these types of opportunities are throughout this book. If you are not looking for opportunities everywhere in your life, you will fail to see what might be right in front of you, right now.

Another point from Dr. Hoomans' post is that choices compound. He says, "We see this most evidently in the choices we make with our spending and the way they collectively impact our personal balance sheet or how we balance everything in our lives. These accumulated choices all work together over a lifetime to take us to various outcomes. Individual choices that concern only us—such as what to eat for lunch—will seemingly only impact us personally, as they pertain to the time they require, the cost, the impact to our taste buds, energy level, and health, etc. However, in business, a leader's decisions always interact with others' choices and actions. These leadership decisions create a ripple effect for spouses, families, teams, business units, organizations, communities, states, nations and even the world-at-large."

As we read about the decisions leading up to the founding of the new company we started in the tire industry, we are also reading about the thousands of decisions that cumulatively lead to the successes and or failures of the business. Everyone makes good and bad decisions, it is just that often we do not know which is which until after the decision is made. In some instances, the knowledge of a decision being good or bad is not known for a long time.

Life involves a series of choices every day. The choices you make today have an enormous impact on what you do and where you might end up in life. For example, if you decide to drive after drinking too much, there can be a lifetime of consequences. A close friend lost a daughter to a drunk driver on a sunny afternoon as she was driving to have dinner with her fiancé. The drunk driver's decision impacted several families for the rest of their lives.

I once heard someone say, "If nothing changes, nothing changes." You, and only you, have the ability to make the choices that lead to changes, and consequently, to the opening of opportunities and doors. Your choices might be conscious or subconscious, depending on what lead up to them in your prior life experiences. A simple decision to complete an assignment at school or work by going beyond what might be expected has a direct impact on your career or school grades. Maybe the change related to that decision happens that same day, or maybe it doesn't happen until many years later; however, opening your eyes to "what might be" is an essential part of making the right choices today and every day.

When we are asked to complete something, many would not see that as an opportunity—some will, and complete it successfully. We make that choice to have the self-discipline to complete what was asked, and even exceed an expectation. We have the option to jump on it and get it done early. We can always keep learning how to see differently, ask ourselves the right questions, and better understand why some succeed while others do not. The more we practice the self-discipline to follow through, the more it becomes like driving the car. We just do it naturally.

What is that perfect job? How do you get to that next level? If you are already a CEO or other leader, what breakthrough will it take to increase revenue, profits, returns or create a new business, or even expand your markets through purchasing another business or a competitor? The answers to questions like this are in front of you, but you have to learn how to recognize the opportunity prior to discovering the answer. If you do nothing, of course nothing will happen. You get to make the choice on what to do and how to do it best.

You have choices to make about how you study and learn, how you spend your spare time, and how you invest in learning. You, no matter where you find yourself at this time in your life, have the same opportunity as the person next to you. It is what you see that others might not, that can make all the difference, as long as you develop the discipline to follow up on that vision.

Most of us are not Einstein or possess a genius IQ, but millions of people have started successful businesses, often from nothing more than a simple idea or passion. Let's take the example of Starbucks. Most people drank coffee every day, but did not see there was an enormous opportunity to build a culture around coffee. The opportunity was always there. It was alive all over Europe, although not as a mass-produced enterprise. Howard Schultz saw it when no one else did, or others who may have seen it failed to act. That vision and opportunity had been in front of everyone for years.

Jeff Bezos and the Amazon story again are the perfect examples of seeing an opportunity using technology changes to do something that was not possible only a few years before. But the stories are all the same. Somebody saw an opportunity that many people might see, then they acted on that opportunity, visualized it, thought it through, and applied the life lessons and education they had to make this passion possible. You can do the same thing.

There are today and will be every day from now to eternity, new opportunities in front of every person. If they are not looking for them, or not thinking of what is out there, especially in their subconscious minds, those opportunities will be missed.

While not trying to quote the exact words and who spoke them, there is a short story about the potential marketing demand for personal computers from the late 1970s. The market study predicted the global market to include just ten personal computers to be needed. Today, millions of personal computers are purchased annually. Bill Gates not only had a vision about this, but more importantly, he had the knowledge that personal computers could be small, inexpensive, and have a huge demand. The leading manufacturer of computers at that time only knew what the reality was at that time: that computers took up a lot of space, consumed a lot of power, and cost a lot of money. They believed that there would only be a market for computers in the business world. Today, almost everyone knows the Microsoft story, and more importantly, that it is still growing and evolving.

How do we see these opportunities? Are others seeing them? Consider the U.S. Patent Office. As recently as 2005, they had 7,000 employees; in 2016, that number has grown to over 12,000! The office issues over 330,000 new patents every year. The human mind's ability to envision innovation and change is limitless! We can choose to look for ideas, or we can choose to simply close our minds and do nothing. It is our choice.

Life with no laughter can hinder your ability to see opportunities. Enjoy the pleasures of life! Doing so leads to a better ability to see what might be in front of you already. Life is not always easy. For most people, success and building businesses is not all fun and games, to say the least. However, creating something from nothing, succeeding in your position, or excelling at school brings an enormous level of satisfaction and drives people from all walks of life to do even more. The opposite is also true. If there is a lack of initiative and a person does not make the effort required, or the choices to do more, life will continue to have its challenges. As in all of life, it is your choice to be happy, enjoy life, accept challenges as opportunities and make the best out of all situations.

CHAPTER 8

THE TALENT WAS ALWAYS THERE

SEATTLE IS THE birthplace and home to many global companies already mentioned such as Microsoft, Boeing, Amazon, Expedia, Starbucks, and Costco. It was also home to a basketball team called the Seattle Supersonics, or Sonics for short. In the middle of the 1977-78 season, they were ranked last in the entire NBA. Their management fired the coach and replaced him with one of the players, Lenny Wilkens. Lenny was still playing on the team, so he became a player/coach, which was a unique position.

Lenny Wilkens was also unique in that he had a vision. He could see an opportunity missed by the recently fired manager. Under his leadership, the team soon started winning a few games, but still, nobody considered them as a contender that season. After all, they were in last place halfway through the season. Going on to win a few more games, they started slowly creeping up from the bottom. They wound up squeaking into the playoffs, but the odds of getting past the first round were bleak.

Coach Wilkens did something which was highly criticized at the time. He drafted an unknown player from an obscure small college called Illinois Wesleyan. The new player's name was Jack Sikma. The fans booed the decision. The head office did not like the decision, and even Jack Sikma told Coach Wilkens he preferred to play for some other team. What was it Coach Wilkens could see that no one else could?

That season, they not only made the playoffs, but kept winning and made it to the championship round! While they lost the NBA title in the seventh and final game against the Washington Bullets, they had almost taken the championship. In that game, Jack Sikma scored 33 points. In just one season since they had been the worst team in basketball, they wound up number two in the world.

So, what did that rookie player/coach see in those players that brought them from the worst team of the season to a few baskets away from the championship?

Lenny Wilkens was not only making thousands of decisions an hour while playing, but he was also making decisions on larger strategy—the bigger picture, with a focus on the long-term. He did what was seemingly impossible by believing he was making the right choices (that were obviously not being made before the change in leadership). Keep in mind, Coach Wilkens was playing with the same team that had been in last place, with the same players. What was the difference? How could they complete what all thought impossible?

The following year, the team again made it to that seventh game of the NBA world championship. They went on to win that game. The Sonics were the NBA World Champions!

Again, what changed? The team consisted of mostly the same players when Wilkens took over, so it wasn't because an all-star joined the team. What was it? Did somebody forget to tell the players they could not win? Or did the coach, who was on the court with the team that first year when they almost won it all, explain his vision and the opportunity to the players? Did they all already believe they could win, and did the new coach convey this to the players, gain their support, communicate effectively, and start working together to overcome their obstacles and start winning? The obvious answer here is as follows: the talent was always there, it was simply not realized until someone else took over that had the ability to see the opportunity and help the whole team also share that vision—to believe in themselves.

Coach Wilkens could see something the management, the previous coach, and even the players just could not see. He then went on to convince management of his vision and successfully explained how he could make it work. He knew one of the problems preventing success was that the players had not shared this vision, and he had to convince them also. Coach Wilkens believed the players had the talent to be the best, and he went about sharing that vision, getting the players to see that they could win. More importantly, he got them to see that each player could add value and share what they thought needed to be done as teammates, not individual competitors. So then, was the problem that the players lacked vision of what they could be? I don't think so. I'm sure the team really wanted to be the best; they just could not see or visualize how to get there until Coach Wilkens opened their eyes. The ability and the skills were already there; it was the vision and opportunity Coach Wilkens shared that transformed them into champions.

After all, doesn't anyone in sports, whether amateur or professional, have an inherent desire to win and be the best that they can be? The choices this team now made turned them all into believers. They could finally see something they did not see until Lenny helped them see it. They could now execute the vision with the talents they already had and be the best in the NBA.

The decisions and choices made by the Sonics' leadership, while not successful at the beginning of the year, were drastically changed. The year-end results changed significantly as well as the incomes of players and owners. This story can relate to anyone in any situation, regardless if you are in school, running a business, starting a career, or a seasoned professional. You are constantly engaging in self-talk in your subconscious mind, and only you know what is being said. Coach Wilkens helped change the self-talk of the Sonics into positive talk. He helped them realize and believe that they could be successful.

You, and only you, make the choices you make. Believing in opportunity, and believing that opportunities are in front of you all the time, helps you make better decisions and look for what is in front of you yet often not visualized.

We all make wrong decisions at times in our lives—some are important, with immediate consequences, while the effects of others are not realized for years. Regardless of how they play out, all of our decisions have consequences, even if we decide to do nothing! The important thing to remember here is to not give up. If you are enduring the consequence of a poor decision, work hard simply work to recognize the error and not blame someone else for your problem. Make a correction or change of course and try again. Never give up. If you believe in what you are trying to do, and you can demonstrate it makes sense, keep trying. Remember, Colonel Sanders tried 1,000 times and failed before finally succeeding at age 66.

So many companies have people who can prove everything will not work. Do not be one of those people. Successful companies (and individuals) are those who are willing to try, not give up, are persistent, and have a vision for success. Experience, at any age, also plays a factor into the wisdom behind many decisions. Believe in yourself. Step out and think outside the box. Open your mind. Keep reading materials and taking classes that help you see what opportunities are in front of you and learn how your mind works. Be a part of the solutions and never join those who simply add to the negatives.

Every company wants great employees, and they want to be great employers. It can be easier for some people to see the negative and find fault. It is the leaders—those who see the opportunity disguised as a problem—who think through solutions and become partners in the positive changes needed. You can make that decision to be part of positive change, and you can start today.

One of the best-known prayers relating to making decisions was coined by the American theologian Reinhold Niebuhr. In its most common form, it states: "God, grant me the serenity to accept the things I cannot change, the courage to change the things I can, and wisdom to know the difference."

Think of that story of a downtrodden, last place basketball team in 1977. They had everything they needed, but the team and the coach lacked the vision to see how it could best work. Change was made and that same team, with the same players, excelled. This can happen in any business just as it did for the Seattle Supersonics. You can be that coach, or one of those players, and you can be the one to visualize what is needed if you believe it can be done.

CHAPTER 9

SELF-DISCIPLINE GETS THE SALE

NOW, LET'S GET back to the story of our business launch. Our company continued to grow rapidly, gaining market share, and expanding capacity. That growth, in a fairly stable market, meant some of the larger, legacy companies in the same industry were losing market share. Now we were becoming a dominant competitor with hundreds of employees. Understanding why one company keeps growing in the same market where several other companies are not growing is important. Just as shared in the previous chapter about a basketball team that went from last place to world champions, the lessons learned can be applied to any business, and any individual. The creation of a team, the fulfillment of a vision, and the ability to communicate what can be achieved to each employee are all part of this important equation.

We trained our employees on much more than just knowing our products and services. Most companies focus solely on that type of training. We went far beyond that by educating our employees to understand the customer's business, the customer's needs, and how our products and the services we provided could meet and exceed those needs. Several other companies could sell the same products we carried, but no competitor could match our service offering. We also trained staff on what the most efficient trends were in our customers' businesses, and how best to educate those customers in the ways they could improve operations and reduce costs. Our team would be considered more like consultants helping customers improve operations as opposed to simply trying to make sales.

The simplest denominator in our equation for business was that the customer desires to find ways to reduce costs and be more efficient. Our company sold mostly the same products as the competition. How could we add value and rise above the norm in a mature industry where nearly every company sold similar products? By continually training on the customer's business, far beyond just training on our products. We offered more value to that customer. We could educate our sales and service people to understand how to help customers spend less, while at the same time increasing productivity. Think about that a litter harder: we were training our staff how to educate the customer on ways they would spend less money with our company!

Every week we made a point to hold well-organized training meetings for service staff as well as sales staff. We would often bring in outside professionals to assist in training on a whole variety of subjects, including what was happening in our customers' worlds. Some of that training included how our staff could not just improve at their work-related activities, but how to better their own personal lives.

Balance in life is important. While in the early days, I was the only one available to organize the training, as it was my vision we were sharing and communicating to the staff. We knew we needed to expand this effort. Just as the story in the previous chapter about the Sonics, it is not the individual, but the team that wins. We were building a team that would go on and build other winning teams as we expanded, and we now had multiple locations in three states.

One of the most important aspects of success in all of life, if not the most important, is self-discipline. It is the trait you develop to follow through, to finish what you start, and to do what you say you will do. In the weekly training meetings, we would share some successful outcomes as they related to self-discipline and following a plan. Following the plan was not always easy, but resulted in significant success. The staff started referring to some of these examples as "Kim's wheel-jerk stories," as they were real stories. The reason why they coined "wheel-jerk" will become evident shortly.

The examples served as sometimes humorous proof why some succeed while others simply stay stagnant or fail. These simple short stories can be applied to anyone, in any situation or industry. They mostly pertain to following through and sticking with a plan, even when you are the only person who would ever know if you did not. By simply doing it, as statistics will prove, at some point, the endeavor or object becomes achievable. But on the other hand, if you do not try, you are *guaranteed* not to succeed. Results are predictable, based on logic, statistics, and experience. The people who practice self-discipline, in any walk of life, will succeed more than those who don't.

All through life, we see the same two sets of people: the ones who follow through, doing what they are asked and exceeding expectations; and those who fall short and do not make the effort. You make this choice. In your self-talk, start right now to remind yourself to follow through and to complete every task.

In every time-management course I ever attended, they categorized tasks as A, B or C, with A being the really big ones that take time. All of us tend to tackle the simple C tasks first to get them out of the way. We learned that instead, we should be putting the most effort into getting the A priority tasks done so they could be completed.

While still in college, I started my career. The boss made a statement in a sales meeting that I'll never forget: "On average it takes five to seven face-to-face calls on a prospect before you get an order. The average amount of calls made to one client by a typical sales rep is less than two."

Think about this: everyone reading this book has received an unsolicited call, which usually feels like an interruption. What the caller wants to talk about, or sell, is something we are either not interested in or already have. When I would visit a new prospective customer, they most likely already had the service we were trying to supply. In most cases, they also indicated they were happy and not interested in considering a change. Any excuse could be used to get me out of their office and stop me from taking up their time.

There were about 50 other representatives in the market at that time trying to sell the same thing—commercial tires and related service. So, if the statistic was correct, it would take time, patience, and self-discipline to eventually gain each customer's business. Of course, you also must have a product or service that you believe would be of value to that customer. It takes self-discipline to make the plans, and then even more to execute those plans, no matter how impossible they might seem.

Keep in mind that while the story here is about our start-up company, we eventually ended up growing massively, gaining dominant market share and enjoying the rewards of the hard work. But it all took time. Success is not easy and has to be built on the principles of self-discipline and planning. These principles can be applied to any company or individual willing to follow the steps and take the risks. Regardless of industry, success is mostly related to each individual doing their best, as well as the leadership having a genuine desire to grow themselves while growing others at the same time. Whether you are growing individually, or growing a department, company or agency, it is all the same. The leadership traits mirror the results in any application.

The statistics cited above were factual, taken from real data from a survey published in our industry by The Firestone Tire Company. While there were many statistics in that survey, the one that caught my attention the most was that a person needs to make five to seven calls on average before they can expect to gain business from a prospective customer.

The process of implementing the knowledge and self-discipline to plan and follow through with that plan will result in greater success across the board. Every industry has their own statistics similar to those used here. I charge you to learn them, believe them, and work to maximize your results. Developing habits that contribute to consistent practices enables greater self-discipline to be implemented. In other words, make a plan, follow the plan, and when it seems hopeless, do not give up.

The habits I developed early in my professional career were simple and basic. Every time I called a customer, either current or prospective, I would write down notes and what follow-up was needed, as well as what the next step was. I developed a habit of not touching the car keys to leave that customer's location until I completed this simple task. It took less than a minute. I would write down when the next call should be, often in just a month or two months. Sometimes a simple, quick follow-up thank you note was needed or an answer to a question. This is a step often neglected by sales reps.

I also quickly learned the importance of listening to the customers and finding their underlying needs. Most people will inadvertently disclose additional information as they are talking. Remember, there are opportunities in front of us every single day that are up to us to see and capitalize on. This is no different. You have the opportunity to think through what a customer needs and see the potential for how you might be a perfect solution for satisfying those needs. Consider the next short story and the outcomes that were drastically different than anyone could have expected. At the very least, you'll get a good laugh out of it!

I stopped and made a sales call at a large tanker company that recycled oil in the industrial area south of Seattle. It was the first call I had made to this firm. The site was a less than stellar facility. In fact, it was shabby, to say the least, but they had a lot of trucks and bought a lot of tires. I made my way into the shop where they work on the trucks and asked who was overseeing the purchase of truck tires. I was directed to a small office and was met by a gruff, foul-mouthed individual named Bob. He quickly made it clear that he hated salespeople, especially tire salespeople. He then physically pushed me towards the exit while bellowing loud enough for all to hear him. It was very clear he never wanted to see me again, and that returning could actually prove to be dangerous.

I went back to my vehicle, and before starting the car, I did what I always did. I logged the information and planned my next visit. But instead of planning the next call in a month or so, I penciled it in for six months later. Granted, I did make sure I was a safe distance from the raving maniac! I recorded the person's name and a few details of the call, but I knew I would not forget the circumstances.

A lot can change in six months, and I hoped it would before the scheduled next call on this maniac. Our company had grown enough to successfully land the account for tires and services to the United Parcel Service facility in South Seattle, with some 7,000 vehicles running tires. They were located a few blocks from the oil recycling firm. United Parcel Service had clean facilities, exceptional management, and was part of the world's largest transportation services company. I had just completed a call with them and was about to turn the vehicle to the right and head back to the main store where my office was located. I was ready to call it a day, and a good day at that. As I glanced at my schedule before turning the car, I was alarmed to see that I had scheduled a call at the oil recycling firm just down the street! It was about 3:30 PM, and it had been a long day. On top of that, it was summertime, and there was still daylight to enjoy. It would have been so easy to let my self-talk convince me that a call at that company would be a complete waste of time and to skip it.

But self-discipline, belief in the statistics, good habits, and experience prevailed. I jerked the steering wheel to the left, and in a few blocks turned into the shop area at the oil recycling company. I walked in the shop and asked the first person I saw where I could find Bob. The reply almost knocked me right off my feet!

"Bob was fired last week. Jim took over his position, and he is in the little office over there. Feel free to walk right in." What an encouraging call so far. At least my fear of physical abuse and danger was evaporating. I walked over and knocked on the door.

"Come on in!" Jim said cheerily.

I introduced myself and why I was there.

"I am so glad you decided to stop by, Kim. We have had a terrible tire supplier for far too many years. I want to fire them. Tell me what you can do, and when you can start!" Jim said, matter-of-factly.

If I would have listened to all my internal self-talk excuses that day, I would have missed the opportunity to land a new account. Instead, I beat the statistical odds (as this was only the second call) and landed the customer! We went on to have a successful business relationship for many years. In this case, had I not practiced the self-discipline, to turn the wheel, go the opposite direction and make the effort, nobody would ever know. As J.K. Rowling says, "Anything is possible, if you've got the nerve."

Here's another wheel-jerk story that can be applied to anyone. It does not matter if you are a salesperson, an attorney building a client base, a rainmaker partner for a CPA firm, or selling jet aircraft, the important element is simply having a plan, then making the choice to take the next step.

There was a very large contract school bus company in Seattle, a national firm operating throughout the U.S. They operated thousands of buses, and all buses use tires. The shop manager, who was also in charge of purchasing tires, was named Howard. He sat at a small metal desk, inside a small, nondescript office with barely enough room for anyone else to sit when talking with him. Rarely would he even make eye contact, as he was always consumed in the endless mass of maintenance and regulatory paperwork. Don't get me wrong; he was a great person. Even though he was always incredibly busy, he wasn't rude.

On my first call to the firm, he explained that all decisions on tires are made at their corporate office in Los Angeles. I thanked him for taking the time and asked for the name and address of the decision-maker in L.A. Keep in mind, when somebody tells you something, it is not always the truth. When I got back in the car, I simply wrote myself a note to send a letter to Mr. Smith in L.A. the next time I was in the office. Remember, computers and email didn't exist yet, so snail mail was our only option. The next day I wrote and mailed the letter, then took a copy of it to Howard and left it with him.

A month passed with no response, so I again made a visit to see Howard and asked if he had talked with Mr. Smith at corporate regarding the letter. Howard quickly mumbled "nope, not yet," as he kept shuffling, signing, and moving papers from the endless piles. As usual, he was too busy to make eye contact, and I simply thanked him and left. I made myself a note to call Mr. Smith in L.A. the next day and planned another personal visit with Howard in a month.

I got Mr. Smith on the phone that week, telling him that I would send another quote and letter as well as an explanation of the services and why they should consider making a change. You can see the trend here. I made sure to always be polite, follow up, and never give up. This cycle was repeated over the course of about nine months, and still, nothing changed. Instead of the five to seven call average, by this time there had been around fifteen contacts made with Howard in person and Mr. Smith via letters and phone.

Then one day out of the blue, Howard called my office and left a message.

"I need Kim to get over to my office as soon as he can," he conveyed to our dispatcher.

I had a two-way radio in the car (before cell phones, this was the way to go for business calls), and the dispatcher radioed me.

"Howard from Laidlaw called, and he wants to see you right away."

I headed directly to Howard's office. He was brief, as usual, but this time he handed me the copy of the quote I had sent to Mr. Smith in L.A. a few weeks earlier. He said they wanted to change suppliers, and asked me when we could start. This was a huge account. They operated thousands of buses, each with six tires. It was a major win for our company! We started doing business with them the following month.

But why is this seemingly boring story of any interest? Who cares that it took nine months and multiple calls to get a new account? Is there a point to telling this story?

On a follow-up visit a few months after we started working together, I asked Howard, "What was it that made you change vendors and do business with us?" For the first time that I can ever remember, he stopped handling papers, leaned back in his chair, looked me in the eye and said, "I am glad you asked that question, Kim." He then opened his top drawer and pulled out a stack of cards. They were business cards from all the tire salespeople who had called on him over the years. It was a large stack, well over 50 from several competing companies, as well as a few from the same company I was working for at that time.

Chuckling a bit, he said, "These are all the people I told the same thing I told you: all buying decisions are made in L.A. Kim, not a single one of them ever followed up. You know, Mr. Smith finally called me and said, 'If you do not change tire companies so this guy will stop sending me quotes and calling, I am going to fire you,'" he chuckled. "Both Mr. Smith and I figured it would be hard to find anyone else who would follow up and take care of details and service as you would, so we agreed to change vendors to work with you."

We ended up becoming friends, and even went fishing together in Alaska. Howard was a great person and friend. What a great lesson to beat the statistical odds. This one was maybe fifteen calls and included several steps over nine months, but we secured a great customer! All the other sales-people simply gave up. They did not follow through. They demonstrated no self-discipline and provided a poor effort. They gave up after the first or second call when Howard told them decisions were made in L.A. As it turns out, Howard made all the decisions, not Mr. Smith. He simply knew how best to blow off a salesperson.

Persistence pays off, and it was really not that much more work. It was not a waste of time, and it goes to show what can happen when you make the effort that others fail to do. Just do what you really know needs to be done, and when it needs to be done. You and your company will all benefit. Had I not developed the habits and been trained on follow up and self-discipline, there would be hundreds of good accounts that would most likely have never done business with us. Train your staff accordingly, and communicate that vision starting today. There is no better time than today!

CHAPTER 10

THINK OUTSIDE THE BOX

A PERFECT EXAMPLE of what happens when you think outside the box took place with a sizeable family-owned transportation company in Seattle. The owner and his son-in-law were very hands-on, hardworking people who operated in a small, old building in a tough part of the industrial area. The two of them ran the whole operation and shared a tiny, cramped office. Don, the owner, gave salespeople little of his time and was very good at getting them out the door. When I would make a call, he would either be loading a truck and tell me he didn't have time to talk, or he'd be at his messy desk, saying he was too busy and there was nothing he needed. Two things were at play here. First, I really did believe I could save him a lot of money. Second, my belief in the statistic that it takes an average of five to seven sales calls worked well with my determination and self-discipline. There was one additional observation here: they ran beautiful equipment. All of their trucks were Peterbilt, the top of the line brand. They were always clean and appeared well-maintained.

This was during my first year of a new career, and before we had started our own business. I called on Don's company every month for an entire year to no avail. Every time I would get brushed off, I'd just write it down in my book and schedule another time to call the following month. Don was a real blue-collar guy; he was hardworking, what I would call a "salt of the earth" type of person. It would be next to impossible for me to know that he was worth $50 million at that time. The office was in an old gas station. Both Don and his son-in-law worked outside, loading and unloading the trailers, pallets, and freight.

All I wanted them to do was simply try Michelin tires and let me show them what could be achieved. I knew if I could just get them to try those tires, I could provide significant savings in tire costs and fuel consumption, thus improving their bottom line. But they were always busy, giving me just a short amount of time and turning me down. At least they were always polite, although I suppose I never gave them a reason to be rude. I think they were actually starting to enjoy, or at least respect my tireless efforts.

December rolled around, and I decided to try something I had never tried before. Having learned a month earlier from his son-in-law what Don enjoyed as a good drink, I walked in as usual. As expected, Don did not even look up when I said "Hello." He just replied with his predictable, "Hi, kid." I placed an expensive bottle of Scotch on the desk, saying, "I just wanted you to know that there are no hard feelings that you never did any business with me this year. I hope you have a Merry Christmas." With that, I simply turned around and left. I could tell, though, that he had a huge smile on his face as he said, "Thank you" as I walked out the door.

Even at my young age, I was simply thinking outside the box. The typical, accepted ways of calling on this customer provided no results. The holidays provided a small opportunity to differentiate myself from the other 50 salespeople selling tires in the area. It was worth a try.

In early January, Don called me out of the blue and said, "Get me 100 of those tires you have been trying to sell me. I don't care when they get here, just get me an invoice dated in December, and deliver the tires when you have them." That order preceded many years of a great relationship and thousands of tires.

Some years later, there was a large international chemical company I was calling on, and I noticed they used many of Don's trucks for their shipping. I stopped by Don's office and asked if he knew anyone there that he could connect me with as they also operated a lot of their own trucks. Don, uncharacteristically, stopped what he was doing, leaned back in his chair and smiled. He went on to explain that 30 years earlier, two young guys were renting a small space from him. They struggled to pay rent, so they would give Don company stock as they were starting their fledgling enterprise. Over the years, that company grew exponentially and was acquired by a Fortune 500 firm. Don then said, "Today, I own 33,000 shares of that stock!"

I went home and looked up the share price that night, and the stock was valued well over $50 million… and that was in the 1970s. Don reminds me a bit of Warren Buffet, one of the world's wealthiest people—worth well over $50 Billion—who still lives in the small, simple home he purchased in 1958 for $31,500. Don also had an appreciation for young people, like me, who demonstrated persistence, self-discipline and made the effort. He made the introduction.

There is a lot of information packed into this story. Most salespeople would make a call or two and give up. After all, it was a small, dingy old office. The company consisted of just a couple guys doing lots of hands-on work. There were only a few trucks there at a time. Why keep trying? The owner constantly blew you off, not giving you the time of day. But it turned out they owned a large fleet of exceptionally well-maintained trucks and trailers. When John and I started our company some years later, Don was one of our first customers.

Things are not always what you see. Opportunity is in front of us all, but not all see it, and not many have the self-discipline to keep trying to maximize it. Seizing opportunity requires out of the box thinking and creativity.

Following is a simple illustration of "out-of-the-box" thinking. See if you can figure out how to solve it!

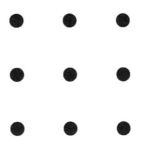

Look at the nine dots evenly spaced. Attempt to connect the nine dots using only four straight lines WITHOUT lifting your pen or pencil, and without retracing over any lines.

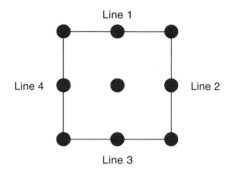

Perhaps your first attempt looked something like this, missing the middle dot.

So, you try again. Here is another example that still misses the mark (or the dot!).

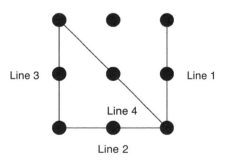

Then the lightbulb comes on, and you give it a third try. The Solution.

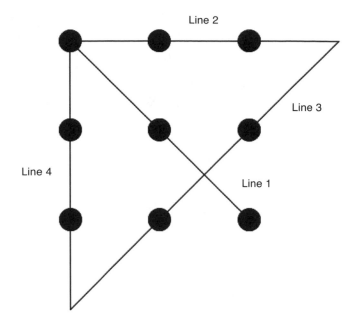

You see, only by going "outside" the box can we connect all nine dots. There was no instruction that said you had to stay "inside" the box. There are unlimited opportunities if you can develop the ability to see alternative ways to solve a problem, which opens your mind to see things differently.

Again, early in my career, before we started our own company, Alaska was part of my territory. At the time, the Alyeska Pipeline was in full construction mode. Both Anchorage and Fairbanks were incredibly busy; hundreds of large contractors had moved in, and things were booming. When planning any trip, I made a habit of always booking the flights in the late evening to not waste the daytime flying as many of my competitors did. I wanted to be able to spend as much time in front of customers as possible. Others missed out on a lot of opportunities because they chose to travel in the middle of any trip, I made a habit of always booking the flights in the late evening to not waste the daytime flying as many of my competitors did. I wanted to be able to spend as much time in front of customers as possible. Others missed out on a lot of opportunities because they chose to travel in the middle of the day. Just this action alone is a form of thinking outside the box combined with the common sense of using the daytime to your advantage. I could make many more calls on a trip than my competition.

All of us, in any vocation, have the same amount of time every day to get things done. When the day is done, it is gone forever. Personally, I always felt a high level of personal satisfaction by planning and then doing what I planned by the end of the day. Waking up each day knowing I had a plan helped me get up with more vigor and execute what I had planned to do.

On this particular trip, I landed late the night before in Anchorage, where during the summer, the sun would rise about 3 AM. My plan had me making 13 calls in that one day before an evening flight to Fairbanks. There was a nice restaurant at the airport in Anchorage, so I included in my schedule a nice steak dinner with a glass of red wine before my late flight.

It must have been about 5 PM, and the day was still sunny and warm. I had already finished several meetings and made the most of my planned calls. It was a tiring day, non-stop but productive, and I had received several orders. It was now time to relax, as I had exceeded my goals. The thought of that relaxing dinner and glass of wine at the airport had been in the back of my mind, subconsciously distracting me from the tasks at hand.

After what I thought was my last call, I hopped back into the rental car and pulled out the schedule. Much to my dismay, there was one more call to make. It was a new and used truck distributor. They didn't do much business with companies like mine, but they did provide leads to other opportunities, as well as knowledge of who was buying what and what contracts might have been signed recently. This particular truck dealer was the largest in Alaska, and it could be a great contact to have. Reluctantly, I jerked the steering wheel in their direction and headed over to Alaska Sales and Service, putting my steak dinner and red wine on hold.

I arrived, parked, and made my way into the office area. The door was wide open, but nobody seemed to be in the office. It looked like everyone had already gone home for the day. Everything in me wanted to bolt to the airport! But the knowledge that you should never give up and always make that extra effort ingrained in my subconscious kicked in. I called out, "Is anyone here?"

A voice boomed from up a stairwell, surprising me. "Come on up!"

Up the stairs I went and was greeted by the friendly face of a man sitting at a large desk. It was the Sales Manager, Don Howell. Holding out his hand, he introduced himself, "Hey there! The name's Don Howell. What brings you in?" I told Don my company had offices in Seattle. Almost all of his new trucks were shipped through Seattle, so I let him know how I could be of service to him or his customers.

He was a great guy; easy to talk to. We chatted about what companies were putting together contracts. I also found out who had been awarded recent contracts for work and who was buying equipment and trucks. Also, I learned who was not paying bills (always important), and who else I should be calling on in the area. I gained a wealth of information in that one visit alone. At the end of our meeting, we exchanged cards, and Don said he would remember and use me if they ever needed anything. It was a good call, as this was not intended to get an order from them, but instead to network and lay the groundwork for a future opportunity.

As I walked back to the car, I was still dreaming of my solo dinner date at the airport diner, but I was also satisfied that I followed through with my plan for a day that started at 6 AM and ended after 6 PM. My flight was at 9 PM, which would put me in Fairbanks late in the evening. I would do the same thing the next day. Even though it would be almost midnight before I landed in Fairbanks, the sun would still be up. Imagine that: even at midnight in June, you can drive with no headlights on!

About a year later, I received a call from the State of Alaska Highway Department. It was a man named Bill, and he explained that they had 100 large new dump trucks. They were going to have snowplows added to the front of these trucks for winter snow removal work and had just discovered the front tire capacity was not correct. They needed larger tires and wheels, but they also needed to keep the diameter and tire height equal, as all the snowplows and engineering were designed around the current height of the front end. The trucks would be coming through Seattle, then shipped to several different Alaska ports. Bill asked, "Is there a solution you can help us with in Seattle before they are shipped?" The trucks would be delivered by ship because so many Alaskan cities are only accessible by water. The work really needed to be done in Seattle, and it needed to be done very soon.

Thankfully, I knew of a solution and went right to work. I presented him with a new low profile, larger capacity tire and wheel that would work perfectly. The tire would meet the load demands and match the height. Bill was thrilled and ended up giving me a purchase order for 200 new tires and wheels on the spot. He mentioned he would be in Seattle in a few months and wanted to get together.

When Bill came to Seattle, he called me, as promised. We met in a hotel bar downtown. We had a great conversation, and I remember thinking to myself, "What a great guy he is. You know, the kind you would expect from Alaska. Just good people." Bill eventually explained how they had discovered the error on the front tires for the snowplows, and that nobody was able to come up with a solution... that is, until he called me. I asked him how he got my name and number, still unsure of how the connection was made.

"Well, we bought the trucks from Don Howell at Alaska Sales and Service, the truck dealer in Anchorage. I explained the issue to Don, and he handed me your card. He said, 'Call this guy in Seattle. He can figure out anything!'"

The deal with Bill and the State of Alaska was a very large sale, generating revenue of over $200,000. Even better, our company continued to do business with the State for many years. When we started our own company, we continued this relationship and opened stores in Alaska as we grew.

The story here is again about thinking outside the box; finding a solution few others at that time could have figured out. It all came about because of self-discipline, tireless effort, good record keeping, and a little planning. Had I failed to do any of these four steps, many millions of dollars in revenue would not have been made, and nobody would ever know.

Continuing to develop the ability to think outside the box to find solutions others missed was a trait that earned us the respect of many customers. These are habits that you can expand on in any business. My success with this customer was all because I had the self-discipline to make sure I followed through with the things I told myself I would.

Positive self-talk is available to every one of us at all times. Use it to reinforce doing what you know "should" be done, even when the outcome might not be immediate. I simply made the choice I knew was right while making calls in Anchorage that day. While everything inside me told me it was probably a waste of time, that the steak and glass of wine at the airport were way more appealing, I stuck to the plan. Nobody would have known if I had not made that last call. Nearly all of the other salespeople I know or worked with would have said something like, "Why waste your time on calls like that?" They would make excuses to not make the effort. Just think about what their self-talk sounded like! They likely convinced themselves through negative thinking that it wasn't worth it. Again, in any vocation, we see these same naysayers while we also see those who rise above average and excel.

You make the choice for yourself every moment of every day. Had I not made that last tough decision to follow through, nothing would have happened. Once again, this is proof of the statement shared previously, "If you do nothing, the results will equal what you do."

Statistics do not lie. While we do not know every outcome in advance, we do know that if you do nothing, you can expect nothing. While my competitors and other salespeople were sitting in the bars, enjoying happy hour and flying in the middle of the day, I was out making calls. The difference between my success and their failure was made up of small decisions leading up to an incredible outcome. I didn't just get lucky. I made things happen, and that same choice is one you can make! The little extra efforts you make will pay off—sometimes much later in life, but the impact is made at the moment of decision. Doing what you know should be done, or can be done, builds your character, and helps you create more positive self-talk.

Note: I did enjoy the bars when my work was done, especially listening to the stories of others that made it even more clear they would not ever succeed.

All of us have the same amount of time every day, and your success hinges on how you invest it.

Here is a little poem I often used in sales meetings while training our employees. I discovered it when I was first starting out and have found it to be as applicable today as it was back then.

The Salesman written by James Cahill

And in those days, behold, there came through the gates of the city a salesman from afar off, and it came to pass as the day went by, he sold plenty.

And in that city were they that were the order takers and they spent their day in adding to the alibi sheets. Mightily were they astonished.

They said one to the other, "What the hell; how doth he getteth away with it?"

And it came to pass that many were gathered in the back office and a soothsayer came among them. And he was one wise guy.

And they spoke and questioned him saying, "How is it that this stranger accomplished the impossible?"

Whereupon the soothsayer made answer,

"He of whom you speak is one hustler. He ariseth very early in the morning and goeth forth full of pep. He complaineth not, neither doth he know despair. He is arrayed in purple and fine linen, while ye go forth with pants unpressed.

"While ye gather here and say one to the other, 'Verily this is a terrible day to work,' he is already abroad. And when the eleventh hour cometh, he needeth no alibis. He knoweth his line and they that would stave him off, they give him orders. Men say unto him 'nay' when he cometh, yet when he goeth forth he hath their names on the line that is dotted."

He taketh with him the two angles "inspiration" and "perspiration" and worketh to beat hell.

Verily I say unto you, go and do likewise.

Every day, no matter your vocation, you have a choice of how you spend your day. It is easy to find fault, complain, make excuses and accomplish very little. Or, you can choose to think outside the box, be creative, and find new ways to do what others do not think can be done. Study how your subconscious really works. Make your self-talk positive. It is amazing how much better you will feel. And, when you follow through on your plans, you will join the elite few who become known as the go-to people in your vocation.

CHAPTER 11

THE GOOD KIND OF TALKING TO YOURSELF

THE 50,000-PLUS WORDS we speak to ourselves every day means there is seldom a time during the day that we do not have an opportunity to improve ourselves through positive thinking. It is rare that you don't have a thought racing through your head during waking hours, either consciously or subconsciously. Think about it: when you are reading something, you are thinking about what you're reading. You likely have an immediate reaction to the things you're reading. The same goes for when you are listening to a podcast or to someone speaking, when you are driving… you name it. Daydreaming is also part of these conversations. The movies and television shows illustrate self-talk often by letting the audience know what the actor is thinking while the other actors do not hear those thoughts.

Your daily inner monologue is referred to as self-talk. Additionally, the majority of what you are saying to yourself happens without conscious thought, and you have no control to stop it. For example, if someone is talking to you and says something in jest like, "I like your shirt; I remember when that used to be in style," your subconscious will have an immediate reaction that you cannot stop. You might have negative thoughts related to that comment racing at a hundred miles an hour, but you laugh anyway. This is a subconscious reaction. Then, anytime you see that shirt in your closet, you will be more apt to think about that comment and that person in some negative way (or question your choice in fashion). Of course, this is a *negative* subconscious reaction, but the same thing applies if you receive a compliment about something you wear. Every time you wear that piece of clothing, you'll likely think about that person and feel good about wearing it again.

Most of us know very little about the subconscious. We all receive thousands of inputs, learning a wide range of lessons during our lives, and develop beliefs based on this acquired knowledge. We can be biased without conscious knowledge. Our opinions might be wrong, but they are ingrained in the brain until we learn something new that changes how we think.

Your subconscious is a powerful part of your life, and the more it is understood, the more it will benefit you. Realizing how it works and why will better prepare you to "see" those opportunities right in front of you. Your subconscious is part of your psyche; in fact, you say the many thousands of words a day to yourself as a result of what is contained in your brain. Every day you are looking at opportunities, signals, or warnings, and not really seeing them or recognizing how they could be of value. Unless you better understand how your subconscious works, all opportunities can be missed. Developing a positive outlook, knowing there is opportunity all around you, opens your eyes and brain to different things.

Here's a simple example: before you purchase a car, you might have seen, but never really *noticed* a specific car brand. But once you identify that is the car you want, you will then see them everywhere. They were already there, but you did not notice. Driving on a city street focused on getting home, you may not notice the reverse lights on a car leaving a parking space two blocks ahead. But, if you have your eyes tuned to finding a parking spot, you will immediately see those reverse lights as an opportunity, simply because you were looking for it. The subconscious mind helps us find what we choose to seek.

Here are some comments from a short piece written by Jim Jensen for a website called Get Motivated[5]:

What we say to others is not nearly as important as what we say to ourselves. All day, every day, our minds are flooded with thoughts that direct us to leading the lives that we live.

What we tell ourselves determines our successes… and our failures.

If you want to make an improvement in any aspect of your life, it's essential to always start by changing your self-talk if you want to succeed.

How? Well, when there's a will, there's a way.

---

5 "The Importance of Optimism: How to Think Positive Thoughts." *Inspiyr. com*, 13 May 2015, inspiyr.com/think-positive-thoughts/

We talk to ourselves at the rate of 150-300 words a minute, or nearly 50,000 thoughts a day.

While you are reading these words, you are having a simultaneous dialog about what you think of this writing while also being distracted by the most important items on today's 'to do list,' as well as other pressing matters.

The internal thinking, or self-talk, occurs through the conscious area of our minds. What most people are unaware of is our self-talk becomes instructions to our subconscious whose duty is to carry out 'orders' given to it by the conscious area of our minds. The subconscious is our own personal servo-mechanism that works on our behalf 24 hours a day, 7 days a week."

In the same vein, I heard a study shared on the radio that applies to how you might think about your subconscious. The story can also serve you concerning what self-discipline can do to improve your outlook on life. Combined with learning to understand both open your eyes to opportunity.

The study said of those who make their bed every day, 62% of them have a more positive attitude and enjoy their work (and life in general). Of those who do not make their beds, 72% are not happy in their workplaces or lives.

Think about your attitude; how you think about work and life. Aside from the making your bed example above, think of all the little (or big) things in your life that need to get done, but you ignore or do not do, as a result of your subconscious. When you make the conscious decision to start doing some of these tasks, your attitude will begin to shift. You will likely start to feel better about yourself, and this feeling carries over to life, work, and relationships.

If you practice waking up with the mindset that you're going to accomplish things today, and then follow through with your intentions, you change yourself as you change your attitude. Most of this change starts with the subconscious at work, for good. Choose not to allow distractions. Avoid others trying to pull you away from your goals. It is too easy to choose to take a short cut or only do part of what needs to be done.

As our business grew and we had hundreds of employees, we would train managers on time management and getting done what we all knew was needed. I believe anyone can get things done, but we find that plenty of people fail the test. The choice is up to each individual.

Let's consider how you feel about working in the first place. Consider *why* you even work. What is it that you want to accomplish? In your mind and subconscious, if you view work as your choice—as a way to better yourself and family—and vow that you will make the best out of it, then you will succeed. If you hate work and spend all your time wishing you didn't have to do it, then you will likely stay that way and not succeed.

Consider a short comment written by business advisor and author, Price Pritchett many years ago when referring to people being frustrated in the workplace:

"We work because we choose to; because we desire some standard of living that affords us a home, car, or social status. Do not take it out (frustrations) on the workplace because you choose to work."

All of us know and see the many who choose not to work and live on the streets instead. There were choices made by many of those less fortunate that resulted in their being homeless. The homeless form their own communities, reinforce their own self-talk and logic (or lack of) that resulted in their situations. Most of the time, it was not their choice to be homeless, and there is no intention in this book to explain that issue. It is that their choices in other aspects of their lives led them there.

Homelessness is a serious problem in many communities and has yet to be solved or totally understood, just as there are many people dependent on drugs, alcohol, and more. In our business, we often dealt with rehabilitation and recovery efforts to help those who fell victim to these diseases. The point is, there were many decisions that had they been made differently, might have resulted in a different situation.

You make the choice to work, have a job, or get an education, and whatever it is, make the best of it, for yourself and your health, as well as the well-being of those you work with or associate with.

Never stop learning, no matter what your age might be. When I started my first business, I had not yet completed my undergraduate education and was still going to night school. I did go on over the years to earn a Master of Business Administration. However, at the time we started the business, I had not even completed an Associate of Arts degree! Early in our business, I always felt like I was missing something, especially as it kept growing. Decisions involved more strategic planning, and the numbers were much bigger, as were the risks. I knew there were better tools that could be applied when making decisions on expansion and growth or entering new markets, and I sought them out.

One day, years after we had started, one of my college business professors, and subsequent friend from the school visited our corporate offices. By this time, our company had 300-plus employees, 13 locations, and a new corporate office we had developed and built with warehousing and one of the manufacturing facilities. The professor had recently retired, and we had kept in touch ever since I took his classes. We met for lunch, and after we had finished our food and spent some time catching up, he made a comment that would open my eyes to a possibility I thought was long gone.

"You know, Kim, you were the most successful student I ever had," he said, looking me dead in the eyes.

"Jim, while that is certainly a high compliment coming from you, I regret never completing my undergraduate degree. I realize now that I should really have a master's degree as our business keeps growing," I replied.

"Well, you still can. Just walk into the City University office and slap your credit card down. Just get started!" he said, almost casually.

My self-talk, most likely fueled by my subconscious, sounded a lot like thoughts gravitating towards my desire for a higher education. We all have these thoughts of things we *think we should do*. However, some people are much better at moving forward with those thoughts than others. I had always wanted to complete my undergraduate studies and possibly earn a Master's degree. It was one of those things that always sat in the back of my mind, but it was mostly in my subconscious.

I had developed the habit of self-discipline over the years, and it helped me believe that anything was possible, at any age, if you just apply yourself.

So, I walked into City University that same afternoon and enrolled. A few days later, after obtaining and providing the transcripts they needed related to my high school courses and Associate degree, a counselor laid out an evening school plan. Off I went again to night school. Since I travelled a lot to our company locations, especially the more remote areas of Alaska, I had plenty of time on flights to study and read. This happened at the ripe, young age of 45. It took a bit of time to get into the swing of things and iron out my study habits. I had to work a little harder than the average student to find the times that worked best for study while balancing both family and work. Thankfully, my travel gave me some time to study and use the internet for the assignments during the later evenings.

I kept studying and chipping away at school, completing my undergraduate work at City University. Then, I got accepted into the University of Washington Foster School of Business for the two-year MBA program. We had started an additional new business by then that we called JIT Inc. The letters stood for Just In Time. We launched this venture with Paccar Inc., one of the world's leading manufacturers of large trucks. We had been planning on taking this company global, but more on that later.

The timing of the MBA program coincided with our decision to launch JIT Inc. internationally. We had planned to open facilities in Australia, Europe, Mexico, and Canada. The whole process—completion of the undergraduate, then completing my graduate degree late in life—all started as a result of that visit by my old business professor.

This is just another example of the fact that if you put your mind to something and practice the self-discipline to follow through, anything is possible. It doesn't matter how old you are or what circumstances you find yourself in. In my self-talk, I always kept thinking I needed and *should* get a higher education. When the opportunity was made clear to me, I knew what I wanted to do, so I made it happen.

At the time, we were running two large corporations with hundreds of employees, multiple locations in three states, and looking to expand internationally. While we were doing well and growing, we also knew we needed more depth in strategic planning, especially entering international markets with different regulations and unknown risks.

In the company, we would continuously send our people out or host classes for employees in many different venues. These included classes on time management, organizational skills, goal-setting (and attainment), and similar subjects.

Every day is a learning opportunity if you are looking to improve. Earlier in this chapter, I included part of a comment from Price Pritchett. He published several books that we used as part of our trainings. Most are short, one-hour reads that we would go through page by page, using examples, and having the employees take their own copy home. Sometimes we would do these short sessions at 7 AM on a Saturday. Most grumbled about the time and the day, but after they had invested that small sacrifice, nearly all the employees commented on how much they appreciated the education. Price Pritchett books are not all business-related; they address your life, how you live it now, and how you can improve. They also illustrate different ways to look at work as your choice and make the best of it.

The next time you think you or your company has a problem, try to think of what opportunity might be hiding in that problem. How did the problem develop? What is the cause? What solution might correct it and make you or your company better than before? Life throws many obstacles, twists, and pain into our lives from time to time. Learn to tell yourself you can make it through, and that you will be stronger for doing it.

The easy way out for many is to blame someone or something else. They will say that whatever happened was not their fault and refuse to accept the fate associated with it. Teach yourself to never fall into that trap. Forget who or what was at fault (if it really wasn't you) and think through the solution. Look for the opportunity and step outside that box. Ask others whom you respect as positive influences for advice, and separate yourself from the naysayers. Notice that you are talking to yourself right now as you read this. Be the person who sees opportunity in this writing; something positive. There will always be those who can only see the negative, and you have the choice to do the opposite.

CHAPTER 12

HOW YOU TREAT PEOPLE MATTERS

IT IS IMPORTANT to build your own "brand" as well as your team, regardless of whether you are working for somebody else's company or it is your own. Work to develop the relationships with both those above you and below. So many people pay little attention to those in lower positions as they start to move up, especially if they are recruited or hired to take over a top job. Mind the arrogance in words you might use as well as your body language, as they are evident to *everyone* around you. Even in meetings or one-on-one conversations, talking about other staff with any air of indignation will eventually hurt your career. Remember how we talked about the way that negative comments stick with you and influence the way you speak to yourself? Everything you say with your words or your body language has the opportunity to influence the way others feel about and talk to themselves about you. Make sure you are building up those above you, below you and next to you with empathy and sincerity.

I have worked with many people who have stabbed others in the back and talked down to the people around them and thought they were getting away with it. In my mind, they're not fooling anyone, and I know they rarely succeed in the long term. Develop the attitude of helping others, and in doing so, you will help yourself learn and grow. As a business owner, and before as an employee who started at the bottom, I witnessed many employees who were insincere, and they rarely got the promotion. They simply did not garner respect, and most often moved to another company where they tried the same tactics.

There is an anonymous quote I still have in a file that explains this so much better than I'll ever be able to. I've kept it for over 35 years—that should give you an idea of its importance to me!

It goes like this:

Something to think about…

Sooner or later, a person, if wise, discovers that life is a mixture of good days and bad, victory and defeat, give and take.

They discover it doesn't pay to be a sensitive soul – we need to let some things go over our heads like water off a duck's back.

We learn that carrying a chip on our shoulders is the easiest way to get into a disagreement. Move on and concentrate on the future and positive improvements

We learn that all people occasionally have burnt toast for breakfast and do not take others complaining too seriously.

A wise person learns the quickest way to become unpopular is to tell negative tales about others.

We learn that most people are human and that it doesn't do any harm to smile and say "good morning" even when it is raining.

Wise people learn it doesn't matter so much who gets the credit so long as the company wins, shows a profit. It is also wise not to point blame on others on the team if you falter.

Wise people learn that most of the others we work with, are as ambitious as we are, with brains as good as or better than our own. That hard work, not cleverness is the secret to success.

It is always wise to realize that the business could run perfectly without you.

A mature person, of any age, learns to have empathy for those below them, the newer employees coming into the business and remembers we were there and as bewildered as they might be. It is wise to remember we were also in the wondering and blundering stages of our careers.

We should not worry when we do not make a hit every time, experience has shown if we always give it our best, the law of averages will break even.

Wise people realize we do not make it to first base alone, that it is through cooperative effort that we move on to better things.

Lastly, we should learn, that most all others are not any harder to get along with in one place or another, and that getting along is 98 percent on us.

Read this again, and re-read it often. There are several valuable lessons we all can learn in this short excerpt. The more you lend a hand to others, the more you grow personally. The fact that you are reading this book is an indication you have an interest in personally improving and learning.

Another gem of a quote I've used for my personal growth and shared with others hits the nail on the head when it comes to leading people. It is also from an anonymous source and reads:

The wish for the supervisor...

Please help me accept human beings as they are, not yearn for all to be perfect;

To recognize ability—and encourage it;

To understand shortcomings—and make allowance for them;

To work patiently for improvement and not expect too much too quickly;

To appreciate what people do right—not just criticize what they do wrong;

To be slow to anger and hard to discourage;

To have the hide of an elephant and the patience of Job;

In short, help me be a better boss!

As you continue to use self-talk and strive for positive ways to think, make sure to reflect on finding an opportunity to help another person. When you see an employee or co-worker struggling, maybe even failing, find ways to encourage and help them.

This brings to mind a funny little real-life experience. When I started my career while still in school, the store manager had some traits I found somewhat insulting. I did not care for the way he treated some of the staff. Several years later, after we had started our business and the company he worked for had failed, he ended up working as a manager in one of our stores. Now, he was working for me. I drove a company vehicle, which I washed myself at home on weekends.

One day, he looked at my car and said, "You know, you should have the service people wash your car."

"Bill, I would never ask an employee to wash my car."

"But you're the boss. You don't have to ask; you just tell them to do it!"

My answer to that caught him a little off guard. I replied, "Bill, you never know when you might end up working for that employee."

Improving your mental attitude opens your eyes to better opportunities and allows you to visualize positive steps that you might not otherwise see. We all hear the glass is half-empty to some, while half-full to others. Thinking along the more positive, "half-full" scenario leads to looking for the rest of an opportunity as opposed to thinking negatively and waiting for the remainder of the negative. Your subconscious never rests, so it is important to be aware and try to use it as a positive force. Look for the opportunity that *is* there. Your self-talk is with you all the time. Make it positive. Only you can make the choice and set the direction for your self-talk.

Having worked with or employed thousands of people over the years, I have noticed how some people can always just "get it done," while others are more likely to think of reasons why something *cannot* be done. Obviously, as managers or business owners, we gravitate towards those who *can* do it; who never seem to let the little obstacles get in their way. These people see what can be done and push aside the obstacles that others stumble over. They see the obstacles as opportunities for improvement. These people are the ones with positive attitudes.

I have a small gem of information that I saved for years from the book *You Can Become the Person You Want to Be*, written by Robert H. Schuller. This is a classic book with mental strategies that empower you to succeed. The piece below is on nine principles to build and keep a positive mental attitude. As you read these principles, remember that when the author speaks of changes in the mind, this refers to your self-talk, our sub-conscious and how we perceive what is in front of us every day.

1. *Say something positive to every person you meet every day, no matter what the actual situation may be.*

2. *See something positive every day in every situation. Look for the good and try to find it.*

3. *Habitually think, "It might work." This feeds the mind with enthusiasm-generating positive thoughts.*

4. *Appoint yourself president of your own "Why-Not Club."*

5. *Activate every positive idea that comes into your mind with the D.I.N.—Do It Now degree. Never let a positive idea wither on the vine. Catch it. Keep it. Don't*

let it die in the limbo of inaction. Activate it or it will evaporate.

6. *Practice positive expectations. Why do some people always seem to be enthusiastic? Because they expect enthusiastic things will happen.*

7. *Exercise the power of positive. Count your blessings, not your troubles, and with this attitude, your spirits remain strong.*

8. *Discipline yourself to become a positive reactionary. Misfortune never leaves you where it found you. You make the change. You will become better or worse. You make the choice. Life is ten percent what happens to you and ninety percent how you react to what happens to you.*

9. *Keep your positive emotions charged and recharged. Allow your personality to be guided by positive emotions, and enthusiasm will flow through your being.*

I encourage you to go back and read that list again and again. Save it and look at it daily, as many others have done for years. Pay special attention to number eight: discipline yourself, for you make the choice. Life is 10% what happens, and 90% how you react.

Let's say you choose to work. Maybe you choose to start a business. Only you know what's going on in your head and what your self-talk sounds like. Only you can choose to use positive thoughts and self-talk about your work. Practice improves the process, which also takes some self-discipline. It all ties together. Be one of those who sees obstacles as an opportunity and tackles the big jobs. Be the person who knows anything can be accomplished, even big things. Follow your dream or your vision with a positive attitude. Combined with positive self-talk, understanding your subconscious is a key to your success. Only you can sway what lies in that self-talk. Develop the good habits of making plans, communicating and implementing those plans, and following through. Set goals and accomplish them in the areas of business, family, and personal growth.

As you practice these positive-thinking skills, they will apply to all relationships: family, co-workers, sales, management, on the shop floor, or in the field.

- Consciously choose to be the person who follows through on what they say; who does what is expected and then some.

- Be the person willing to go beyond what is asked in every area of life.

- Develop the positive self-talk to keep disciplined habits at home, work, and play. Everything improves with a better attitude, including those you interact with.

- And always be the person that others can depend on, in any situation.

In saying this, unfortunately, there are a few out there who will never understand the positive and always have a hand out for help, advice and sympathy. Give them your best, but stay attuned to when it is time to let them walk and grow on their own and in their own way. There is a great book titled *Good to*

Great by Jim Collins. In it, he says: "Good to Great Companies first got the right people on the bus, the wrong people off the bus, and the right people in the right seats. And then they figured out where to drive it."

Our little company started without even a single customer, in a small, eight-by-twelve rented office trailer. But starting with that first employee, we hired great people and got them on the right seats on the bus. I knew where the bus needed to go, but I also knew it could not get there without the right people. Today, the company has thousands of people and a huge market share. Our teams all shared the vision of how to get that bus to reach each goal, then set new goals to do it again. Our people then went on to build great teams and grew professionally and personally. You can choose to be the person others want to work for, or the person companies want to keep. It is always your choice. I guarantee you will never look back when you see the world in a positive way, accomplish your goals, and keep growing.

CHAPTER 13

WONDER, BLUNDER, THUNDER, AND PLUNDER

A CLOSE FRIEND once remarked that our entire lives can be broken down into four stages; *Wonder, Blunder, Thunder* and *Plunder*. These are various stages of life and stages of our careers. Keep in mind that any of us can repeat this cycle more than once.

1. **Wonder:** Early on, when something is new to us, we might experience the Wonder of what we might do and how. This might include dreaming of a career yet to be found, or just starting a new job, position, or opening your own business. This applies to changing careers, as well.

2. **Blunder:** As we learn the ropes and obtain more experience, we are prone to mistakes. Learning the business and landscapes can be difficult, and as we grow, we are bound to screw up.

3. **Thunder:** This is when we are, hopefully, heading to the top. We are succeeding, making our livelihoods

matter, getting promotions, growing our knowledge base, and increasing our net worth. This is when we might start to think we are at the top of the pyramid.

4. **Plunder**: This is likely to be when we retire or sell a business but can also apply to those who learn how to better enjoy what they worked for while still being productive and continuing to grow. One might envision more golf and lounging around, but at the same time, this can be a time to invest in other endeavors, giving back, humanitarian work, or coaching others. It is a perfect time to do what you might have dreamed of doing and make a difference in the world. The "Plunder" might be realized when we can see the fruits of all the work, decisions, risks taken, and investments made in both time and treasure for many years.

It makes no difference which of these four stages might define you as you are reading this. All four stages can be experienced with any opportunity. Often, the difference between success and taking advantage of the many opportunities we have is simply taking that first step past *wonder*. It involves taking the *blunder* risks you must take to see something you are thinking of pass from a dream to a reality.

In most cases, and throughout history, we see famous people *blunder* before they can *thunder*. However, this shouldn't make you afraid of taking the risk and stepping out. It simply involves thinking beyond your comfort level. This is not saying to go blindly into any new endeavor, but instead recognize that no matter how much you might plan and study, there can be surprises in anything new you try.

Hopefully, as you read this, you can visualize where you are today in one of these four scenarios of life. Make some mental notes about what stage you might be in, and how you can keep moving forward.

Rarely do you hear or read a story of someone who went from nothing to great success without spending a significant amount of time in each of these stages. The exceptions are people like Bill Gates, who we might imagine, spent a relatively short time in the blunder stage. He may also have spent a short time, comparatively speaking, in the thunder stage before entering plunder. He and his wife, Melinda Gates are still very much in the thunder in different endeavors, giving back to the world in ways few can. They are incredible people who seem to almost be living in a fairytale world, but rest assured, it is a world of commitment with a recognition that they can make significant, lasting change by bettering humanity. Their journey could be a book (or several books) by itself.

The Gates' may be an exception to the standard progression through the stages, albeit, one that is not yet concluded. As they entered the plunder stage, the path they chose was to give back through The Bill and Melinda Gates Foundation. They went through some blunders as they started it. Few in this world have made an effort with as much commitment as Bill and Melinda Gates. Even Warren Buffet came to the conclusion that there was a steep learning curve when doing humanitarian work, and he gave billions to the Gates Foundation. He is incredibly intelligent to realize he did not have to reinvent the wheel they successfully pioneered. His funding will have greater impact through their efforts.

John and I founded, ran and sold two successful companies to Fortune 500 firms. We both also started working at young ages. Looking back at our early beginnings, John and I quickly discovered the top three traits of successful entrepreneurs— even though at the time we weren't as successful as we thought we could be. We were both committed to 1) hard work, 2) constantly striving for excellence, and 3) being 100% honest with each other and our customers.

Throughout our wonder, blunder and thunder years, we committed to never stop learning, whether on the job or through formal education. We were also committed to helping our employees learn, both lessons related to business as well as their private lives.

The following quotes from Henry Ford have stuck with me through every stage, and I believe they apply to all of us:

"Anyone who stops learning is old, whether at twenty or eighty. Anyone who keeps learning stays young. The greatest thing in life is to keep your mind young."

"If you think you can do it, or think you can't do it, you are right."

"Obstacles are those frightful things you see when you take your eyes off your goals."

Notice how Henry phrases this as "your goals"—only *you* can set goals specific to your life. These goals do not just pertain to work. They can be personal, relational, business-related, or all of the above. Your goals are what you are wondering and dreaming of doing that only you can formulate.

We all have dreams of something that might be (and *can* be), however, it is what you do to make the dream a reality that helps you take the steps to reach and exceed those goals. This applies to everyone, whether you're a CEO, management person, employee, or student. The same reality also applies throughout your life. When you reach that goal, set another one and follow through. Developing the habit of following through will make a positive difference for you your whole life.

From a young age, one of my goals was to always be the best at whatever I did. Whether it was earning money mowing the lawns in the neighborhood, washing the windows on customer's car at a gas station, or school endeavors, I made it my aim to pursue excellence. As I worked at the station and sat through my school classes, I often daydreamed about ways I could make a million dollars. My self-talk often was asking the same questions to myself, "What could I do? How can I do it?" I knew there just had to be a way.

This daydream wasn't some far-fetched, unreasonable aspiration; I could rattle off dozens of names of people who had far surpassed this dream of mine. I read every story about successful people and how they achieved success. Knowing what so many people had done gave me the confidence that I could do the same.

There's a story of an obscure quarterback from a small school that was drafted by the Seattle Seahawks football team. His name: Russell Wilson. Wilson was not tall or well-known, but he was creative and able to think fast on his feet. He grew up believing he could be a champion, and his father kept telling him, "Russell, why not you?" A few years after he joined the team, the Seahawks won the Super Bowl.

I wasn't dreaming of winning the lottery or getting lucky while gambling to earn my millions—although let's be honest, sometimes those thoughts cross most of our minds! Rather, I knew that if I worked hard enough, I could accomplish this dream on my own. I just did not know what work might open up my path of success. I knew that simply working at the gas station and graduating high school would not guarantee me the success I so deeply believed I could achieve.

Looking back, I was fortunate to have succeeded at all the goals I set for myself. I was able to do so many times over because of the principles presented in this book. I also discovered that many people either do not set goals or simply do not try hard enough to accomplish them. They have not accepted that they can succeed far beyond where they are if they would only try, believe, work hard, and learn.

Achieving success was not easy. It was a lot of work, yet almost anyone could do the same thing and go even further than I did. I was tireless in my self-talk, wondering and blundering. At a relatively early age, I was thundering because I had invested in learning, worked hard, and never gave up. You have that same ability inside you; just apply it!

I hope you never lose sight of the value of learning through continuing education and hard work. Working hard and smart at the same time will accelerate your success by leaps and bounds. Neither John nor I had parents that were in any position to provide a formal education after high school. Since the 8th grade, both of us held some sort of job. As I mentioned earlier, I had a part-time job at a service station, while John helped his father with the carpet business he worked at.

When I was about 15 years old, after breaking several pairs of glasses, I decided I wanted contact lenses. However, my parents would not agree to buy me them because of the expense. They did not have that kind of money then as contacts were much more expensive than glasses. So, off I went on my own to meet with the optometrist without telling my parents. The doctor told me the cost was $160 for both the exam and contacts; a fair sum for a young boy of 15. I looked the doctor in the eye and said, "I have a job. I can give you $40 now and $40 a month over the next three months to pay it off." The doctor looked at the assistant and said, "I think we can work this out." This was one of my first experiences in financial negotiations, and I am thankful for the learning opportunity at such a young age. I still chuckle as I realized at a later date, the doctor had winked at the assistant as he agreed. I was so serious, and he obviously enjoyed the determination and grit I displayed.

While maybe just a cute aside, it's worth mentioning that 35 years later when I was 50, I found myself at another optometrist getting an exam with those exact same two contact lenses! I had never lost either of them over those 35 years. That is the kind of value I placed on something I worked hard for. The optometrist had never heard of anyone keeping the same pair that long without losing or scratching them! There is something to be said for the value you place on things you achieve as opposed to things simply given to you.

In high school, I signed up for the yearbook class my senior year and had the opportunity to take on the role of business manager. My job was to produce revenue from advertising sales to offset some of the costs associated with creating and print-ing the school yearbook. The production of the yearbook was a significant expense to the school, but the school had never broken even or made a profit on it. The yearbook was always a loss and a cost to the school budget.

The first thing I did was ask the instructor why the yearbook wasn't raising more revenue from advertising, as that didn't make sense to me. The instructor explained, "The advertising does not even cover the cost of printing the yearbook, so the school has a budget in place to cover the balance." From what I could see, the school or students working on the yearbook simply failed to see the opportunity to sell more advertising, raise more money, and cover all the expenses. So, although the yearbook had never made a profit before, in my mind, a profit was attainable. I had looked at all the expenses and revenues from the past and knew it could be done. It would just take more work.

I was 17 at the time and had my driver's license. Any excuse to leave school with permission was a good thing in my mind. So, off I went during the class period time, selling advertising to the local Coca Cola bottling company, sporting goods stores, grocery chains, burger joints, and many more. I used my time wisely, worked hard, made all the cold calls to businesses, and followed up with the print and advertising designs to be approved. Many of the places who bought advertising, such as Coca Cola, had their own art departments and provided ads for us. I set the advertising prices, selling full-, half- or quarter-page ads, and even took the pictures when needed and obtained the copy for every advertisement that was sold.

For the first time in the history of the yearbook, the school made a profit. The instructor was baffled, saying, "I was told that it could not be done, so I just accepted the fact and created space in the budget for the loss." I guess she forgot to tell me *it couldn't be done!* Over 50 businesses signed up for advertisements, and I had the opportunity to meet some brilliant people in the process. I learned many things about being unafraid to ask for business, selling and being persistent while still being polite. When I look back, it was almost as if it was my first opportunity to run a small business. Getting enough advertising sales took getting out there and just doing it, making the effort, setting aside the time required, leaving my comfort zone and simply asking.

Looking back, I remember many of those who said yes to a simple, small advertisement were also appreciative of this young, polite high schooler making an effort. It took a little planning and some hard work, but it was a win for all involved. After all, every business in our town was a potential customer. I think almost all would have said yes if there had been time to call on more people. I did get a few rejections, but I learned that even those are beneficial to learning. In that small microcosm of business, I went from wonder to a little blunder to thunder.

Sometime later in my career, I headed up an initiative and raised the funds to complete the building of large truck trailers designed for hands-on Driver's Education safety training that would go into every high school Driver's Ed class in our state. This was coordinated with the Washington State Patrol for hands-on safety training about trucks on the road. It is an example of talking about something, thinking it through, and then executing a plan.

Several people thought it was a great idea, but nobody was willing to do anything to make it happen. It just takes step after step, learning what to do and how to do it, and asking for what is needed—which were companies to donate goods and services in this case. When I asked, the local power company donated a generator and wired it, a large semi-trailer company decided to donate a whole trailer, and a truck engine company donated an engine. The goal was to show student drivers the dangers of driving in a truck's blind spot and how long it takes a truck to stop, how much a truck weighs and how to drive safely around large trucks. On the side of the trailer, it read, "If it saves one life, it was worth it."

The examples here illustrate simple discipline: instead of just thinking, "This might work," discipline involves making the choice to get off your butt and do something. That "doing" could be learning and applying that knowledge, trying something new or going full-out on a business idea. Simple discipline can be applied to any person, in any situation. Simply put, it is developing a habit of questioning everything; not accepting things as they seem to be and asking yourself why they are not.

Whenever I was told "we tried that once and it did not work," I asked, "why?" By asking that question, I learned how they tried, what they did and gained an understanding of what caused the failure. Discipline also involves taking initiative and taking the first steps to imagine and create what you think might be possible. As the Nike slogan says, *Just Do It*! When you are dreaming of something you really want to do, start thinking about what the first step is and take that step. You will not only feel better, but you will also likely commit to accomplishing more. Only you can choose to strive to do more in any situation. Do not worry about what blunders might ensue. Work through them and find the opportunity that results.

There is so much we can learn every day; so much we still do not know, both personally as well as within our global community. Never waste a day. Even when you need a vacation, make sure and do it. Just do not waste your time. In science, new discoveries are made daily, advances in chemistry, in business, in relationships and how we can work and live together better. There are advancements in education. Create a desire for lifelong learning; an attitude of always desiring to grow, learning the why, the how, and the reasons things are done a certain way and how you can change them for the better.

Always work toward developing your self-discipline. You can do this. Anyone can. It is simply that few do it. Habits "they" say are hard to break. Consciously develop good habits. Put them in place of the bad ones. Start with positive self-talk and start following up or following through on everything. This helps reinforce the good habits. Keep practicing and do not allow yourself to have negative self-talk. Strive to create positive self-discipline and a get-it-done attitude.

We all have 24 hours in a day. What we do or don't do in this time is our choice. We cannot go back and retrieve that time; rather it is lost or invested as you choose. But, luckily for you, if you are reading this book, you are still able to do something going forward! You are gaining knowledge of how to spend and invest your time as you read through these chapters.

It's important to remember that the lessons in this book are not just relevant to a career or work, but also apply to relationships, family, friends, and co-workers. When you learn how to manage your time and invest in that which will be fruitful, you are creating a balanced life and setting yourself up for success in all areas. Remember, "If you do nothing, nothing happens." If you get up in the morning and have a plan, you will accomplish much during the day. If you wake up with no set plan, you cannot expect to accomplish much. As was mentioned in the beginning of the chapter, make your bed. It starts the day off on a positive note. You accomplish something immediately at the start of your day!

I really got a good laugh while visiting my nephew in Abu Dhabi. He was a two-star Admiral in the Navy stationed there, working with governments and intelligence. He asked if we wanted to visit his apartment downtown, which we did after getting through a ton of security. His mother is my sister, and as I walked through the apartment, he said, "Make sure you tell Mom that I made my bed."

It is said the definition of insanity is doing the same thing you have always done and expecting a different result. Again, it makes no difference where you are in life, career, or school. Many who have made it to the top sometimes get into a familiar rut, going through each day the same as the day before. They made it to the top position, perhaps as a CEO, and then their goals to achieve and do more are just not as appealing to them. At the same time, other CEO's continue to improve, add value to the business, expand, and do great things. They too must continuously improve and find new ways to do business. We all put on our pants the same way, after all. The difference is what you mentally establish regarding what you need to do and your level of follow through. Continual success requires the tireless discipline to do it; taking the time to write down the goals. This is what makes the difference between the ordinary leader and the exceptional, growing leader. If you can form some vision around what something *can* be, then take the first steps to get there, your visions will start taking shape.

In the early days of our business, we had a store manager named Jim. He was always on time. His desk was neat and tidy, and it seemed he had his own way of doing things. He always kept busy. So far, he sounds like a good employee, right? However, as time went on, we discovered that Jim often had problems following through on what we wanted. He seemed to consistently fail to implement new ideas, or programs even after we had all talked about them and agreed to them. For example, when we had agreed to buy a new piece of equipment, seeing that the need was there and it was something that would enhance service and increase profits, the equipment did not get ordered. Whenever he was asked when the equipment was to be delivered or installed, he would tell us that it had not been ordered yet, but he was *planning on doing it.* This sort of pattern happened often.

One day, I asked him point blank, "Why do you always procrastinate? Why don't you just pick up the phone and place the order? What is holding you back?" He looked right back at me and said, "You are just a super achiever." I was struggling to find the correlation between what I might be doing and his lack of follow through. Many things ran through my head that I did not say, but what I did say was, "Jim, I simply write down what I want to do each day, then follow through. I do my best to make sure all my tasks are completed."

This small example of follow through—or lack of it—reminded me of a quote from Lewis Carroll: "If you do not know where you are going, any road will get you there." Jim never seemed to get to the thunder part of his career. He would go hunting, fishing, camping and do many other things that he excelled at. He just seemed to freeze when it came time to make a decision, such as a large purchase. We had a store in Juneau, Alaska—a hunting and fishing paradise for someone like Jim. He was a perfect fit, so we moved him to this location. He hunted and fished with about every customer, and the business ran fine with him there. Jim did well there, the customers enjoyed him, and I believe he still lives there today.

The point is simple. Just plan for each day and follow through! You will feel better about yourself, develop a reputation of a person who gets it done, and people will trust you as someone who comes through on their word. You will also be adding to your positive self-talk and self-confidence.

Most people who have successfully accomplished something difficult found obstacles and failures along the way. Building something from nothing is not without challenges. Learn from your history and the lessons of others and keep asking why.

Achieving success in growing from wonder to blunder comes with knowledge. Then, as you reach thunder as a result of determination and hard work, take care to learn from the blunders. In your thunder, do not be afraid to encounter a few more blunders. A person who has never failed is a person who never tried to create something new. Hopefully, as millions of others have done, you will find the ability to plunder, which can be carried out in many ways. I chose, like Bill and Melinda Gates, to give something back to the world, working through Rotary and World Vision in developing countries. There are thousands of opportunities to spend your plunder time for good, it's simply your choice.

CHAPTER 14

I WANT TO HELP OTHERS THE WAY YOU'VE HELPED ME

THERE ARE MILLIONS of successful people who did not run their own businesses yet became successful. The percent of failure while working for a company you do not own is many times lower than the risk of failure when starting your own company. You might find that by changing your outlook about where you work now, you will see opportunity there to be very successful. That opportunity may have always been there, it was just not recognized.

Knowing we all blunder from time to time, it is best to wonder and blunder while working for a company as opposed to doing so in a company you start. Often, the blunder encounter can cause bankruptcy and failure, which can be a really expensive lesson. Starting your own business is not for everyone. There are thousands of business owners today who would have been better off working for someone else's company.

Solid and successful employers realize most employees want to grow and excel, improve their value, and increase their earnings. These successful employers embrace this reality and help the employees reach those goals. At the same time, there are those employees who are never satisfied and always find fault, looking only at the negative. In your self-talk, avoid those negatives and strive to find the good. If it is simply not there, look at alternatives or start your own business.

We started our company because our employer was failing financially. I could not see any other company in the industry that I had a desire to work for. I had a reason to start my own business, but I strongly advise you to think through all the alternatives before doing so. The old saying "The grass is always greener on the other side" lulls many a person into making only lateral moves—not up, nor forward, just side-to-side in the same company or changing companies and never being satisfied.

I remember a time when I was first out of college and working at my first job. It was a very busy day for us, as we were having a sale. No matter how busy we get, I believe most of us have a sense when somebody is watching us. I had that feeling on this particular day. I turned around to see a well-dressed man watching me work. As soon as there was a lull, the man pulled me aside, sharing a few words of wisdom that I'll never forget: "Son, I have been watching you for a while. I am a friend of the owner of this company, and I also own a very large company here in town. I have seen many of my friends who were bright and ambitious jump from job to job, always chasing something they thought was better. But they made poor choices because of it. Had they stayed in one place and developed their roots, they could have followed in my footsteps and eventually owned their own businesses."

His business was a large lithograph company located not far from our building. I learned he had started working there out of school and worked hard for years. Then, he bought the company from the owner who wanted to retire. There are many thousands of very good, profitable companies with owners wanting to retire. Many of them do not have family in a position to take over. The majority of these companies are small, but profitable and specialty-focused. There is no end to the various vocations they cover. It pays to do your homework and follow a passion. Your opportunity could be in retail, manufacturing, engineering, automotive or in the boating industry—whatever industry interests you. If you do not look for opportunities, they can be hard to find.

Everyone, from time to time, will likely be frustrated with their jobs. When that happens, we all have choices to make: quit, look for a job elsewhere, or complain and be negative. On the other hand, you can realize management might benefit from having you explain why you think something is not working as well as it could be. It is amazing what your mind can do when you start to focus on what *could be* instead of dwelling on the negatives. If you think there is a better way, how is it going to get better if you don't say anything? It is your choice to be part of the solution instead of being part of the problem.

Every manager, in every business, has made decisions that could have been better. Sometimes the decisions were downright terrible. However, unless someone steps up and shares an opinion regarding how it could be changed for the better, these bad decisions will continue. Choose to be a part of the solution that improves the company. And please, always make sure you have the facts correct. I used to get proposals from employees only to find I was given nine-tenths of the information. That last tenth made all the difference in the decision. Do a thorough and complete job.

Whether you're a truck driver, working in an office in an entry-level position, or already in management makes no difference regarding your ability to add value to any business. What does make the difference is not what position you hold, but instead, how you look at and recognize opportunities and act on them. Are you going to take the opportunity to be a positive agent of change in your current position and company, or not? Often that decision is already in your subconscious mind. You just need to make your plan, then act on it.

From the very start of our company, John and I put a strong emphasis on helping employees succeed. Over the years, we have helped hundreds of employees, many of whom we keep in contact with today. It gives us immense pleasure to see how each of them grew and succeeded in their own ways. Many of those employees now pay it forward to others. We helped get employees into night classes, and coached them on steps to take in order to get a certain position they wanted in our company. We also sometimes realized what the employee wanted was not something we could fulfill in our company, but we still helped them take the next steps to achieve what they wanted and land a job elsewhere. Rarely, if ever, did we lose an employee to a competitor, although many from other competing companies applied to work for our firm.

As our first company was acquired, some 20 years after we started it, our employees sponsored a large party to honor us. John and I were both given a large notebook with cards and encouraging words from many of the employees. A man named Tony wrote the following words in my notebook that still choke me up to this day, "My goal in life is to help others the way you helped me."

A number of years before, we had fired Tony. He was a young, hot-headed service truck driver and service rep. No matter how hard we tried to work with Tony, it didn't seem to help his attitude. He was a handful! Tony constantly saw the negatives instead of the opportunities, and we eventually gave up on him as a lost cause. If that seems harsh, keep in mind that the driver or service person is the one your customer sees more often than anyone else from the company. The drivers, technicians, and service people are the face of the company. It seemed Tony could never be happy, and we did not want his attitude to negatively impact our customers.

Six months or so after being fired, Tony called me and said, "I have never worked for anybody who sincerely seemed to care about my personal growth and well-being like you did. Would you consider giving me another chance? I am really sorry about the way I acted while working there."

Since John and I had adopted a policy not to re-hire anyone who quit or was fired, I knew I had to talk to him before making any decisions. John said, "Absolutely not!" Remember, we had an agreement that if we disagreed with each other on a decision, we would always talk it through. If one of us felt strongly about something, we would present it, and we would only proceed if the other said OK.

Though John originally said no, I felt strongly about the situation and brought it up again. I explained that we had already invested so much time and money into training him, and that it might be worth the effort to give him another chance. I had also spent some time talking to Tony about what our expectations would be and that he would not be given any slack. John begrudgingly agreed for us to re-hire Tony, and I am so thankful he did. It turned out to be a great decision, both for the company and for Tony. He moved up from driving trucks to sales, and eventually became one of our top producers! It took a lot of coaching, but it was worth it. The investment we made in helping him excel was paid back well. Soon Tony was making well over $100,000 a year in commissions. Customers really liked him, and he loved his job. We are still friends to this day.

If you are not willing to invest in your employees, you will not see positive outcomes like the one we saw with Tony. We could tell countless stories like this one that happened only because somebody made a choice, took a positive step, and envisioned some sort of opportunity. Don't get me wrong; it doesn't always turn out positive. But the same thing is true as we've talked about before: if you do not try, or if you give up from the get-go, then the outcomes are certain to be nil.

Tony was able to see an opportunity and go for it. He blundered in the job the first time around. He really wanted to be in sales, but as with most, he couldn't see the path to get there. He eventually thundered, and is still in sales and management—and all of us are the better for it.

How many people go to their jobs every day wishing they were in a different position—either at a higher level in their company, or another company altogether? The sad reality is that most of these people will never go after the things they want. In this case, Tony wanted more, and we wanted successful, motivated employees. It was a win-win all around. As can be the case, sometimes we need to fire someone, or they need to quit before they can see the grass actually *was* greener where they were. Blunders and failure can be a great lesson to learn from.

How you treat your co-workers—both those above your current position as well as below—is a major reflection of your character. The more empathy and sincerity you apply to others, the more personal growth you will experience. To clarify, empathy is not the same as sympathy. Rather, it is making a sincere effort to understand the other person. Imagine you are standing in their shoes and think through their current circumstances in order to better understand them. If you are not sincere in your actions and words, it will be obvious to those around you and cause you to be viewed as untrustworthy.

Just let the reality of this sink in for a moment: here was a young person, Tony, doing hard, physical work. He had no formal education, but what he did have was the desire to improve himself and better support his family. He closely watched successful people who were making it in the business and decided that he wanted to learn from them and grow into his own successful career. Shortly after he started as a sales representative and stepped out of driving a truck, he was earning well over $100,000 a year as mentioned, but that was some 25 years ago! Today as we write this, it would be closer to $180,000!

There are thousands of "Tony's" out there; every company has them. At his worst, his self-talk was so negative he could only see what was wrong with everything. This is what led to his being fired! As he thought about his circumstances, he realized that the problem was with him, not the company. He had the initiative to make a call that, frankly, few would make. He swallowed his pride, confessed that he was wrong, and asked for his job back. We could have easily said no, but we gave Tony that second chance he asked for, and it was worth it. Tony was one of the people we had to "get off the bus," as mentioned in Jim Collins' book, *Good to Great*. When we put him back on the bus, we risked setting a poor example to many other employees if nothing had changed. We ended up putting Tony in the correct seat, and he helped us drive that bus to further success.

Tony's is just one story of the many employees we invested in and coached. John and I were sincerely interested in the personal growth of every single person, and we wanted them to know it. We encouraged continuous education and self-development, and often provided the means for the employee to achieve such. If that meant the next steps were to move on to another career or company, we would help them with that also, no hard feelings. Most people find it hard to appreciate what they have until it is gone. The more you help yourself and employees to see, literally, see and understand what can be, the better we all are as a result.

A few employees went on to top executive positions in Fortune 500 firms (and one Fortune 100 firm). Part of the risk we accepted by helping employees was when helping them achieve higher success, large international firms would recruit them away. That is simply a cost of doing business. We moved on and did it again and were proud we were part of their dreams being realized.

In both business and personal relationships, the bottom line is the same: how you treat people is always a reflection on you. A genuine, self-confident person treats all people the same, regardless of position, gender, race, or social status. Every person has their own story, their own struggles, and their own hopes and dreams. While we realistically cannot listen to all of them, we can make a better effort to get to know the people around us. To this day, I love seeing the look on the face of a service employee while travelling or at another business when I look them in the eye and ask, "How are you doing today?" Maybe it's a TSA check person at an airport, a mail delivery driver, bank teller or barista. They all appreciate being treated like human beings. Think of how many people either ignore or are rude to these hard-working servants. What would happen if you simply took the time to hear them out or compliment them? If you just take the time, I guarantee you will be astounded at the stories you hear or the ways that a simple gesture can brighten a day. These people also wonder, blunder, dream of thunder, and hope to retire someday better off than they might be right now.

CHAPTER 15

HOW QUICKLY OUR WORLD CAN CHANGE

OUR BUSINESS WAS still growing—by 50% or greater—even after we had been in business for five years. We had grown to have six locations to service our clients, and it didn't look like things were going to slow down anytime soon. Business was good.

Until the unthinkable happened.

The day began much like any other day. I had many appointments booked, including an hour at the bank that morning. There was no indication that this day would be different than any other, but soon, my entire life would change drastically.

As I've already mentioned, John and I had made the decision to leverage the banks for cash flow needed to cover the gaps between making purchases of inventory and receiving payments from customers. We had added second mortgages to our homes and established credit lines with the bank. We understood the importance of maintaining a close relationship with a bank, and even more important, with the individual banker assigned to our account.

A fast-growing business can often run short on cash. We made it a point to meet with our banker at least once every quarter to go over the company's financial needs and look at the income statements and balance sheets. Often, we would fall outside of the bank covenants agreed to. In these instances, the bank would usually make adjustments to the credit lines so we could maintain a good relationship.

At this time, we were not with the same bank as when we started the company a few years earlier. That bank had been sold, and our trusted banker and friend Andy Clark had gone to work as a CFO in a private company. He had left the banking world. We knew Andy well, and he knew both of us and our character. Andy's assistance was a significant help to our success when the business started, and he had guided us through the rapid growth and turmoil. After the bank was sold and Andy left, we had to find another bank capable of handling our continued growth needs. The people at the new bank were okay, although they had not yet created the personal and helpful relationship we had previously experienced.

That morning, John and I arrived at the bank a little early. However, instead of sitting down with our banker in his office as we had always done, he met us at the front door and escorted us to a conference room. When we entered the room, there were four other people there that we had never met. The banker must have noticed our confusion and said, "Jim and his team here will be taking care of you today." It quickly became obvious he was not going to join us in the meeting. The meeting now felt ominous and very uncomfortable. Something was wrong, and we had no idea what it was.

As our banker disappeared, closing the door behind him, we sat down. Jim proceeded to explain that the bank was "calling our note," giving us just a few days to pay it off, and even went so far as to ask for our company credit cards! Our entire bank line of credit and long-term financing was being recalled, cancelled. The bank was essentially firing our company as their customer. Without a bank, we would be out of business in a short time, unable to make payroll or pay our vendors. Without the credit line, we would be out of cash in a day!

My life suddenly started flashing before my eyes. How could I tell the hundred or so employees who had worked so hard with us building this business from scratch that the business had failed and we could not pay them? How would I tell my wife that we might lose our home, car, and income in one fell swoop? These thoughts raced through my mind in seconds. My self-talk was not positive; in fact, it was far from it. I was terrified.

There had been no previous indication of any issues with the bank, so both John and I were completely taken aback. What we did not know at the time was that our bank had been working closely with another company in the tire business that recently failed. The company that had failed was nothing close to the business we were in, but somebody higher up at the bank made a decision based on that company's failure, and now the staff had to carry out their marching orders to stop doing business with us.

The bank did not allow us to make it clear why the other company failed and why we were far from failing. We did not believe our business was a risk in any way. Both John and I knew we were heavily leveraged due to growth and other factors. We were growing too fast. Our suppliers *loved* the growth and kept providing better terms and higher credit limits. Even though we knew we were a high risk, we carefully managed and planned all the details of the operations every year.

Looking back on the scenario, I can see where we had gone wrong. We had failed to develop a close working relationship and open communication with that bank. More importantly, we had failed to develop a relationship with the individual banker. And, we had no other banks in our network as backup! All this added up to a huge mistake—a mistake that could cause our still fledgling enterprise to fail quickly.

One might call this a company blunder phase indeed. We went from wonder, to blunder, to thunder, and in a few minutes, we realized we were back in a huge blunder position. We had depended too much on bank credit lines and bank equipment financing. We had not developed or thought through any options or alternatives should we need additional help. We were operating a profitable venture, albeit one that required high levels of financial leveraging in order to maintain required cash flows. Our company had never operated at a loss. From the get-go, our profits far exceeded our projections, which we would adjust every year. The bank simply made a decision to limit their losses, taking a position to liquidate the company believing they would never recover all their investments in us. Their decision would also cost hundreds of jobs.

The bottom line of this situation was that the bank had also failed to understand us as business owners, and never made an effort to understand our business. We never learned who made that decision at the bank, and likely never will. I have to believe they made the decision without all the data and knowledge that could have led to a different outcome. Whatever the case, at this point, both the bank and our employees would lose. John and I were facing imminent failure. Something had to be done, and it had to be done quickly.

We left the meeting in shock. The bank had made their decision, and there was no room for appeal. So much for the plans scheduled that day! We had just over 48 hours to find a solution before we would lose the business, and eventually, our homes and cars. This was looking like the worst-case scenarios we had shared with our spouses some five years earlier when starting the company.

I was terrified, feeling sick to my stomach. In fact, it felt like my legs were refusing to work, as if they had been cut off at my knees. My physical body was responding to the cruel, devastating blow John and I had just been dealt. One minute we were on top of the world, working very hard with little play time, building an enterprise. We were growing, working hard to succeed, focused on the business and success. The next minute, it was all taken away. We were struggling to even think straight. Stress can wreak havoc on the body, and any thoughts of positive self-talk had not kicked in yet.

However painful it was, we knew that timing was important, and we needed to devote 110% of our time to this issue and take steps to resolve it. First, we called our CPA, Dennis, who had also been with us from day one. Dennis had been recommended to us by Andy Clark, our original banker. He answered his phone almost immediately. John explained what had happened. "Dennis, our bank just called our notes and fired us. We need some help. We need to find another bank. Can we meet to discuss right now?" He agreed to meet with us during lunch. He knew our situation well and had been a trusted advisor for us thus far.

As we arrived at his office and sat down, Dennis got straight to the point. "There is really something wrong here, gentlemen. Most bankers in the area would jump at the chance to work with your company. Sure, you are highly leveraged, but both the balance sheet and your income statements are solid, consistent, and showing positive trends. I just don't understand!"

"Where is Andy when we need him?" I said half-heartedly.

What we did not know at the time was that Dennis had stayed in contact with Andy. It caught both of us a little off guard when he said, "Actually, Andy is back in the banking business! He is working with a new bank now as a VP in commercial. Let me get him on the phone while we're here."

He called Andy while we all sat there in the office. Both John and I were still in a fog from shock, trying to make sense out of everything that had happened in the last few hours. Andy picked up right away, listened to what had happened, and told us he could meet us first thing in the morning. Dennis agreed to send Andy our current income statements and balance sheet that afternoon so he would have enough time to review them before the morning meeting.

That afternoon and evening seemed to drag on for an eternity. The stress, fear, and shock had piled up and tried to convince me that my life as I knew it was going to end. I was about to lose it all. This was around the time my wife and I welcomed our third child, and I was the only wage earner. All I could think of were all the bills I wouldn't have the means to pay, and the fact that our whole lives were on hold.

As I laid in bed, I couldn't help but think about all of our employees as well. It added all the more stress and ill-feeling to think about how all these valued employees would handle losing their incomes, uprooting all their plans and lives. Our employees were hardworking and dedicated; some had been with us almost from day one. They also had bills to pay and families to take care of. Our blunder was going to wreak havoc on all *their* lives—not just ours.

Fear of the unknown can block clear thinking. Saying that John and I were concerned or scared about the future is a gross understatement! Fear changes the mind: it clouds decisions, causes doubt, and cuts you to the core. If there was any bright side to what the bank was doing, it would not be clear until after this crisis was resolved. John and I were both fighters, focused and not willing to quit, but afraid just the same. Our real concern was that, other than Andy, we did not know a single banker to call.

Andy was ready to get started as soon as we arrived at his new bank the next morning. Because we had worked together previously, he knew he could trust us. He knew we were honest people, which is of utmost importance in the banking business. Though Andy had only been apart from us for a couple of years, he was surprised by the excellent growth of our company. He knew that we were the type of people who did what we said we would do; always laying out annual financial plans and carefully-crafted budgets. We were also cautious every time we took steps to expand. Andy was well-aware of the cash flow issues that rapid growth can cause, especially in a legacy, low-margin business such as ours. Andy was an excellent banker who knew the business well.

That being said, we went over the numbers and updated Andy on where the business was currently and where we were, hopefully, headed in the future. After spending only about 30 minutes with us, he had already come to a conclusion. He said, "I am fairly confident I can help you. I have a loan committee meeting this afternoon, and though I am fairly new at this bank, I really think we can have you back in business by the end of the day tomorrow. I can see an increased line of credit and will suggest a few other changes and improvements. Let's meet again tomorrow morning, and hopefully, I will have some documents for you to sign." We wanted to believe him, but it seemed too good to be true.

Andy called late that afternoon. We had been approved by the committee! His new bank would pay off our old bank, handling all the details. We would have higher credit lines. We were to be in his office early the next day and sign the papers. In a period of just over 24 hours, we went from being successful and focused on our business, to almost complete failures, focused on survival, and back to the top of the world! We were back in business!

The lessons learned from this situation were many. One of the most important was something that had been told to me by a very successful, company founder: "Banks are not your friends." There are many great bankers out there, like Andy; bankers who take the time to learn your business, acting as partners in your financial decisions. The lesson here was to stay close to the ones who genuinely advise you and help you with major decisions.

After this experience, we made it a point to develop relationships with several banks and their bankers. We would remain loyal to the bank we dealt with, but still meet and get to know other bankers as options for the future. Never again would we experience a bank calling our notes, which almost cost us everything.

In banking schools and the industry as a whole, although it might be considered "old school," I am not sure enough effort is placed on developing the relational skills necessary between the individual banker and clients. People deal with people. A good banker will take the time to know you, know your business and provide honest, frank, solid advice, and feedback. Your banker should advise you when you might be at some elevated risk or if the bank has some concerns that might lead them to discontinue business with you.

Nobody can predict the future. There is always risk in any venture where you take on debt, and there are always market changes that can adversely affect a person's or business's plans. It is critical to listen to your banker's advice and have proper exit plans should markets and conditions change.

To have a bank, with no warning, make a decision that would cost hundreds of jobs, shut down a thriving business that, unfortunately, was so dependent on a single bank, proved very wrong. From that day on, we developed relationships with a few solid bankers who always followed through on what they said. Over the years, we really had some great bankers, and kept our business growing. This blunder directed us to a higher level of thunder, albeit with additional caution and planning. Thankfully, not a single employee ever knew what we had gone through in that 48 hours. I think I aged a few years during that time but ended up better and stronger as a result.

CHAPTER 16

THE EXIT STRATEGY

AFTER THE BANK crisis, we rarely missed a beat. We continued to expand and grow. Even so, those 48 hours were a defining moment in our company history and made a significant impact on my life. Our growth was still at or near 50% annually, a difficult level of growth for any privately funded enterprise. The bank leveraging continued, and for the remainder of the years we owned the business, we never experienced a similar situation with another bank.

Banks make a lot of money on highly-leveraged companies like ours as the bank assumes a higher risk. In addition to high interest rates, the banks also charge large annual fees, similar to some credit card annual fees, but in the thousands. The banks were rightfully spending a lot of time with us, monitoring all aspects of our business. They were entitled to the higher fees as they were, in essence, partners in the business. The bank has a responsibility to their shareholders to understand the risks involved in various partnerships and ensure their loans could be repaid.

From the time of the original late-night planning session John and I had before we started, we had planned on buying our own buildings and land when we were able to do so. This was largely because we envisioned eventually selling the business to the employees. (Who else would want to buy a tire company?) We both felt commercial real estate would be our retirement income after we exited the business, whenever that would be.

This is called an *exit strategy*. At some point, every business owner will need to start thinking about the future. We can liken this to how an individual might think about retirement and prepare for an income after they stop working. We had set up 401k accounts for the employees as well as ourselves, and provided a match to help encourage employee planning.

A few years after starting up, we did start buying facilities, keeping them outside the business in limited liability corporations (LLCs) and leasing them back to the business at market rates or lower. So, when the banks financed these property acquisitions, we would have very minimal down payments. The banks would charge high loan fees every five years when the property loans had to be re-negotiated. They also gave us a fixed interest rate for five years with payments based on a 30-year amortization. Sounds simple, but if you were to buy a house this way, after 30 years, you would have only paid about 9% of the mortgage, not to mention racking up very high fees every five years to re-do the loan. Of course, this deal was great for the bank, and if the property appreciates, it could work for the owner, too, but it was incredibly expensive. Almost all our payments to the bank went to interest expense. A deal like this is the result of the borrower not having enough clout, knowledge, or cash down payment to negotiate a better way to purchase.

Our company growth also came from the acquisition of other similar companies in the industry; some already in currently-served markets. Others were in new territories that made sense for us to serve. As the company kept growing, John and I were both juggling multiple responsibilities. John was now managing three retread manufacturing facilities in two states, and I was managing operations and sales in both states with eight locations.

Any sort of growth can present challenges that oftentimes the founders might not see as clearly as someone from the outside. The founders can get so caught up in the day-to-day operations that they are somewhat blind to their own limitations or company needs. Also, the founders' mindsets can be biased. Since they were the founders, they must know how to do everything better than anyone. They think they know what the needs are. After all, it is *their* company, right? At least that was the self-talk we heard, which was coming from a lack of knowledge. I am mostly talking about myself here. You'll see soon enough.

The Alaska operations had been growing consistently. We were dealing with two different banks: one in Alaska, and one in the Seattle area. At the time, we had an Alaska Corporation as well as a Washington Corporation. Most banks, due to various state regulations and laws, operated as separate entities, even if they had the same bank name. This was the case with our banks. The Washington bank would not bank with us in Alaska even though they had branches there. The Alaska bank we were using was not located in Washington. While we had an excellent relationship with the large Washington bank, and continually asked that they would allow us to deal with them in Alaska, they would not budge. It was getting to be a hassle having separate lines of credit, financing, and completely different individuals to work with in each state. However, we got the same answer every time we asked: "It cannot be done."

Here's where having great relationships with other banks can come in handy. The other bankers we had stayed in contact with were still calling on us, wanting our business as we had now grown to over $30 million a year in sales. One of these banks seized the opportunity and presented a solution for us with a single banker, and one bank that operated in both states. It was a total company solution for us. We spent a significant amount of time making sure this could work for both corporations, and that the bank had the capacity we needed. After much deliberation, we decided to make the switch and take the bank up on their offer. It was a really tough decision, as we really liked our current bankers. They just would not accommodate the need for a single contact for banking in both states.

On the day the new banker showed up to sign the final papers, we met in our conference room inside the corporate office. The table was loaded with papers, legal documents, and agreements. It would take an hour to sign them all. Right in the middle of signing, a staff person opened the door saying, "I hate to interrupt, but Kim, your banker is on the phone wanting to talk to you." This was the banker representing the bank we were in the middle of replacing. I picked up the phone, curious at his timing and what rumors might have led to his call.

"Hi, Kim. We have thought long and hard about this, and our bank has decided that we will bank both corporations in Alaska and Washington with a single contact, just as you have wanted us to do." His voice was firm and full of conviction. We had enjoyed a close relationship with both the banker and the bank, so we really did not want to change, but we had already made an agreement with a new bank.

"Well, as we speak, we are signing the papers to change banks. If you had called just a day earlier, we probably would have stayed with you. Unfortunately, this change is being made only after your refusal to combine the banking as we had been asking for over a year."

I told him how much we had appreciated all his work for us and that we would stay in touch. One never knows when you might need another banker, right? We went through with the change, and it ended up working out very well for all parties involved.

Several months later, the same banker we had replaced called me out of the blue.

"Hey Kim! I'm playing golf at Sahalee Country Club, one of the premier golf courses in the northwest. Would you like to play? This is the same golf course that hosted 1998 PGA championship."

"Geeze, if I knew that changing our bank would have resulted in playing golf with you there, we would have done it sooner!"

We did play golf that day, and it was refreshing. We pledged to keep in contact, keeping the communication lines open. A smart banker keeps the relationship open for a future chance to get the business again. A few years earlier, we were fired by a bank. Now we had great relations with another great bank, and another banker wanted our business. What a turnaround!

It was also important to us that we treat all the suppliers, bankers, customers, and employees with respect. In the book, *Beach Lawyer*, the author, Avery Duff says, "What goes around comes around." It serves as a reminder to always treat others as you would like to be treated, even though it can be difficult at times.

I will guarantee you that every successful person has, at some time, encountered obstacles. However, it is how you overcome them that is a true measure of your fortitude. We have all likely read and watched stories about many wealthy, successful people who created large successful businesses. Rarely do you hear that they were born into wealth, created nothing, and died just as wealthy. The stories that stick with us are the common ones: the ones who were born with nothing, started from nothing, took a risk, realized a dream, and made history.

What is important is to recognize that many successful people have also failed—many more than once—before tasting the fruits of their labors. Look at our story: we had already overcome two serious events that might have caused others to give up. We are just two average people who took a risk and vowed not to let the hurdles stop us from pursuing our dreams. Ours is a story of hard work, continual learning, perseverance, tireless efforts, and great success.

The Wall Street Journal often prints obituaries exampling successful individuals. They once wrote about a man who grew up in abject poverty but died a multi-billionaire. This was a man who grew up with no indoor plumbing! Just as all parents want what is best for their children, this man's father started out as a low-paid teacher, but knew he wanted a better life for his son. The father made choices that would eventually lead to a better life for his family, and even enrolled in graduate school in order to increase his income and be able to send his children to school.

One of his children, Jon Huntsman, was then able to attend Palo Alto High School. There, even with the sting of poverty still fresh in his mind, Jon became class president. He was awarded a scholarship to Wharton, one of the most respected business schools. Even though he struggled with his studies, he made the choice to commit himself to studying and succeed.

Jon went to work in his uncle's egg production company and was tasked with creating a better egg carton—one made from polystyrene, which was a relatively new invention. The technicians at the time told him it could not be done, so he fired them! He then found other out-of-the-box thinkers who, through trial and error, came up with a solution. Jon went on to create the clamshell cartons we are familiar with today. Not only do we see eggs in these cartons now, but the clamshell design is used for all sorts of take-out food. Jon went through all the stages of wonder, blunder, thunder, and plunder. His story is just one of thousands of stories of an ordinary person deciding to capitalize on an opportunity, even when the people around them say it can't be done.

In another case, one of our country's greatest presidents struggled with failure much of his life. However, he was not easily discouraged, and pushed through to realize his ultimate success.

Consider these facts about him:

- Failed in business: 1831
- Defeated for the legislature: 1832
- Again, failed in business: 1834
- Sweetheart died: 1835
- Had a nervous breakdown: 1836
- Defeated in election: 1838
- Defeated for Congress: 1843
- Defeated for Congress: 1846
- Defeated for Congress: 1848
- Defeated for Senate: 1854
- Defeated for Vice President: 1856
- Defeated for Senate: 1858
- Elected President: 1860

That man was Abraham Lincoln, one of the most memorable and revered men in the history of the United States.

Every day, there are thousands of opportunities in front of us that others have thought impossible. Often, we don't try to take advantage of them because we are told it isn't feasible. Imagine if Abraham Lincoln had listened to the voices that said, "Just give up. You'll never get elected." Imagine if Bill Gates let discouragement stop him. Imagine if you and I never got to indulge in Amazon Prime because Jeff Bezos gave up before seeing the opportunity realized. Think about what the self-talk sounded like for these people, especially Abraham Lincoln!

We all have decisions to make when it comes to taking risks or trying something new. We can choose to step off the ledge and attempt to do the "impossible," or we can stay "safe" and never realize true success because of it. As President Theodore Roosevelt stated in his famous quote, "The Man in the Arena":

"It is not the critic who counts, not the man who points out how the strong man stumbled, or where the doer of deeds could have done better. The credit belongs to the man who is actually in the arena, who's face is marred by dust and sweat and blood; who strives valiantly, who errs, who comes short again and again. Because there is no effort without error and shortcoming; but who does actually strive to do the deeds, who knows great enthusiasms, the great devotions; who spends himself in a worthy cause; who at the best knows the triumph of high achievement, and at the worst, if he fails, at least fails while daring greatly, so that his place will never be with those cold and timid souls who neither know victory or defeat."

In any vocation, it is only you who can enter that ring when seeing an opportunity.

About what we do not know, Confucius said, "To know what you know and what you do not know, that is true knowledge."

When considering self-discipline, Tony Robbins said, "It's not knowing what to do, it's doing what you know."

When it comes to hard work and following the vision, David Sarnoff says, "The will to persevere is often the difference between failure and success."

Many times, people succeed because they simply followed up on a thought or took the steps they noticed that no one else did. Or, as John and I experienced, simply getting back up after being knocked down and staying in that ring made all the difference.

No one has said this process is easy. Most of us can attest to this quote from Germaine Moody, "There are some things in life that may come easy but most things worth having or achieving will only come with dedication and tenacity to get it."

The difference in your life, whether successful or not, is often simply how you apply yourself. It involves the discipline to follow up and follow through on any goal. Just as exampled in the "wheel jerk" stories earlier in the book, nobody would have known if I had not followed up on what ended up being those last calls of the day. They were scheduled as the last calls because either consciously or subconsciously, I thought the odds were low of any positive outcomes.

Statistics clearly tell us the odds are in our favor if we simply follow up. We should all know if we do nothing, nothing would be the result. The story here is about not giving up, believing in yourself, getting back on your feet after a fall. Never let a failure—a blunder—stay with you. Learn from it and get right back into the arena.

CHAPTER 17

NEVER LOSE YOUR WONDER

WHILE OUR BUSINESS (and our lives) have changed drastically over the past 30 years, try to imagine the changes in the next 30 years. Change is a part of life. Technology changes rapidly. Markets change. Demographics change. What has not changed is the human brain's ability to wonder; to ask why, to always strive to improve and find better ways of doing things. As you read this, you, through your mind, are actively talking, thinking, and wondering. You do not have the ability to stop your self-talk, or the formation of opinion and thought. Although some of it is conscious, much of it is subconscious.

Our wonder starts in infancy. It is innate. Wondering is an inner part of the conscious brain that absorbs the education we experience as we grow in thought and study. Back in the 300 BCs, the Greek philosophers Plato and Aristotle said that the principle of philosophy was wonder. So even though many will be into the blunder and thunder stages of life in their twenties and thirties, we still never outgrow the wonder aspect of our *psyches*. Your brain was made to wonder, to assist you in looking for answers and learning new things. As you learn, what you learn changes the way you see the world. The more you learn, the more you will recognize opportunity that has always been there for you to see.

What follows are short stories about a few individuals that share a common theme. As you learn about these individuals, notice that there was an important point in their lives when an opportunity appeared to them and they were in a position to act. Their stories show us that while our brains might reach peak potential at age 25, they still continue at top potential for many years.

After covering these few stories of global proportion, we drill down to the more common, down-to-earth stories from mine and John's company that allowed dramatic change in others whose stories are still unfolding. Every story is about an individual who wondered about how they could improve and found a higher level of success. Improving our lives is ingrained in us, but how we do it is up to us. Believing we can is a big step.

Howard Schultz, one of the key persons behind the success of Starbucks, grew up in a housing complex for the poor. He was quoted once as saying, "Growing up, I always felt like I was living on the other side of the tracks. I knew people on the other side from me had more resources, more money, happier families. And for some reason, I don't know why or how, I wanted to climb over that fence and achieve something beyond what people were saying was possible. I may have a suit and tie on now, but I know where I'm from and I know what it's like."

There are many people in similar circumstances with similar dreams. Most of us would like to succeed in some way. We are always wondering how.

Howard ended up getting a scholarship to attend college. He graduated and started working for Xerox. He then went on to purchase and run a small coffee shop in Seattle called Starbucks, and the rest is history. Starbucks' success credits also go to the other two original executives. They were Howard Behar and Orin Smith. Howard Schultz eventually became CEO of the company and developed the chain to a global entity, opening thousands of locations around the world. Both Howard Behar and Orin Smith served as company presidents at different times.

Starbucks has also been a global force in recognizing the needs of their mostly part-time employees—many struggling as he once did. Starbucks was one of the first major corporations to provide health care and assistance with education to all employees, including part-time workers. This was a direct reflection of Howard Schultz' character, remembering his path to success and desiring to help others do the same.

Howard Schultz may have grown up poor, but like most people, he had a desire to do something meaningful. He kept on wondering. His first step? Get an education and start that first job, while still holding onto that dream of something bigger. Howard saw something in a small coffee shop that many of us had seen in Europe but did not see the opportunity. We saw a small, simple place to enjoy coffee in a relaxed setting, a sort of coffee culture that did not exist in North America, but few attempted to act on it.

Howard took the next steps and risk by buying that small coffee shop in Seattle and learning the business, then launching it on a global scale. Before the beginning of Starbucks, millions of people used to work in coffee shops, donut shops, and small cafes. What Howard Schultz did was something anyone might have done, but he is the one who did it! Every one of us today has this same opportunity. The opportunities are in plain sight, and there are literally millions of them. It is the choices you and I make that determine where we will be tonight, tomorrow, next week, or next year.

Larry Ellison was born to a single mother and adopted by an aunt and uncle in Chicago. He dropped out of college after his adoptive mother died and moved to California. He worked at various odd jobs over a few years. He founded the computer software company, Oracle, in 1977 at age 34. Oracle is one of the world's largest technology companies, and Larry Ellison is one of the top 10 wealthiest individuals in the United States. At the time of this writing, his net worth was above $54 billion, and it is continuing to grow. Oracle continues to expand as well, taking up new opportunities as they come and creating new technology. Today, they are one of the leading companies in cloud services along with other big-name players such as Amazon and Microsoft.

These stories about how these two individuals grew up and acted on opportunity are similar. These men saw something many others probably could also see. The difference is they wondered about those opportunities, then acted to create something. The opportunities are still there. The decisions you make will lead you to success or failure. The decisions are only yours to make. When you believe there is something different available to you, your vision can shift towards recognizing it exists, and then see the opportunity as it might unfold. And even if you fail at first, or many times, you can still try again.

Consider Colonel Sanders and Kentucky Fried Chicken. Did you know that Harland Sanders retired from running a restaurant at age 65 with nothing to his name? Stories claim that all he had were his social security checks of about $105.00 a month. He had developed a recipe for chicken that he thought was great, so he started going door-to-door to homes and restaurants, looking for someone who would partner with him. He was met with 1,009 rejections before he finally got a yes. Think about that: he failed to make any progress after trying over 1,000 times, but his tireless efforts never stopped. He believed he had something people wanted. He simply could not find the way to get it to the public.

Sanders finally made a deal with a restaurant on the 1,010th try. The deal was that for every piece of chicken they sold using his recipe, he would receive a nickel. He supplied his spices in packets to the restaurant so they would not know the ingredients. He wanted to keep the recipe secret. His story goes to show you that you're never too old to realize a massive success, and that sometimes it takes a whole lot of closed doors for the right one to open at the right time. It was obvious from his relentless efforts that Harland Sanders was ready when, after failing so often, he realized that opportunity. Few start their thunder at his age after so many years of blunder, but his story shows that wondering is alive and well as we age.

At all our company locations, we made it a point to regularly hold short communication meetings with all employees, as well as sit down with each employee one-on-one at least once a year. Often, I would use one of many small handbooks written by Price Pritchett. The books could be read in an hour. A couple of them we used most used were: *You 2: A High*

Velocity Formula for Multiplying your Personal Effectiveness in Quantum Leaps and *The Employee Handbook of New Work Habits for a Radically Changing World: Thirteen Ground Rules for Job Success in the New Information Age.* Price Pritchett has several other books, but these two served us well. We gave each employee one of these handbooks. They each had a variety of lessons on different topics; some motivational, but more often philosophical. Our meetings were designed to help both employees and management expand their vision, hopefully seeing opportunities and goals to strive for together. They helped create a paradigm shift in how many employees viewed work; to see it as an opportunity that helps them as opposed to simply something they "had to do."

Our employees knew that it made no difference if these opportunities were inside or outside the company. More than once, I met with an employee who desired to expand in a career outside our company, and I would strive to help them get that job. We worked hard to establish a culture where all the employees knew that management and the owners were sincere and cared for their personal well-being, whether that meant they stayed with our company or not.

I once had a service person who expressed interest in a career outside the company. He wanted to be a truck mechanic and work regular hours inside a shop. After a few calls, we were able to get him an interview with one of our best customers. He was one of our best service people, and I'd be lying if I said it didn't sting just a little to lose him. However, several years later, the owner of that company thanked me, saying, "He is one of the best employees we have ever hired. Thank you for helping us both."

That former service person went on to have a successful management career because of that move! We helped him realize the opportunity he had wondered about, even though it was a loss at that time for our company. Doing so proved to the other employees that we meant what we said. We practiced what we preached because we had a genuine concern for all employees. It also proved we wanted all employees to wonder, to think about opportunity and let us help them achieve it if we could. Of course, the ideal is to promote and help those that stay with us, but it does not always work that way.

One of these small handbooks explained having a job something like this: "You work, because you choose to work. You desire to have a home, a car, a lifestyle." The point was to help all employees understand it was their choice to work. Nobody forced them. Working is part of the opportunity in our free country.

A tire company can be a difficult place to work as a technician or service person. It is not very glamorous, and most often, it is physically tough work. The handbooks helped us communicate with all employees that since they chose this line of work, we wanted to make ours the best company in the industry to work at and help them achieve their goals. Then, together we could be the best in our industry.

As the great motivational speaker Zig Ziglar used to say, "You can have everything in life you want, if you will just help enough other people get what they want." There is a unique satisfaction in helping others up the ladder, or down, where everyone gains. In the same vein, a wise person once said, "You meet the same people on the way up that you meet on the way down." Let that one sink in.

To me, there was great satisfaction in seeing any employee grow personally, in both knowledge and job satisfaction as well as in their own self-confidence. Most of us business owners or CEO's who started from nothing share that same desire to help others. As a result, our actions paid back dividends far beyond the financial statements. So, while these small stories do not equal Starbucks or Oracle fame, they are all still big wins in the lives of those involved. Besides, who knows how those individuals might pay forward what they learned?

Both my business partner, John, and I have always had a desire to serve others and help them succeed, finding at some point in each of our careers that it was actually a huge benefit to us and our families. It helped us develop character.

There are many quotes defining "character." One of my favorites is by an unknown author, and states, "Everyone tries to define this thing called 'character.' It's not hard. Character is doing what's right when nobody's looking."

I can only hope every reader of this book can appreciate and protect at all costs the importance of developing their character. In both personal and corporate life, people immediately recognize character. People, especially employees, know who can be trusted, who is going to be honest. As an employer, recognizing character shows you who you can go to when you need help and who to give the promotion to. It's also often easy to see who the slackers are—the employees with all the excuses. The slackers are not likely to be the ones who desire to serve and see others succeed.

As the Price Pritchett handbooks pointed out, you do not have to work for a living or strive for a higher education. You choose to. We would make the point to employees that since they had made the choice to work, to do it well—not to be negative about it or take it out on your boss, teacher, or company that you choose to work or continue your education. We kept illustrating that it is how you look at things and what you see that can make a significant difference in your well-being, success, relationships, and income. As an employer, the benefits of having employees come up with so many ideas on ways to improve the company provided immeasurable returns to all involved.

Over the years, I've kept a file of quotes and stories that have meant something to me in my life, especially the ones that have helped me develop my character and core beliefs. Both John and I have found that there were often employees that strived as hard as we did to succeed, and this quote by Carl Helman sums up this type of person—the type we both hoped we could help.

And Then Some…

These three little words are the secret to success. They are the difference between average people and top people in most companies. The top people always do what is expected… and then some. They meet their objectives and responsibilities fairly and squarely… and then some… they are good friends and helpful neighbors… and then some. They can be counted on in an emergency… and then some… I am thankful for people like this, for they make the world more livable. Their spirit of service is summed up in these three little words… and then some.

CHAPTER 18

COURTESY PAYS

FOR MANY YEARS I carried a little clipping around with me that told a simple story about courtesy. I cannot confirm or reject the story. I can tell you that it taught me a lot about attitude, perception, and how you project yourself to others. How you want people to treat you is often mirrored in how you treat (or appear to treat) them. The title is "Courtesy Pays," and the story goes like this:

Many years ago, a nondescript couple visited the office of the president of Harvard University. The president greeted them tartly: "You will have to be brief. I'm a very busy man and can only give you a few moments." Not wanting to impose on this important man, the couple left immediately. They had planned to give Harvard several million dollars, but instead they donated it to start a new university in California. The new university was named for its donor, Leland Stanford. Discourtesy costs much.

I researched the validity of that story on Leland Stanford, something that today is easy to do with internet and the proliferation of applications to see what is true or fake. I decided to print the story, as it was written on my little piece of paper. The story reminds me of other stories of a similar nature that lend credence to the phrase, "you can't judge a book by its cover." The facts that are important are how we treat others, and that courtesy is always the best path to take.

On that same paper I kept all those years, there is another story dealing directly with how others perceive us through our expressions, body language, and words. Again, regarding our self-talk, our subconscious can be swayed to generate a more positive attitude and outlook on life, work, and family, which in turn is projected in our attitudes towards others we interact with. That perception, or attitude we project to others, both consciously and subconsciously, is the reflection of something we are thinking of or thinking about the person we are interacting with. How we act is a result of what we perceive, what we have convinced ourselves is factual. But always keep in mind that what you think you see might not be what it seems.

As we move further through this book, you will find references to how you can change your self-talk and perceptions, how you can change the way you make decisions, and how reframing can help you look for the positive instead of the negative. All these things can drastically change your trajectory. They also influence how others perceive you when it comes to your sincerity.

Consider this next section from the "Courtesy Pays" piece:

Basic Courtesy influences all of human relations. It also begins at home. Members of a family who treat each other with consideration at home will be courteous in their contacts outside the home, for the home is the testing ground for courtesy. A wife once complained to her husband that he gave the dog more attention than he gave her. The husband replied that perhaps the reason was that the dog showed more signs of genuine welcome when he came home in the evening than his wife did.

Everyone appreciates courtesy, as one businessman discovered. On his many trips to New York City, he concluded that all the city's cab drivers, as well as hotel and railroad employees, were impatient and bad tempered—all difficult to get along with. Then one day he read the words of William Thackeray, 'The world is a looking glass and gives back to every person the reflection of their own face.' The man began to check up on his own attitude, and on his next trip he found he did not encounter a single discourteous person. New York had not changed. He simply found that the quickest way to correct the other person's attitude was to correct his own.

As we can see through this excerpt, you are the only person who makes the decisions regarding your attitude or how you relate to others. A simple smile, removing a chip from your shoulder and acting on the fact that you control your own attitude can have long-lasting positive results. This applies to business, home, friendships—everything you do, anywhere and anytime. If you own a business or manage employees, this includes how you interact with them and correct your own attitude before attempting to correct theirs.

A valuable piece of advice I received was from a chief financial officer we hired. The advice related to how I interacted with an employee when I was angry with him or her. His simple suggestion was to smile and no matter how much I was tempted to cause bodily harm to them, to just contain myself, walk away, and let him deal with the issue and individual. It was not easy, but proved to be an important lesson, as he was a very sharp person who could deal with situations from a different perspective than I could at that time.

Remember, you are talking to yourself all the time, mostly without the ability to stop the comments in the moment. Make an effort to learn what you can do to maintain positive self-talk, which will result in positive actions and comments. How you channel and direct your self-talk is totally dependent on only you and is a result of the efforts you invest.

When I think back to the day we found out the bank had called our note, or the day we were served a federal lawsuit by that Fortune 500 firm, it would have been easy to let negativity creep into our thoughts and self-talk. There were, at first, horrific negative thoughts brought on by sheer fear of failure, but my self-talk soon turned toward clear and positive thinking. I would persevere. I would not give up. There had to be a way to survive; to overcome this obstacle. We had poured tireless energy into building this enterprise, and we were not going to give in to doubt and negative thoughts. John and I were both intentional about flipping the scripts in our minds, thinking instead about how this would only make us stronger and prove our business to be strong.

As you read about the famous people early in this chapter, they also went through difficult times in their lives and in building their businesses. Rarely does anyone succeed without some degree of failure or obstacle to overcome. We all have to deal with occasional doubt. It is how we overcome those feelings that adds to our character, success, and achievement, both personally and corporately.

A man named Don Bennett always comes to mind when I think of tough times and bouncing back from tragedy and failure. Don was a management coach when I first met him. He schooled us when my courtesy (or lack of) needed an adjustment. Don had an incredible history. He founded a business in sales training that eventually went nationwide. It was called Sales Training Incorporated, known by many just by its initials, STI. The tuition for the majority of Don's students was paid for by the G.I. Bill. Don realized that every company had salespeople, yet many lacked professional training. So, he capitalized on that opportunity and was very successful.

At one point, the government decided to stop allowing the G.I. Bill to be used for non-traditional education. It would not be difficult to envision some of the largest universities lobbying congress to make this happen so more funds would go to the universities. Politics aside, STI failed almost overnight. In 1972, Don fell off his yacht while it was underway, and the propeller cut off one of his legs. He came very close to dying, but survived to not only succeed again, but excel at everything he did. Don had a positive attitude all the time. It exuded from him in every situation.

His story was amazing. Here he was, a very successful man with a seemingly unlimited amount of opportunity. First, he lost his business. Then he almost dies and needs to have his leg amputated. He even wound up in bankruptcy court. Just when he thought he had it made as a highly-respected business person who was improving the lives of thousands, he lost almost everything. Despite all this, Don had many friends and was known for always having a positive attitude. He also had an insatiable drive to succeed. Giving up was nowhere to be found in his subconscious or self-talk. Don was the epitome of courtesy at all times, even through that near-death experience that would have broken the spirit of most people.

In 1982, Don became the first amputee to climb to the top of Mount Rainer. He also started another business called Video Training Centers, known as VTC, and marketed his services to businesses to train all employees, not just salespeople, including the owners, company presidents, and CEOs. This was when we first met Don through his training centers and video library. I had enrolled in VTC as a young commercial sales rep when I first started my career. Then, after starting our first company, we enrolled our entire sales force as well as our support staff. Each session consisted of a 30-minute video once a week that could either be played at Don's offices and training rooms, or we could rent the video and play it in our company conference room. Our company held a weekly meeting with staff anyway, so adding a 30-minute video on a whole host of subjects was educational for everyone. So, we decided to rent the videos and incorporate them into our weekly meetings.

I remember a few were videos by Lou Holtz after he was done coaching football at Notre Dame, as well as Vince Lombardi from the Green Bay Packers. Those motivational and educational tapes were about never giving up and giving your best at all times. Successful sports teams are much like company teams, and we gleaned useful insight from their stories. Much like the story about the Seattle Supersonics, these stories about how effective leadership and a belief in yourself can make significant, positive changes for all concerned.

I recall a time when Don was in our corporate office to do some hands-on training in addition to the videos. During his time in the office, he noticed what most of our staff thought (or at least I thought) was simple comradery between some of the sales and service people: slamming one another with smart-alecky comments, always ending with a good laugh. Don pulled me aside, and I'll never forget what he said to me: "Kim, you really should stop these kinds of comments among your staff. This type of 'humor,' as you see it, is not positive at all. In fact, those negative remarks, even if they're meant to be funny, lead to negative thoughts implanted in your employees' subconscious minds." I was taken aback. I thought they were all building comradery, maintaining levity in the stress of daily work. However, I realized that Don was correct. I just couldn't see it even though it was right in front of me. We were acting discourteously to each other with those negative comments we (I) thought were funny. Stopping that habit did not mean we could not have fun in our environment; it was simply not through acts of discourtesy.

Today, in an increasingly "politically correct" climate, many are now realizing the impact of their actions and words. The negative impacts of the past had not been clearly understood when off-color comments or jokes were practiced at the expense of others.

When you think of another person, invariably, you have some sort of observations, and your subconscious and self-talk keep working. Others have the same self-talk when thinking about or seeing you. For this reason, it is increasingly important to notice and celebrate the positive, both in yourself and others. Understanding how our words and actions affect others made a significant difference in many parts of our business. As the saying goes "all ships rise with the tide."

Always remember that courtesy pays. While it is positive to have fun in our work environments, we need to be careful at the same time. Try to understand what your comments might mean to others, whether you say them out loud or not. What could your words create in their minds? What self-talk could you be suggesting to co-workers and friends? Those memories could last many years, so it's always best to have them be positive memories. You can learn to be positive, talk to yourself positively, and maintain a more positive attitude toward other people. When you do, watch as, just like the businessman who visited New York City, the whole world changes. It begins with us.

Practice courtesy at home, work, and in all aspects of your life. Keep learning about your subconscious and self-talk, as that knowledge can be put to work improving your life as well as the lives of others. The results are positive and beneficial to all. Set a goal to learn to be more courteous. Open your eyes to opportunities to give a compliment to another person, at home or at work. Find the positive to dwell on. Look for the good and let others know by being sincere and appropriate. Day by day, you will improve, and your view of the world will expand. Your vision for opportunity will become clearer. You will see better things in other people, as they will see in you. How people react to you is really is a mirror reflection of how you treat them. Remember, you only get one chance to make the first impression. Strive to always make it your best.

CHAPTER 19

WHAT ARE YOU LOOKING FOR?

ALMOST EVERY DAY, you can read a story about someone who saw an opportunity and acted on it. Or as is the case here, someone who saw a higher potential for a company started by someone else. The Wall Street Journal printed a short obituary of billionaire titled, "A Cop Bought a Coffee Shop and the Result was No Joke." This "Cop Billionaire" story was about Ron Joyce who passed away in 2019.

Ron's father was killed when he was just a few years old. At the time, his pregnant mother was only 23. As a boy, Ron was a below-average student. He dropped out of school at age 15. After working at various jobs, he became a police officer in Canada, but was not making enough money to support his family. He was looking for an opportunity to earn more and to be successful. Where he lived, a couple of people had converted a former gas station into a coffee and donut shop. The business had been started in 1967 by a Canadian hockey player named Tim Horton and his partner, Jim Charade. Eventually, Ron bought in as a partner as well. The small shop was called Tim Horton Donuts. The name was later changed to Tim Hortons.

Tim Hortons grew as a fast food restaurant chain, specializing in coffee and donut items. It became Canada's largest quick-service restaurant chain. Ron assumed control over operations after Horton died in a car accident in 1974. He expanded the chain into a multimillion-dollar franchise. Ron sold the business to Burger King in 2014 for $11.4 Billion.

The stories are all so similar: someone who has decided to search for something, finds it, sees the opportunity, and capitalizes on it. All of the stories I am sharing have one thing in common: the people had a mindset of trying to find something better for themselves and their families.

You can see things easier when you are looking for them. For when your mind is open to understanding the why and the what of things you see every day, more becomes visible. Even though you might not be clear on exactly what you are looking for, you will still develop an eye for opportunity and open your mind to thinking outside the box.

Another common theme in these success stories is that the individuals acted on their visions; they took the next step. The story around the Tim Horton enterprise and Ron Joyce, while similar to Howard Schultz and Starbucks, is actually very different. Starbucks went global almost overnight, while Tim Hortons grew slower and more consistently, replicating a model they perfected. The Starbucks leadership team felt that unless they grew very fast, some other large, well-financed chain could squash them and beat them to the market.

Earlier in the book, I made the case of seeing something as you looked at it only because you were focused on finding it. Imagine you are driving home from a downtown area during rush hour. Ordinarily, your focus would be on the traffic, the lights, the car in front of you, and the time of day, as well as some of the other 50,000 self-talk thoughts going through your mind. But now, imagine yourself in this exact same location, but this time, you are going to make a stop to meet someone for dinner. Now you want to find a parking spot.

In the first scenario, you would not notice the turn signal or back-up lights from a parked car two blocks ahead, signaling that they are preparing to leave a parking space. In the second scenario, from the same location, you immediately see this opportunity and focus on it. You might click on your turn indicator, showing you have found a place to park (even though it is still two blocks away).

The main point we take away from this example is that if you are not looking for an opportunity, you will not see it. Both Howard Schultz and Ron Joyce were actively looking for opportunities, and they both saw something that could work for them and acted on it. If you keep your eyes open to the things happening around you, you might just see a business opportunity or something at your work you could improve upon—something no one else sees. You see it simply because your mind is open to seeing it.

John and I started another company just a few years after starting the tire company. We were always looking for opportunities within our business, but this new company was started as a separate entity, and it went global after a few years. Here's how it came about: as our tire business was growing, we developed several manufacturing efficiencies. We had learned to focus on better ways of running our business. I had also been studying Dr. W. Edwards Deming, and how his operational and statistical expertise had helped companies like Toyota become one of the world's leading car makers after World War II.

Deming had a Ph.D. in Statistical Analysis. Studying Deming and our manufacturing processes opened my eyes into what a complete system should look like. Another way to say this is I learned how to view, or "see," our operations from a perspective that included the total supply chain, not just our part of it. My vision included our suppliers and how we could work together to perfect processes that would benefit us all.

There are many books written around Deming's work and focus on quality and management. I was fascinated by his work and fortunate to spend a week in person with Dr. Deming just a few months before he died at age 93. He was an incredible individual who helped change the world.

The result of our continued focus on quality and better systems led to the founding of JIT Inc. JIT is short for Just In Time. According to Wikipedia, Just-In-Time (JIT) manufacturing, also known as just-in-time production or the Toyota Production System (TPS), is a methodology aimed primarily at reducing times within the production system, as well as response times from suppliers and to customers. Its origin and development was in Japan, largely in the 1960s and 1970s, and particularly at Toyota.

The story of our new company began with one of the world's largest truck manufacturers, Paccar. They build Kenworth and Peterbilt trucks in North America, as well as a few other brands in Europe. They have factories in several countries. Paccar is a very large, sophisticated global manufacturing company. They have many very bright people working for them, yet there was an opportunity right under their noses to improve production, increase efficiency, and significantly reduce costs that were being missed. Nobody in the company had their eyes open to the opportunity that we could see for improving operations and significantly reducing their costs.

In addition, the process we thought could be changed would improve many of their supplier operations and reduce their expenses. Yet none of the suppliers, also Fortune 500 firms, could visualize how to do this. It was a perfect scenario for better "Optimization of a System" as started in Japan and taught by Dr. Deming. The largest supplier who did eventually save millions annually from our new venture, was also, ironically, a very large Japanese company called Bridgestone.

As you read the story, keep in mind how you might apply this thinking in your own life. Inside many companies, there are several departments that often do not work as a team, even though they are all paid by the same employer. This "stovepipe" style of organizations, as it is referred to, can be a result of many contributing factors:

- Management style that is hierarchical, very much top down

- Dictatorial styles of management

- Too many layers of management with too few lines of effective communication between them

- Departments that do not work well together or strive to understand the roles of others

- Culture of competition between departments, often made worse by management that fails to understand "Optimization of a System"

A stovepipe activity or style in any organization can be far from productive and allows for added expense and waste. It harms the corporation as well as suppliers. Such was the case we discovered and then remedied by forming our new business around it. In our case, it would appear Paccar was failing to work closely with a valued supplier to optimize a system. One of the key suppliers, Bridgestone, along with Alcoa, Goodyear, Firestone, and several others, found it difficult to push back on Paccar to better the supply chain. I suppose it was in fear of losing them as a customer. The system, or lack of it, inside this Fortune 500 firm was allowing many millions in annual expenses to be wasted.

Paccar had a plant in Seattle that was producing around 40 trucks every day. That meant they were using about 400 tires and wheels every day on these new trucks. These are the large trucks you see on our roads for highway transportation and construction-type trucks. They had additional manufacturing plants in Texas and Ohio, as well as plants in Mexico, Canada, Australia, and the Netherlands.

Every week, the factory would call our company store in Seattle as they needed to have special tires mounted on special rims which were used on trucks that went off-road in the oil fields and other remote areas. We had developed a close relationship with their factory and the people involved in the tire area. Our company would send out a service person to perform the work at their plant, and all was well. This was the norm with many companies who supplement their operations with small contractors, as they needed work done that they were not equipped to do. This meant that while the Paccar employees were mounting some 400-plus tubeless tires on tubeless wheels every day, they might have ten or so of these special tires and multi-piece wheels that required special handling. So, they contracted with us to do that work. Initially, we didn't see any hidden opportunities, but the excellent relationship we had established would help us, as you will see below.

A few times a month, Paccar would call our company and buy a single tire. Then, like clockwork, about a week later they would return a tire of the same size and brand (not the exact tire they bought but a replacement), and we would give them a credit. Do you see what was happening here? Essentially, Paccar was borrowing $400 tires from us for a short period, then returning a tire for credit. This same cycle had been going on for years. While there was a logical explanation as to why Paccar was doing this, nobody was asking the right question: what created this need to borrow a tire from the little tire company down the street in the first place? They had international contracts with Michelin, Bridgestone, Goodyear, and others, and bought their products direct from these manufacturers. Why did they need us?.

One day, I was walking through the dispatch office. Customers were in and out, and there was a lot of activity all day long. One of the truck drivers walked into the dispatch office to turn in paperwork, and he said to one of the dispatchers as I was standing there, "I have the return tire and paperwork from Paccar for the tire they bought last week."

I was aware that this happened occasionally, and I had always wondered why they borrowed tires in the first place. So, I turned to Rick, one of our dispatchers, and asked him, "Why does Paccar borrow and return tires to us like this?"

"I don't know exactly, but I know they do it several times a month."

I really wanted to know why, as I had developed that habit. I asked Rick to get an appointment for me with the person in charge of the tire program at the plant. The main thing on my mind was the enormous cost for both our tire company and Paccar, especially regarding the paperwork, handling of the tires, billing, accounting, inventory control, and follow up. This had to be a huge inefficiency, and we might see something we could do to help them (and ourselves).

This borrowing and returning of inventory was not only a disruption for our tire company, but more so for Paccar. Imagine the amount of paperwork and people involved in the exchange! I wanted to know why they were doing this. What was the thought behind the process?

As mentioned previously, I had been studying W. Edwards Deming as we continued to open additional manufacturing plants. The work and study of Deming is far more than just a study in manufacturing—his philosophy can be applied to everything we do, from office efficiency to quality of products and systems. More importantly for me, it was a philosophy of continual improvement, leading us to always question, ask why, and find better ways to do everything. It would be worth your time to further study the work of Deming as well. He taught the value of asking questions and always looking for ways to improve any system, to understand the lack of a system, or to point out the existence of stovepipe styles of management.

Here is a short Wikipedia piece on W. Edwards Deming that sums up his legacy:

> **William Edwards Deming** *(October 14, 1900 – December 20, 1993) was an American engineer, statistician, professor, author, lecturer, and management consultant. Educated initially as an electrical engineer and later specializing in mathematical physics, he helped develop the sampling techniques still used by the U.S. Department of the Census and the Bureau of Labor Statistics. In his book, The New Economics for Industry, Government, and Education, Deming championed the work of Walter Shewhart, including statistical process control, operational definitions, and what Deming called the "Shewhart Cycle." Deming is best known for his work in Japan after World War II, particularly his work with the leaders of Japanese industry. Many in Japan credit Deming as one of the inspirations for what has become known as the Japanese post-war economic miracle of 1950 to 1960, when Japan rose from the ashes of war on the road to becoming the second-largest economy in the world through processes partially influenced by the ideas Deming taught:*

1. *Better design of products to improve service*
2. *Higher level of uniform product quality*
3. *Improvement of product testing in the workplace and in research centers*
4. *Greater sales through side [global] markets*

Deming is best known in the United States for his 14 Points (Out of the Crisis, by W. Edwards Deming, preface) and his system of thought he called the "System of Profound Knowledge." The system includes four components or "lenses" through which to view the world simultaneously:

1. *Appreciating a system*

2. *Understanding variation*

3. *Psychology*

4. *Epistemology, the theory of knowledge*

In 1980, there was an NBC documentary written by John Huner titled, "If Japan Can, Why Can't We?" At that time, the Japanese auto industry was capturing more and more market share in the U.S. Dr. Deming was "discovered" in the U.S., still being active and consulting in Japan and in other industries. As a result, Ford, General Motors, and others started talking to Dr. Deming about his research. If you are old enough, you may remember the Ford advertisements in the mid-1980s where they used the phrase "Quality is job one." Much of the significant changes in U.S. manufacturing, especially our auto industry, are a direct result of Dr. Deming and his teachings.

I once watched a video of Dr. Deming at a seminar with executives at General Motors, and I think it is relevant to the story here, and a bit humorous. The General Motors CEO, when made aware of "this Deming person," asked his staff to bring him in. The staff flew to Virginia to meet with Dr. Deming and learned he would only meet with their CEO if the

CEO came to his small office in Virginia. In addition, Deming would only work with GM if that CEO was personally committed. Upon return, they informed the CEO he needed to go to Virginia to meet in The Deming Office, which was in the basement of his old home. The CEO replied in the video, "Does he know I am the CEO of the world's largest automobile manufacturer?" The reply was, "Yes he does, that is why he makes this demand. He will not work with GM unless you, sir, are 100% on board and engaged." Deming firmly believed that unless his teachings were clearly understood by top executives, it would be a waste of time teaching the rest of the staff.

The CEO made the trip, saying, "I have to meet this guy." He recalls having to duck his head entering the old basement along with an entourage of other executives. At 5 PM, Deming stopped the meeting to enjoy his daily gin and tonic.

There was a sea change required in the way people were thinking, not just in the auto industry, but in any application. You might call this thinking outside the box, or some new philosophical theory, but it was not. Deming had a Ph.D. in mathematical physics. He was one of the world's leading authorities in statistical applications. He taught the Japanese that if they built quality and consistency, with continual improvements, they would realize higher customer loyalty and increased profits. They also would see increased market share. This was all happening with the Japanese auto manufacturers, and the U.S. automobile manufacturers were feeling the results in decreased profit and loss of market share. Remember, this meeting was in the early 1980s, while Deming had first started his work in Japan in 1950.

I was working hard to apply the Deming principles to all applications of our business during the same time that Paccar was borrowing tires from us. So, I ended up meeting with the Paccar plant manager, who was also in charge of the tire program. The Paccar manager proudly explained the modern, efficient system they had developed for the receiving, staging, and mounting of the 400 tires and wheels that were mounted on the 40 trucks a day they were manufacturing at that Seattle plant alone. All I could see in what they did was huge inefficiency and the introduction of errors—which we already knew existed—along with increased expense.

I left that meeting and set out a plan to change their whole process, utilizing a broader scope that would encompass all their suppliers. It was apparent that Paccar was focused internally and not seeing the whole picture or how to optimize the system and improve quality while reducing expenses. I, on the other hand, saw an entirely new business that could be started around these inefficiencies.

Smart companies outsource processes they do not have the knowledge to do themselves. What I could see were the effects of all that was happening outside of the Paccar Kenworth plant, the effects on their many suppliers, the double and triple handling of products, and the added risks of error. We knew there were errors already, as they were borrowing tires from us. By investing the time to ask the right questions, I was able to see a new opportunity. It took two years of planning to launch, but proved quite successful. Our new company JIT was launched to fulfill a need, and my partner John took over as president of this new venture.

CHAPTER 20

JUST IN TIME

AT THE TIME we met with the people at the Paccar plant to understand why their process had errors, we found they were requiring their suppliers to handle and ship product multiple times. The suppliers all complied, even while knowing they were adding significant cost to the process. Sometimes a tire supplier would have to handle and ship tires three times before final delivery to the Paccar plants.

Paccar was proud to show me the "efficient" system they had in place, but I was well aware that there was a problem with the way they were doing things. It also became very apparent there was a stovepipe mentality where the suppliers were left out of the planning.

As mentioned, every other week or so, the day before one of the 40 trucks was on the Paccar assembly line, one of the 400 tires received from the suppliers turned out to be the wrong one. It was either the wrong size or the wrong ply rating. The added handling and shipping incurred by the supplier simply added variation, introducing errors into the system.

The plant was forced to borrow a tire quickly, either from our company or some other company, or the truck would roll off the assembly line with only nine of the ten tires and wheels installed, then get parked in a holding yard waiting to be corrected.

It was hard to imagine the cost this process was racking up. The people in the tire department had to requisition a tire, then purchasing had to locate the tire and issue a purchase order immediately. Once that was done, purchasing needed to advise the original supplier of their shipping error and issue another purchase order to have the correct tire shipped to the factory. When that tire arrived, they would return it to our company and a credit had to be issued. There were several people involved, and, in our case, we made zero profit by simply loaning out tires.

What may come as a surprise to you when you see a big rig truck running down the road is that there are over 280 different wheels a customer can order (or individual Stock Keeping Units, part numbers or SKUs), and over 500 different tires. It was not difficult for the supplier to ship the tires in stacks of ten tires per truck as Paccar required and have one of those tires be incorrect. This was often not discovered until the day before the tires would be mounted on the wheels to be bolted on the new truck going down the assembly line.

Immediately, it was clear to me there was great added expense with double shipping, and the triple handling of the tires could be simplified. What if they had a vendor that could receive all the tires and wheels from the many suppliers at one location with a single shipment? Then that vendor would mount the tires on the wheels and would deliver them to the plant, "just in time"—the same day they would be installed. The shipping expense alone could be reduced by an estimated $3 million per year, not to mention the handling and warehousing. We had not even yet considered the amount of time and paperwork required by the purchasing departments!

The root cause of the plant's problem was one we still see quite often in different businesses and operations. It happens when an organization focuses internally on what they *think* they need to do to improve efficiency without involving all stakeholders or people and organizations involved. They failed to understand how their actions impacted the suppliers or the total supply system. Looking back on the data taught by Deming, it is the appreciation of the total, end-to-end system that has to be the focus.

The Paccar plant managers were sharp people. They were simply not looking at the end-to-end solution. They only focused on their small part of the larger system. Additional handling costs and errors were not intended, but that was the result. The fault could also lie with the suppliers, as they allowed the additional costs and handling to continue. They failed to try to work with the factory as a partner to develop a better system to improve efficiency, which would be beneficial to all partners.

This sort of activity happens in every company; even between departments in the same company as we referred to above. Somebody devises a great idea to help their department, but in turn creates a negative effect on the other departments. I was eyeing an opportunity to be the person solving all these issues for both the Paccar Kenworth plant as well as all their suppliers. We called this a win-win-win.

While deploying the Deming methods in our company over several years, much of the learning was brought to life in the short full week that I spent with Dr. Deming in person. One of the several examples of a company not focused on optimization of a system was at General Motors. Deming illustrated a simple example. Note: you do not need to be a car wizard to understand this.

In the Transmission Department at General Motors, employees came up with a way to save over $300 per transmission and improve quality, but only if the engine department would add $50 for a device mounted on the engine. Both the engine and transmission departments were graded on their department's efficiencies. Departments in this case can actually be competing instead of optimizing the system as a whole by working together. It turns out the engine people decided they would not allow the other department to cause them a greater expense, even though the company would save $250 in cost per car overall. This could add up quickly, as GM builds many thousands of cars and trucks a day. This was a simple, but excellent example of stove piping. It can creep into any organization unless you are made aware of it. It is one of those opportunities so often mentioned in this book that once you have knowledge of, you realize you missed seeing.

Coming back to our Paccar Kenworth plant story, what I saw was a way to significantly improve efficiency, especially for their suppliers, with a focus on the end-to-end total supply system. My vision was to eliminate the entirety of the tire department staff of 43 people, as well as getting rid of the 50,000 square feet of space used for the inventories of wheels and tires, assembly bins, and mounting areas where tires were put on the rims.

I saw a way that the suppliers could reduce the triple shipping, handling, and staging they were required by Paccar, and calculated about $7.50 worth of savings per tire—and that was just for the suppliers! This would amount to over $3 million in annual savings to just one supplier. I had not yet even calculated the savings to Paccar, which would also be in the millions.

Now, imagine trying to present this idea to a plant manager at Paccar's Kenworth truck plant; that you, who owns a little local tire company down the street, could do what they were doing but better and more efficiently. You might imagine encountering some resistance, to say the least! Again, Paccar is one of the world's largest truck manufacturers. They have exceptional people. They are smart, but like everyone else, unless they are aware of and can see the total effects of decisions well beyond their own operations, they will fail to optimize the system or recognize how to improve it. The suppliers also failed to step up and work through the logistics and plan together.

I went straight to the Paccar corporate office, having secured an appointment with the corporate global head of purchasing, Larry Petrovich. From the get-go, Larry's body language and enthusiasm for this meeting was less than enthusiastic. Later, after JIT Inc. was founded and an enormous success, Larry would tell me what he was thinking during that first meeting. He remarked; "I was sitting there listening to you, thinking, 'How in the hell did this guy get in my office?' I deal with global companies like Michelin, Bridgestone, and Goodyear. Yet, some guy from some little tire company is sitting here meeting with me telling me he can significantly improve our business?" Larry and I did, later, become good friends and stay in contact.

So, I gathered the information I needed in that first brief meeting, and Larry agreed to meet a few weeks later to listen to a proposal. He also suspected the proposal would be a waste of his time, but he, begrudgingly, set up a follow up meeting. Like all the other Paccar employees I met, they were sharp, extremely focused, hardworking good people. It was a great company for which I was very proud to be considered a vendor.

The day came for my follow up meeting in the corporate offices with Larry. I sat down and started walking through the what and why and how I was proposing this new company, yet to be formed, to be the outsource logistics and solution for Paccar for all the tires and wheels. Larry started to show genuine interest in what I had to say. His crossed arms fell to the side and he leaned forward in his chair, listening intently with his eyes starting to widen in anticipation. He cleaned off the surface of his entire desk so I could lay out a map of the U.S. and explain why what Paccar thought they needed was not working, and why the solution I devised would save millions of dollars for Paccar and all their suppliers. By this time, Larry was standing, completely engaged. After I finished my presentation, he promptly sat down, spun around in his chair, grabbed the phone on his credenza and called the Seattle Kenworth Truck plant manager. The plant manager (also named Larry) picked up the phone and Larry stated flatly, "I have the man who is going to solve our tire logistics and mounting problems sitting in my office right now, and I want you to meet with him immediately."

Let me remind you of what just happened: some guy from a tire store in Seattle walked into one of the world's leading truck manufacturing plants and told the corporate global head of purchasing that he could do what they were doing, but better. That definitely took some moxie and knowledge, but at its core, I was acting on a vision. I "saw" what could be, and from a global perspective at that.

In the plant, Larry was implementing what his senior staff had devised, and it made sense to them at that time. They did not know, nor did they *seek* to know the disruption and added costs they were causing themselves and their suppliers. No one was looking at the "global" or complete process, or the total system, and thus had allowed added costs and regular failures through the many variations and handling required. My vision—what I could see—was learned from our own manufacturing process lessons as taught by Dr. Deming. Never stop learning, no matter what you are doing or where you work.

As mentioned, Paccar employs some very intelligent people, and both Larrys were no exception. So, when they were presented with an outsource plan that would save all them millions, of course they studied it, found it made sense, and decided to implement the solution I had come up with. My idea would go on to become our new company. We copyrighted the name "JIT." It was formed a few years before the acronym ever hit the college textbooks. But, of course, JIT was in practice many years prior to our name at Toyota in Japan. Today it is an everyday word in business schools and textbooks! Funny enough, a few of the employees at Paccar laughed at the name when we told them about it. They were not laughing when the results surpassed all our estimates on efficiency and reductions of cost, not to mention significantly increasing productivity with absolutely zero errors over several years of our operations.

During this new venture planning time, I met with the Bridgestone tire company staff and explained what we were proposing to do. Instead of shipping the tires two or more times and handling the tires multiple times, which was the source of many errors, Bridgestone could ship entire truck or trainload quantities direct to a new warehouse we had acquired. It was estimated this would save Bridgestone $7.50 per tire. That would amount to about $800,000 a year for *each* Paccar plant, just in the freight costs. Add to that the additional warehousing and handling costs they would save and the additional paperwork and accounting savings... it was a win-win-win.

I remember one person in particular at Bridgestone somewhat scoffing at my number estimates, saying, "We have professionals that can figure out if there will actually be that much savings." About a week went by, and Bridgestone called to share their findings. "You were very close; our folks calculate saving about $7.41 per tire, so that still puts us very close to the $800,000 per year savings per plant," he said. They were now also on board to work towards optimizing the system with our new venture JIT Inc. Both companies, Bridgestone and Paccar, also recognized the advantage of outsourcing this process as neither company had the specific knowledge or core competency to implement it. Paccar had obviously failed to understand it, and Bridgestone had too many other operations, not wanting to get into another business.

It was not easy forming this new venture. A lot went into the planning for this new company, easily thousands of hours. I remember a Paccar senior staff person commenting to me, "Kim, if you err and the result is an assembly line shutdown, ever, it is the death penalty!" Of course, he did not mean literally, but corporately. If we failed to that degree, they would fire us.

In order to make our new company work, JIT would be doing much of the handling and paperwork that Bridgestone had previously done, and we negotiated a fee per tire accordingly. Bridgestone would eventually save well over $2 million a year at just this one Seattle Kenworth truck plant, as production rose to around 70 trucks a day after JIT started. Bridgestone would save over $6 million annually when the new system was implemented at all the U.S. Paccar plants. This was a definite win-win-win opportunity, just as I had presented to Larry Petrovich in the corporate offices that first day.

Paccar would pay JIT for our end-to-end work: the receiving of all inventories, the handling, mounting and delivery to the factory, literally, just in time. We manufactured specially made racks (one rack per truck) and placed each rack just in time at the back door of the plant, very close to the end of the assembly line. The trucks are all built on a conveyor system, and the last process is bolting the ten mounted tires and wheel assembly on the truck, which then rolls off the conveyor and gets driven out the plant door, ready to deliver. JIT would have these racks in place for each truck, perfectly in order with some 800 different SKUs available for the tires and wheels.

JIT had to have bulletproof quality control and systems in place to ensure there was no chance of failure. Bridgestone would even supply the computers in our offices tied to their corporate billing so the tires were billed that same day they were installed, also saving Paccar days of free cash flow as opposed to billing a few days earlier when they used to ship the tire. Every aspect of the total optimization of a system was thought through, implemented, and constantly improved. Think this through in your work—how departments work together, or fail to, and how you can be the catalyst of change. You might even see that elusive opportunity to start something completely new.

JIT was finally founded about two years after the day I wandered into the plant to see why Paccar was borrowing tires. We invested millions of dollars into building the plant, the conveyers, paint booth, mounting, and safety equipment prior to opening. The JIT daily plant work was labor intensive for four hours every morning, so in addition to our full-time staff, we had firefighters who got off shift at 7 AM rotate into the plant to supplement their incomes. I thought this was a genius way to get through that four-hour period. We always had a contingency plan should the firefighters have an actual fire or emergency in the morning. However, this never happened, and there was always a contingent of firefighters there at 7 AM.

In addition to reducing the tire department staff by 43 people and freeing up over 50,000 square feet of valuable plant space, Paccar was also able to disassemble a paint facility used to paint wheels, thus lowering their Volatile Organic Compounds (VOC) levels for environmental gains. JIT was a very profitable, cash-flow-positive operation from day one. All the planning was built on 40 trucks a day (meaning 400 tires and wheels every day), with growth to maybe 60 trucks a day. At one point, the Paccar plant reached 100 trucks a day and JIT still handled it with existing staff and those additional part-time firefighters filling the extra workloads.

My partner, John, had designed and practically hand-built the facility along with contractors. We had even found a small business in Texas that came up and built us a machine that would inflate every large truck tire to 100 PSI in one second. To put this into perspective, Paccar had previously been filling each tire with a conventional air hose, just like many who are reading this might have used on a car or a bicycle tire. To fill a large truck tire from a standard air hose would take several minutes per tire, and we were doing that same work in one second. With the conveyors and systems John designed and implemented at JIT, it took about four seconds to mount each tire on the rims, all automatically fed to the operator, then one more second to add air pressure to 100 PSI. Anyone who came to see the operation was amazed at the efficiency. We had to buy large class 8 trucks with custom-built large truck trailers to carry the racks of tires. We bought special material-handling equipment, forklifts, and installed special computers, tied in with the supplier databases as well as our own systems. We designed the whole facility from nothing. On top of the amazing productivity of the operation, there was not a single time in the many years JIT operated that there was a missing or incorrect tire or wheel discovered in the process. Paccar saved many millions annually, as did their suppliers, and the errors were zero. We never came close to causing a plant disruption, ever.

Our new JIT Inc. facility practiced Deming methods, providing quality control and continuous improvements while optimizing the total system. When we started mounting the first tires a few days prior to the actual first start day, it took us about a day and a half to do the one-day production run.

The day before we were about to start, it took about a day to complete the day's production run. By the time we went live, we were down to less than a day. After just a few weeks into live production, we were doing a full day's production in about four hours. The full-time employees then prepared for the following day with the rest of the time on the clock, and the part-time firefighters would go home.

Here you have another example of a significant new business opportunity that no one else saw. We saw it because we were always looking for opportunities and ways to improve business. We practiced this with all our customers, every day. We trained our employees in the tire company to always look for ways to improve with every customer. Our new venture, JIT Inc., was a tremendous success. And to think that it all started over a simple question: "Why does Paccar borrow single tires from us?"

So, what did this mean for our tire company? Well, John took over as president of JIT Inc., and I remained as president of the tire company. We worked in separate facilities in the same town and continued a close working relationship. JIT quickly became a very successful company with plans to go global with Paccar and expand to Freightliner, another of the world's largest truck manufacturers, owned by Mercedes.

Several years after we started, Paccar and JIT decided to take the relationship to Australia, the Netherlands, Canada, and Mexico to service all their plants as well. At this time, I was completing an MBA at the University of Washington to better deal with our international business operations. Paccar then decided that there was a risk involved in expanding the JIT operations globally with an entrepreneur. Many millions of dollars' worth of Paccar inventory was controlled by these two individuals, John and me, as compared to a large publicly-traded company. They felt they had no control over us. They were looking at the risk if we failed financially, died, got divorced, or sold the company to others with less attention to details. At that time, Paccar retained ownership and paid for the inventories, while JIT Inc. provided the logistics, assembly, and perfected Just in Time delivery. If JIT failed, Paccar could be forced to shut down operations temporarily and put millions of dollars at stake.

The two companies agreed that it would be best if John and I sell JIT Inc. to Alcoa, which was already a large, established Fortune 500 firm that had great relationship with Paccar. When JIT was acquired by Alcoa, John retired. This was after many years of successful operations.

That company could have been started by anyone. I saw an opportunity and could visualize it, but more importantly, I had the self-discipline to actually follow up, do the research, and start another large corporation. You have the same opportunity in your company or industry—just look around. See what is going on around you, and occasionally ask why. Why does your company or your department do things the way they do? What could be improved? More importantly, if you consider implementing something new, or better to improve efficiency, make sure you consider all stakeholders or all who will be affected by your changes. Strive to avoid stovepipe departments and educate those involved, especially the staff who work for you, on the factory floor, or drive your trucks. Billions of dollars are wasted every year due to poor decisions that seemed brilliant at the time they were implemented, only to fail when they actually started because of lack of input from all concerned.

Even governments often find results from what they do backfire from lack of research and data. An example of this from years ago was when the Federal Government sought to increase tax revenues by imposing a large additional luxury tax on yachts and private airplanes bought by wealthy people and corporations. All they focused on was increased revenue. The error here was that they thought the wealthy would keep purchasing those expensive items and at the same quantities. Hundreds of thousands of workers lost their jobs, yacht and aircraft sales plummeted, and government tax revenues actually fell. Everybody lost in that debacle, but it was years ago, so who remembers? Now, they are considering the same path: tax the wealthy, who are the key creators of the jobs that produce the taxes from incomes and profits. We *can* learn from history.

We started something from nothing by creating JIT Inc., but you, in any position in any company, or even while in school, can learn from this story. You can learn a great deal from the stories of others and how to open your mind to see opportunity. In your self-talk, stay positive and strive to learn more, whether it is through Deming's writings or other sources in your vocation. Never stop learning, and start believing you can be that person who sees and acts on an opportunity.

CHAPTER 21

WE SEE ONLY WHAT WE FOCUS ON

IT WAS ANOTHER busy day, like most days. My schedule had me in the office all morning. The focus, as usual, was on my schedule and plans. What happened that morning was very critical in shaping my vision, in seeing what was right in front of me, yet I was oblivious to. I was completely unaware of how insensitive my actions were to others. While it is embarrassing to talk about my failure here, I believe it is important to share, as this story can be related to by many. Some will relate more to what I experienced, either as a person who might act the way I was, or someone who was dealing with demanding behaviors.

Some might call this sexism, as the recipient was our female office manager, although I believe I would have handled the situation the same no matter if they were male or female. My shortcomings that will be illustrated were not reserved to only those who worked in the office. Regardless of what side you find yourself on, the point of the story is to understand the valuable lesson learned. Pay close attention to the words shared here, as you will be able to learn from my mistakes in management as well as how a staff person handled this injustice. A take-away here is how we treat others—above us and below, inside the company as well as the customers—at all times.

There were some significant time-consuming pressures on several members of our staff, including myself, leading up to what happened. A year prior to the incident, our company had made a large purchase of tire stores and real estate from the General Tire Company. It was a complicated multi-million-dollar transaction, as it involved the assumption of their current operations, property, inventory, and employees—many who had worked for General Tire many years. Great care had to be exercised as these employees would be leaving the relative safety of a large corporation and now be working for a private company.

This was also a big step for our growing tire company. In addition to the new store locations, the purchase included an additional retreading manufacturing facility in Spokane. While Spokane is about 300 miles east of Seattle, culturally, it could be a million miles away. There is a distinct difference between eastern and western Washington, divided by the Cascade Mountains.

John and I had both been warned by many sources about the differences between eastern and western Washington. We even decided to change the name of the company so we would be less identified as a western Washington entity.

When we founded our company, it was called *Puget Sound Tire*, which was a reflection of the Seattle region where it all began. We dropped the "Puget" going forward. Even our bank, in a very professional way during the acquisition, advised us that it was not wise to have a company name reflecting western Washington. They knew of other companies that stumbled or failed in their expansion over to eastern Washington when associated as a western Washington entity. At first, we didn't take it that seriously but eventually realized we better listen.

The local Kenworth truck dealer also mentioned to me, "You know, you might consider changing the company name," giving the same reasons the bank had given. The truck dealership operated stores on both sides of the state. They had experience. As time went on, more companies we worked with started to share the same advice. John and I realized there *was* some seriousness to this issue, and we decided to heed the advice of the people around us. So, we filed for a DBA and changed the public name of the company to simply *Sound Tire*. The name change has nothing to do with the lessons learned that opened my eyes and made me a better owner and manager. It just added to the list of all the pressures of growth and excuses for the way people were treated.

During this time of acquisitions and expansion of markets, we were also dealing with the onboarding of many new employees. We were paying close attention to the diversity of cultures we were now encountering. Many departments in the company were busy with the new manufacturing plant, as well as the addition to the large fleet of service trucks we were already operating. Hundreds of new accounts were being added to the receivables, adding a lot of pressure on our corporate office staff. The purchase and expansion brought additional salespeople to manage, and a much larger geographic territory as the store in Spokane covered thousands of square miles of farms. Our staff was starting to get overloaded with work, especially the Human Resources department.

With the exponential growth we were experiencing, I was working 12-hour-plus days, often 6 days a week. I did a lot of travel to our Alaska stores, and was now adding eastern Washington, visiting the many customers new to us and working with our staff who were also new to our operations and processes.

We had a floatplane in Alaska as so many customers were large logging and mining companies on remote islands not accessible by roads. Many of these large remote companies had their own schools in the "camps" as they were called. They had hundreds of employees and expansive, complex operations. We added another plane in Seattle so we could cover eastern Washington and the more remote customers and stores. We purchased another long-term second-generation tire company in Wenatchee, also in eastern Washington around this same time. I had earned my pilot's license and the instrument rating needed to fly over the mountains when covered in clouds. Instead of a five-hour drive over mountain passes that were often closed due to snow, I could fly home in our plane in less than two hours.

I was not the only one who was overloaded and busy. I was not the only employee balancing work, children, a marriage, and family. There were a lot of others, particularly the office manager, who was juggling greater demands in many departments such as human resources, receivables, payables, and accounting, to name a few. The office manager was a huge source of support to me and my demands as I also shuffled multiple responsibilities.

At this time, my partner John was already working as president of JIT Inc., and he was working across town at that new facility. John and I were still 50/50 partners, shareholders of both companies. We both kept very busy daily schedules. My schedule had become overloaded with all the additional burdens placed on us by this new purchase of stores and operations and staff. Our office manager also handled much of the accounting and back office operations for JIT Inc., as well as our tire company. Just to add a little more pressure on our office manager, I was serving as treasurer at a private school our children attended, as well as treasurer of the very large Washington Trucking Association. I must say, our staff always did an excellent job of preparing my reports. To say I was a handful to support staff would be a gross understatement. While I was focused, my vision was on *my* needs, and I did not see the excellence in the work so many others were performing.

Among all the complexities of the agreements with General Tire, we had a legitimate claim for some $50,000 owed to our company. The claim had been circulated for a long time, and General Tire was slow to get the proper people in a meeting to clear this up and pay us. It wasn't a huge issue by any means; just one of those loose ends that needed to be tied up. It is probably obvious I am adding more and more excuses leading up to my life lesson here.

One day, much to my surprise, the "right people" from General Tire finally showed up. There had not been a meeting scheduled, but I was in the office and thought everything should be easy to handle. All that was needed was the claim paperwork which contained the $50,000 credit details they needed to see and approve. The General Tire folks should be able to easily conclude the matter and issue the credit to us. I went to our office manager's office to get the paperwork needed for them.

Susan, our office manager, was out that day because of problems with her children. So, we were not able to handle the paperwork at that time. Now, let me clarify here: Susan was not a single parent, but her husband also had a full-time job. I had begun to notice that Susan seemed to be out of the office often tending to sick children or handling other issues surrounding them.

Now that I'm on the other side of this situation, I will admit that I was only seeing a narrow view of a much bigger picture that virtually everyone else in the office could see. There is simply no excuse for my behavior that followed, and what happened the next day was one of the most important lessons I have ever learned.

I had failed to notice that whenever I needed anything, ever, it was on my desk in minutes, even when Susan was not in the office. The staff all worked flawlessly to fill in for each other if they had needs with children or other important demands. We had great staff.

The next day, Susan was back in the office. As I was passing her after getting some coffee, she mentioned, "I heard the General Tire people stopped in yesterday?"

"Yes, and you were out of the office… AGAIN." I am sure many in the office heard this verbal insult.

That little addition of the word "again" was not received well, as I would soon find out. Susan did not respond at the time, but about 30 minutes later, it was clear she was fed up with my demanding style as well as my poor choice of words.

I was at my desk. My office door is almost always open. Susan walked into my office, closed the door behind her and proceeded to share her thoughts about my comment with tears streaming down her face:

"You are a complete bastard! You have no appreciation that the whole office runs like a clock. The HR department, payables and receivables departments all run exceptionally well. Accounting and financial statements are always on time. You have never asked for anything that was not on your desk in minutes—ever! Even when I am gone taking care of my children, I get these issues handled, especially your requests. You clearly do not appreciate any of the hard work and effort I have put into making this company a success over the years!"

Susan went on with some other examples of why I was a bastard. She was totally expecting to be fired on the spot. I'm sure everyone can look at this situation and appreciate the guts and emotional toll it would take to say this while realizing she may possibly be losing her job.

I sat there, stunned at the truth in her words. I quickly realized that Susan was correct in everything she said. How blind I was at not seeing what was right in front of my face. I had an extremely dedicated employee—not to mention many other faithful, loyal employees in other departments—but my focus was on so many other things that I failed to see their dedication and hard work. It was not easy having someone tell you such horrible things about yourself, but it was all so correct. She was shaking while crying, her emotions were so sincere. I really was a bastard.

And in case you didn't hear me the first time, I know now there is no excuse for the way I treated Susan. My self-talk was active, with thoughts racing around regarding how right Susan was, while realizing the courage it took to confront me. When I was finally able to collect my thoughts and pick my jaw up off the floor, I swallowed my pride and apologized.

"Susan, I am very sorry. I agree with everything you have said, and I am very embarrassed. I guess another concern I have is whether I am able to change—"

"I DOUBT IT!" Susan interrupted, tears still rolling down her cheeks.

"Susan, I want you to go home for the rest of the day. Don't worry, I am not firing you, and I'm certainly hoping you do not quit. I am sincerely sorry for the way I acted and have been acting. Everything you have said is so true—the paperwork is always here; the reports are always on time, and everything is on my desk when I ask for it. I hope you will accept my apology. I promise I will sincerely try to change. Please forgive my incredibly stupid comment from this morning. I have totally acted like a bastard."

Whatever plans I had the day were put aside. I left the office door closed while I collected my thoughts, reflecting on Susan and her words. It was clear I was lacking empathy towards the support staff, as my focus was on retread production and sales with little attention to so many hardworking people who really made the company run well.

I had kept a copy of the Harvard Business Review from sometime in the late 70s. The article that had caught my attention was on empathy and sincerity and their importance in relationships. I read the article again that morning. Empathy, compassion, and sincerity are of utmost importance in any work or family relationship. It makes no difference if you own the company or you are working for someone else, if the conflict is just between departments or with co-workers or management, failing to have empathy will destroy relationships—and potentially an entire company. Empathy means being able to put yourself in the other person's shoes, to understand their world, to help them, and remain aware of your tone and language. Every one of us has pressures, both from work and outside work.

Susan was an exceptional employee. She taught me a huge lesson. I was equally humbled and embarrassed. Just seeing the gumption in her to face me as she did was huge. A lesser person would have probably just quit their job, and we both would have lost. Both Susan and I will probably never forget that day. Admitting and acknowledging I acted like a bastard was not an easy thing for me to do, but I knew it needed to be done. On the other hand, the fortitude Susan exhibited took a lot of bravery and took a toll on her emotions, but it was also the right thing to do. Susan always did a lot of work, and, again, her brazen action towards me that morning were another demonstration of her commitment to the company. She saw that my actions were not helping the company, and she did something to fix it, risking getting fired while trying.

Thankfully, Susan and I are still friends to this day. Many years later, after the company was sold to a Fortune 500 firm and her work transferred to their corporate office, I helped Susan find another job she wanted, and she found great success there. We still communicate from time to time. Susan did such an incredible job. Everybody in the company knew it and could see it… except me. This is another example of something in front of our (my) eyes yet unseen.

Much of this book is about what we do not see when we are not focused on opportunity. I was not seeing, or even attempting to see the good jobs being done in areas outside of sales and production. I was only focused on making *improvements* in our processes and our team members outside of the office while ignoring my own faults. Once I focused on my own attitude, expectations, and the treatment of those around me in the office, just like the New York taxi story, I was amazed how my view of their roles changed. My prior attitude was similar to some old saying you have heard before, that, "One 'Ah shit!' wipes out a thousand 'Atta boy's." From that point on, I started seeing so much more of the good people were doing all the time. I also started seeing where some might stumble and could look past it if they were normally sincere and doing good work.

CHAPTER 22

SIZE DOESN'T GUARANTEE SUCCESS

THIS LESSON IS about one of the world's largest companies, Boeing Commercial Airplane Company. For many years, they were the largest employer in the Seattle region. In addition to being large, Boeing leads the world in airplane design and performance innovation. Boeing, through vision and forward thinking, has a successful history of delivering what the customer (and the world) needs before the competition. They are a leading-edge, innovative company combining vision and a winning strategy.

A few years ago, Boeing made a decision about the future of air travel that surprised many. Their vision of what the future of aircraft travel would be can be seen in the Boeing decision to not develop a larger plane than the world's most successful 747 model they had introduced in 1969. The 747 was the symbol of success and filled the skies all over the globe. Their rival, Airbus, decided to build a bigger plane and introduced the Airbus 380 in 2007 that would have a capacity of over 500 people.

Boeing, at the time Airbus announced they would develop a larger plane, visualized that travelers would prefer a different plane and mode of travel. Boeing felt the future would be more city-to-city, non-stop direct travel, as opposed to the hub-to-hub methods in use at that time with very large planes. The hub-to-hub (big-city-to-big-city) routes in use required passengers take two or more flights to reach their destinations overseas. Passengers would have to go to one hub city, then fly from one hub to another hub city, and then wait and take another flight to their final destinations. Boeing visualized the airline industry future as creating more frequent direct flights and phasing out the big, expensive jets used in the hub-and-spoke model.

The carriers would save money. The passengers would be better served, and the planes could be more efficient. Living near Seattle where I grew up, many of us thought it would be easier for Boeing to extend the upper deck of the iconic 747 and beat Airbus with a bigger plane. Boeing took a completely different direction, seeing an advantage for airline companies in flying these more direct routes. In routes from the U.S. to China as an example, the airlines could (and now do) fly direct to 16 or more cities in China from multiple cities in the U.S. Before, the airlines were only flying from a handful of U.S. cities to only a few destinations in China.

Boeing, as we now know, was correct. Airbus, after losing billions on their bet to unseat the Boeing 747, has now cancelled future production of the A380. At the same time, Boeing has a growing backlog of the new, less expensive 787 composite jets as well as the very efficient 777 that can fly the new point-to-point direct flights. The story here, again, is thinking through what the customer really wants, even though the customer might not know best how to get it. But this was not the lesson. It is just an example of why Boeing is one of the world's largest corporations. The lesson is in how any vendor, such as our company, could teach them a better way to conduct their business and save millions.

Boeing, just like every customer and every consumer, desires the best value for the money they spend. The company has professional procurement staff in large purchasing departments working to help make Boeing more efficient and to control costs. Boeing employs thousands of people in management—all of whom have a focus on production or support roles and work across various departments. Everyone in the company, as in most companies, is tasked with similar objectives of improving operations, improving efficiency, and reducing costs.

Just in the Seattle region, Boeing has several very large plants, manufacturing sites, and offices. As you might expect, they have the most modern systems, manufacturing processes, management methods and training available. They also have some 2,000 pieces of equipment that have rubber tires on them, and that is where this success story develops.

Boeing would request bids annually for their tire contract, which was roughly $500,000 in annual business in our area alone. For many years, the same supplier was awarded that bid based on the Boeing bid process they deployed. Boeing is audited internally as well as externally by the governments and huge customers they serve. The best industry standards were always foremost in the process. Boeing would send out a Request for Proposal (RFP) to qualified vendors based on the tire sizes and usage they expected to need. It was a very logical, well thought out process. Several tire companies would fill in the prices, then a contract would be awarded to the company whose total price, based on all the historical usage criteria, was the lowest.

How on earth could some small regional tire company teach them anything new or improve their processes in purchasing as well as manufacturing protocols? As with all large operations, the overall objective is to be able to buy quality products and services efficiently, reduce costs, and save money.

As I mentioned, Boeing was spending roughly $500,000 a year just on tires. So, you might find it hard to believe that we found we could save them roughly $600,000 a year by changing how they handled the buying and tire management processes. This is not a typo, as you will read, but thinking outside the box using a different focus.

Every tire company in the region would bid on the Boeing contract, but it always seemed to be the same company winning the bid. We attempted several times to illustrate to those handling purchasing a better way to handle the tire acquisition and management with little success. After all, we were just a local tire company—how could we show Boeing a better way to succeed? Our company *was* able to secure a small specialty contract with Boeing. We developed a solid relationship with the maintenance department personnel, and they paid attention when we could show by example how to do things differently with their tire purchases and operations. They had several maintenance facilities all over the region to service their many plants and facilities. From our small contract, we were able to show that even better operator training on the operation of the large airport fire trucks could save them significant expenses. That led to our first Small Business Contractor of the Year Award and cemented our relationship as a trusted supplier.

While we had still not been successful in being awarded the main tire contract, we could clearly visualize a much better way to lower their costs; something that no other competitor (including the one that won the bids) could see. Much of this vision was a result of the "optimization of a system" approach and our studies of Dr. Deming.

To begin with, there were far too many tires sizes used in Boeing's fleet of equipment. They needed to standardize, consolidate, and reduce the number of tires needed. They could reduce the number of tire sizes used from 26 to 7 sizes.

Then I could see they were spending a lot of money warehousing the tires and distributing them to the other Boeing facilities. This required several staff members working in a warehouse and driving delivery trucks. Just the warehouse labor, rent, and related expenses added an additional $500,000 annually that was being spent on the tire maintenance process. You can see where this is headed—they were actually spending well over $1 million annually on tires if you include all the related and unnecessary expenses!

They did not need any of this additional expense. Every tire company in the area had delivery trucks, as well as warehouses, and could replace this obsolete process. But the purchasing staff at that time were blinded by the mindset of "this is the way it's always been." They also operated in stovepipe methods where the automotive department that handled all maintenance and tires could rarely talk to purchasing staff. It seemed impossible to change their minds. However, every so often,

Boeing needed some sort of special tire or something that was almost impossible to find, and I became their go-to person. Headway was slow, but our tireless efforts would pay off. It just took a few years.

One day, the head of maintenance called and asked if I could get them eight special-sized tires for a trailer. He said, "I know you are going to tell me we should not be using these old tube type bias-ply tires, but we have 100 of these trailers, and they all have the exact same tires on them." So, they had 800 obsolete tires and wheels on these very special trailers that hauled the engines to the manufacturing facilities.

I called my competitor, who had been awarded the Boeing contract, and simply asked if they had the tires in stock and was told they had 66 of them on hand. This is the same day they had just told Boeing they were out of stock... something was wrong here. So, I drove a pick-up truck over to the warehouse myself, picked up the eight tires needed and delivered them to Boeing on my own—all in less than an hour.

The VP of maintenance was shocked.

"Where could you have possibly found these tires?"

"Well, there was only one tire dealer in all of the Northwest that carried that exact tire, and it just so happens they are also the company that always wins the bid for supplying you with tires. The tire you needed was one of the largest line items on the bid, so the bidding company has been bidding you below their cost. However, when you order, they have been telling you they were out of stock, which then allowed them to supply a similar tire with a guaranteed profit as allowed by the bid contract."

I paused for a moment to let all of this sink in before I continued, "When are you going to learn that these folks are taking advantage of you? And when are you going to stop buying these outdated, poor-quality, low-bid tires and start switching to tubeless radial tires like I've been telling you all along?" I could see it was finally sinking in that they had a broken system. While we were only finding a remedy for one trailer, one piece of equipment, we were illustrating a symptom of a much larger problem in his operations. There was a corrupt supplier who was dishonest in handling their supply bid, in addition to the overall waste in their mode of handling tires in all areas.

The two of us sat down for an hour as I explained what Boeing was currently doing that should be changed. Keep in mind, these Boeing folks are professionals—they do want to improve, but they also have large bureaucratic systems and processes to work through, which makes it hard to convince them to change. I made it clear to him, again, that they were actually spending over $1 million on tires including the warehousing, labor, and inter-plant delivery. We could eliminate all that, as well as save more with standardization and upgrades in sizes. After explaining my ideas and sharing what I had been seeing over the past few months, I left to give him some time to think.

As you will read in the numbers soon, it should have been obvious, but there were many factors that prevented management from seeing the change I had presented as possible. They needed to consolidate the tire sizes from 26 different tires and wheels on equipment (standardize) and eliminate the warehousing and distribution. In addition, they needed to switch to radial tires to save fuel and cut tire costs.

Sometimes we must paint the picture for the person before they can see it clearly, and it looked as though we finally had that opportunity. But that individual running the maintenance also had to convince corporate executives above him, who in turn had to achieve buy-in from purchasing.

The next morning, the maintenance vice president called me. Apparently, he had spent a significant amount of time mulling over everything I had presented, and he was ready to make a change and do it now. He gave us a purchase order for 800 Michelin tubeless tires and 800 new wheels to change these 100 special trailers over to radial and tubeless. He also then set up a meeting of other maintenance management staff and purchasing staff to listen to a detailed presentation we would facilitate on significant ways Boeing could cut the overall costs of tire use and acquisition.

While the single order on its own was large—nearly $240,000—what was truly important here was that I finally had their attention. They were now willing to listen and open to looking at a significant way to change what they were doing.

They all wanted to find ways to save money, of course, but now I had the opportunity to paint the picture of what change could do for them. We could show them with actual numbers how our recommendations would save them $500,000 minimum per year in just the warehouse, labor, and logistics required because they were doing it all in-house. Of course, this was a shock. They only knew they spent roughly that amount on tires. How could they reduce that same amount and more? Because they were not "seeing" the total end to end system, or lack of it, I had a solution.

I was able to show them what no other competitor was able to show them, simply because none of our competitors could see or comprehend the opportunity we could see. This is a prime example that paying the least amount for a product is not always the best value in the long run. Boeing, like so many companies, was focused on the up-front product cost, while the real savings was on the process and the total end-to-end system. By standardizing the sizes and eliminating the warehouse and labor, they could save more than they were spending.

I had been collecting data, putting together a comprehensive business model that could be shared across multiple Boeing departments—especially purchasing. The changes would require moving forward with a completely different concept, but it was the same concept Boeing was so adept at when building their airplanes: the increasing dependence on sub-contracting to increase efficiency.

To develop accurate numbers for these departments that would illustrate what could be done and the resulting increases in efficiency and decreases in costs, I suggested they pay me $5,000 to do a comprehensive study and a survey of equipment. I did this for two reasons: one, they would have "skin in the game," and two, when presenting the findings, purchasing would view the report as done by a consultant as opposed to one department trying to tell the other what they needed to change. The goal was to eliminate the stovepipe mentality as to who owned the decision. After completing the survey, we could present very accurate numbers.

Boeing agreed to pay me for the study, and I went straight to work. It took me about a month, working a few hours here and there and a few weekends while some equipment was idle to get the survey completed and compile the data. I strived to make a business case anyone could readily understand while providing examples of how this same model has worked for other companies. What I really wanted was for them to be able to act on the recommendations, with each department feeling like they owned the outcomes and could take credit for the result I knew would be realized. Not very many companies have a purchasing department that works well with operations. They can often be at odds. Boeing was no exception. The presentation had to be something both departments could clearly accept.

The following is a summary of the report I developed, backed by the data collected.

Boeing was spending about $500,000 a year on tires. They were running old, tube-type bias-ply tires. By changing to radial, tubeless tires, **we could save them approximately $50,000 a year.**

Boeing had 26 tire sizes on their main fleet when they really only needed 6 different sizes. By standardizing sizes, they would achieve better utilization and require less inventory, **thus saving them an estimated $50,000 a year.**

Boeing had a warehouse leased to store tires with rent of about $150,000 a year. They also had fully-weighted employee and staff costs of over $350,000 for the warehouse, and additional expense for delivery staff of $100,000, including the truck expenses. They did not need a warehouse and inventory, as I already had the warehouse and would be able to maintain the inventory on my own. My company would provide warehousing, weekly deliveries, and maintain small inventories at all facilities for approximately $100,000 a year. **This worked out to savings estimated at $500,000 in annual actual expense eliminating warehouse and in-house delivery.**

This made the total annual savings estimate $600,000.

It was clear, and easy to verify, that by making a change in the way Boeing operated, they could procure tires, maintain smaller inventories at each plant (similar to the JIT model from previous chapters), and spend significantly less money The savings would increase as we switched them to radial tubeless tires and reduced the obsolete sizes over time.

Boeing did change their process of how they went to bid and procure tires. My company was awarded the entire bid, as no competitor was able to demonstrate the ability to provide this broad range of expertise and services. All the competitors had warehouses, and they all had delivery and service trucks. But what the competitors did not have was employees trained in fleet management and inventory control, as well as people trained to work in the customer locations as if they were employed there.

With this success, we continued gaining market share and growing fast. Our competitors couldn't wrap their heads around how we were doing it. I often used the saying, "You do not know what you do not know." There were maybe 15 other companies, including big national operations like Goodyear, Firestone (now Bridgestone), and many big regional tire companies competing for the same market, yet none of them were able to see what the customer really needed. The competition knew the customer wanted a lower cost, but rarely can the customer achieve that objective simply by buying something cheaper. It requires a change in the way they operate. We were able to show a mega global company a much better way to operate, while at the same time, increasing efficiency and safety simply by looking at a bigger picture.

Just as Boeing had the vision of future air travel and capitalized on that vision, we were able to visualize a better way for Boeing to operate, in our comparatively small way. I still laugh to think of the reaction on the faces in the room when we told them we could save them over $600,000 a year in their tire and service costs when all they knew was that they were spending $500,000 a year.

Leadership has an obligation to visualize what can be and what is in the future; otherwise, companies become obsolete. Boeing is not the only company that has successfully accomplished this. We can learn a great deal from all these success lessons. Boeing has over 50,000 small business suppliers. Our company was honored after the success of the changes we had recommended, making it to the top finalists in companies to be awarded the Small Business Supplier of the Year award.

Every company has a desire to improve operations, add business, reduce expenses, and be more successful. No matter your vocation or position, if you think outside the box, ask yourself why things are done the way they are and what improvement could be made, your vision will improve. Our company was on the way to record-setting market share as a result of our continued efforts to focus on training and staff as well as increasing our knowledge of what the customer really needed to change in order to improve efficiency. You can do the same.

CHAPTER 23

A TALE OF TWO CITIES

THE LAST CHAPTER contained information about Boeing, one of the world's largest and most successful companies. The company maintains a very sharp vision and utilizes strategic planning to remain successful many years into the future. This foresight and the constant attention to what the industry needs now as well as what it will need in the future is evident in the examples cited regarding Airbus' strategic failures compared to Boeing's strategic direction and success.

In an article about the Airbus A380 debacle published by The Wall Street Journal, the author asked an analyst where they thought Boeing would be in 100 years. The reply was eye-opening. He said something to the effect of "100 years to Boeing is simply two aircraft model lifespans." The 747 was introduced in 1969 and is still very much in use in 2019. The 737's first flight was in 1967, and they have backorders for it through 2026. There have been well over 10,000 of these planes manufactured. The new 787 composite plane and the variations of the 777 could see production past 2070, and there is already talk of a new model.

Aside from the aircraft production decisions Boeing makes, Boeing also plans where to locate manufacturing facilities to ensure they can continue to operate competitively now, and over the next 100 years. About 20 years ago, they announced they were moving their corporate offices out of Washington State where they had been since Boeing started. The Boeing Company had been the largest employer in the State of Washington for quite some time.

My father came to Seattle from Chicago to work at Boeing during WWII. He worked there for over 30 years. Both my brothers and sisters worked at Boeing; one brother was there 40 years. Growing up in Seattle, many of us have a kinship feeling about Boeing.

A few years after moving the corporate headquarters, Boeing also announced they were opening new manufacturing facilities in South Carolina. These facilities would be a second location for building the model 787 composite airplane. When they opened the new facilities in South Carolina, they did so in defiance of the National Labor Relations Board (NLRB), who was fighting to keep them in Washington. Was their move related to union issues?

While I cannot give all the reasons for Boeing's strategic moves, our company had an experience that clearly illustrated why a company like Boeing would move. Just before the Boeing relocation announcements, our tire business was expanding and needed to acquire larger facilities. The tire company at that time had over $30 million in revenues. We were outgrowing our offices and manufacturing space. Our JIT Inc., Paccar facilities were also expanding. The Kenworth truck facility was producing almost double the number of trucks they had when we started production. On top of that, the Freightliner Corporation, who also built trucks, was talking to us about opening a JIT facility in North Carolina for two of their very large plants who had *almost double* the daily build rates as Paccar. I had been meeting with Freightliner for over a year. They were impressed with our company and the solutions and efficiency we could provide them.

We decided to expand the tire retread manufacturing, warehousing, and corporate offices to Auburn, Washington, where we were already operating and purchased five acres to build the new facilities. Auburn is located between Seattle and Tacoma. Several large transportation companies were establishing operations there, and Boeing also had a large support facility there. It had only taken us a short time to outgrow the Auburn facility we had acquired just five years previously when we moved our manufacturing operations there from the crowded industrial area of Seattle.

Associated with this business growth is the need to hire additional employees as well as adding space. When companies hire more people, it generally lifts the tax base and spending in the city where they are located, which would seem attractive to that city. As we made the final plans to construct a new 60,000 square foot facility, we found out how difficult and expensive it would be to operate in Auburn. As mentioned, we were also looking to construct an 80,000 square foot facility for Freightliner in North Carolina. Freightliner, owned by Daimler Benz, also owns Mercedes. Their U.S. corporate offices were in Portland, Oregon. Freightliner had three production facilities in North Carolina, as well as one in Oregon. So here we were, looking to expand both of our companies, Sound Tire Company and JIT Inc. and in two very different business climates. The differences were eye-opening.

Even though our operations are a small fraction of a company like Boeing, the story of how two cities approach business, their futures and their constituency was stunning. In Auburn, what we experienced, we thought, was simply "government" and the negative aspects of an overgrown bureaucracy. How could we have known differently? Since we started both Washington and North Carloina expansion projects simultaneously, we were able to compare the two and the differreneces were staggering. It became crystal clear why Boeing made their decisions, and why so many large U.S. and foreign companies are relocating to the southern states. We read about these moves and expansions. Now you can read the supporting information that is not shared publicly. This speaks volumes about in which cities and regions companies choose to locate their operations unless the cities change their strategies.

Typically, few if any governments are known as power-houses of productivity or ingenuity. Companies generally look to locate where the tax structure might be advantageous, where the government truly welcomes their presence, and where the company feels they can develop a mutually beneficial part-nership. Forward-thinking cities offer tax incentives geared towards long-term tax revenue growth, lower unemployment, and relations that are advantageous to both the community and the business. This is just common sense, good business, and represents a government wanting to serve the people who live there. Some examples have been made public regarding cities bidding to attract large corporations such as Amazon and others.

At the time of this writing, Amazon's world headquarters are in Seattle. Recently the city council voted to levy a new "head" tax on all large companies in Seattle in order to create a fund to help with the homeless problem even though the city had no plans on how to solve the growing issue or how the funds would be used. To the south of Seattle, the City of Tacoma immediately advertised they would provide an equal tax credit per employee for any business relocating to Tacoma. Fortunately, for all the businesses in Seattle, the "head" tax vote was overturned a few weeks later. Now Amazon has announced they will start shifting their operations east across Lake Washington to Bellevue as a result of the deteriorating business climate in Seattle.

When a state or city maintains a healthy business climate, both the city and the businesses can do well and serve the taxpayer base that supports that area. When the taxing authority (states or cities) lose those relationships and start to overtax or overreach their authority to a point where it becomes less competitive, then business suffers. When a business suffers, they can fail, keep suffering, or find a more suitable business environment. Boeing recognized this over 20 years ago and planned for it.

From the first day we started working towards expansion in Auburn, Washington, we were met with an adversarial environment. We were working with a very time-consuming, expensive bureaucracy that seemed counterproductive but with no other city to compare our experience with, we just kept working through the system (or lack of) towards the construction of our new facilities. It was about the time we completed that new construction project that I flew to North Carolina, accompanied by Freightliner executives who had set up meetings with the City of Statesville, where we were looking to build and start a new JIT Inc. operation. The differences in how the two cities operated were eye-opening. The building sizes were close to the same, as was the property needed. Both facilities would be light manufacturing, distribution, and warehousing, which all had common zoning codes.

In Auburn, we had already received a small variance in order to manufacture retread truck tires. However, it took us 14 months to get the building permit and at great expense. Plans for the building were submitted many times, changed many times; often changing the same thing the city asked us to change months prior. The property we had found required $200,000 or more in pre-work to make it suitable to construct a building. Land in that area is located on thousand-year-old volcanic mudflows from Mt. Rainier that contain old trees and organic materials that have to be compressed. Before a building can be constructed, the owner has to import hundreds of truckloads of dirt, allow it to compress the soils, then export that dirt before starting to build. The process is called "pre-loading," and if not done, the building will settle, crack, and eventually fail.

The City of Auburn levied a $40,000 fee for us to hook up to the sanitary sewer system. They added another $170,000 assessment for future improvements on four intersections since we would be adding traffic and employees to the new facility. It did not seem to matter to the city that we were already located there. They stood firm with their fees.

There were several other fees and permits required over those 14 months before we could start construction. We had to construct the road to our building as well as continue the road past our property for future companies which were expected to buy the land behind our facility. We were told our road had to stay open for anyone to use. This was our private property, and the city was forcing us to build a public road, sewer, and utility area, all at our expense! All of this added additional expense and time. In addition to the sewer permit fee, we had to construct the sewer lines *beyond* our facility for those future businesses on the land behind ours. Just the road, sewer, and utility lines cost an additional $100,000+ and we would not be allowed to collect that back from the landowners who would build in the future.

Contrast this to what happened the day we landed in North Carolina with the Freightliner executives. After driving from the airport to Statesville, we were met by a city employee. Keep in mind, Freightliner already operated two very large truck manufacturing plants near Statesville, so we had jointly chosen and agreed that the Statesville area was centrally located to service both plants with one large JIT Inc. facility. We were driven to a beautifully completed business park. The city employee explained the city had recently constructed this large business park in order to attract new business. All the roads were in place; all the utilities were already underground waiting for the new property owner to build. The person who met us in Statesville was talking the same way any commercial real estate salesperson would. He was trying to sell us an 8-acre building site. I had to ask him, "Are you the real estate person selling this property? I thought you worked for the city." His reply was startling, "Sir, I work for the City of Statesville. We invested our tax revenues and sold bonds to develop this land in order to attract new businesses that would locate here and hire people from our area. We aim to develop a solid, dependable business base in our city."

Having just been beaten down for 14 months while getting our building permit in Auburn, his response came as a great surprise. I then asked him, "About how long do you expect it takes to get the building permits?" This time the reply was "Sir, it normally takes three days, but if we are busy, it could take a week." I went on to explain my question was really pertaining to receiving the whole building permit to construct an 80,000 square-foot manufacturing, warehousing, and distribution facility. He looked at me with a slight smile and said, "Sir, I understood your question the first time. We know how to fast track business here. We want businesses here, especially clean operations, as you have proposed. We can have the civil permits in three days. Before you can mobilize the equipment to start the dirt work, we will have the foundation permits, and before you start the foundation, we will have all your needed permits coordinated and ready. We have three contractors that could start your project construction next week if you have the proper credit."

This was so foreign to me: a city employee, representing a city that welcomed new business and was truly serving the taxpayers. The new business park was exceptionally well laid out. Buildings shared conformity in design. They were all good-looking structures with landscaping and ample parking.

The whole area was a stark contrast to the hodgepodge of different construction, poor overall planning, and sloppy industrial appearance in the area the city of Auburn had zoned for industrial use. The Statesville business park was stunning in appearance, and the forward-thinking city planners obviously shared a very long-term vision for their whole community. As if the city employee had not already sold me on the area and the business environment, he went on to state "The city will also give you tax credits for every employee you hire in this area."

This true story is similar to the Boeing and Airbus comparisons with similar vision and in contrast, lack of vision by leadership. Airbus was run by bureaucracy and government planners; Boeing by executives who had a vision and a focus on what the customer (both the airlines and their passengers) would buy if given a choice.

What we saw in the City of Statesville is a small story repeated all over the country by mid-size cities which desire to build their tax base, improve their communities and exercise excellent control on the type of industry they want located within their cities.

Auburn, on the other hand, had a Boeing facility there already, had been building ever-larger bureaucracy layers, and lacked leadership with any vision. The focus in Auburn seemed to be control and income through fees and excessive taxation. It seems few if any city or government entity ever tries to *control expenses* as every business has to do. The cities and states just keep raising taxes, and if they are not careful, they will find companies like Boeing, Amazon, and others exercising their rights of choice and moving away. A business needs to stay competitive; a city also does. Many just fail to understand this.

By this time in our business, we operated in several cities, both in Alaska and Washington. We dealt with many municipalities and departments. Most all were easy to work with, and I believe most businesses want to be good "corporate citizens." There should be a mutually beneficial relationship between city and business like we had developed in most locations, the same as so many other businesses. But some cities develop anti-business behavior that I believe is simply a lack of solid, intelligent leadership and vision.

Here is a short summary comparing our Auburn WA and Statesville NC expansions;

	Auburn WA		Statesville NC	
Building size	60,000 SF		80,000 SF	
	5 acres		8 acres	
		per acre		per acre
Land	$1,250,000	$250,000	$96,000	$12,000
Sewer fee	$40,000		$ -	included
City Street improvements	$170,000		$ -	included
Additional environmental	$200,000		$ -	included
Building preload	$250,000		$ -	Not needed

Add private road, utilities	$100,000		$ -	included
Total before building cost	$2,010,000		$96,000	
Permit time needed	14 months		1 week	

Important to note, a city is not controlling the land costs. That is market-driven. A decision on where to locate a business is driven by where they *need* to be located, and businesses adjust accordingly to account for the costs. But the ongoing costs, taxes, labor issues, fees, and regulations only designed to enhance a city coffer, cause businesses to move. Boeing can build planes anywhere they can find labor, while our operations were centric to our customer locations. So, while we would operate in both Auburn and Statesville, what a huge difference in the way each city viewed growth, long-term stability and mutually beneficial relations with business while still looking out for the taxpayers and environment!

Leadership starts at the top, we see this in every company, and it is reflected through their employees, how customers are treated, and eventually their revenues and profits. A city has customers, those who pay the taxes that support that city. The leaders of some cities seem to forget the fact they are there to serve the community. They are also there, of course, to enforce the laws, enforce the codes, protect the environment and so much more. How they treat the customer is a reflection of the leadership and vision or the lack of it.

In the tale of two cities here, we felt abused and mistreated in so many ways, with city employees making demands instead of working alongside us. We all wanted the same results, a beautiful, and functional environmentally-safe facility that we, our employees, and everyone else would be proud to see. It seemed instead of focsuing on the customer, some cities only focused on increased revenues and building a larger,   more burdensome bureaucracy.

It is clear why Boeing moved, and now Amazon is shifting. The vision and leadership, the strategic planning, and focus on the customer that successful businesses employ, needs to be emulated in government. Of the millions of individuals who work in governments as employees, many are very sharp, although not so much when we look at the city councils and elected officials. Statesville, North Carolina and hundreds of other future-thinking, well-managed cities are growing while many poorly managed states and cities are seeing businesses flee. Now you know more of the possible reasons why Boeing moved and opened alternative operations. I would predict Boeing will have only a small footprint, if any footprint at all, in Washington State 100 years from now.

CHAPTER 24
CAUSES OF FAILURE

AS YOU LIKELY have gathered by now, most of this book is aimed at learning to exercise your mind by developing habits that lead you to look beyond what you see at first glance. Thousands of people have benefited from looking past what might seem to be the obvious or the first impression and asking themselves "why?" By really looking into what is not seen, and asking questions, thinking through the alternatives of doing something differently, you exercise your mind to seek greater knowledge, to understand the why and possibly come up with a better alternative or process. All of us are in daily situations here we could benefit from having our eyes opened. We are "looking at" something, but not really "seeing" what it is or why it is there. The "something" we see can be an object or an action. An example of this is how we started JIT Inc. ; by asking why a company did something we considered unusual, and then researching what led to their actions.

Here is another simple story that illustrates the idea that things may not be what they appear to be. Something we all see when on the freeway; those pieces of rubber laying in the middle of the road so you have to swerve to avoid them, or littered on the side. Have you ever wondered what they are? Most people assume they are from retreaded tires. However, those pieces of rubber have almost nothing to do with retreading.

The next time you are driving past one of these pieces, just glance at the ends of the rubber piece where you will most often see mangled wire protruding. This short story, once you understand what you are seeing and why, might save you from a similar circumstance with your own tires. If your tires look as if they are low on air, and you drive some distance at freeway speeds, your car tire can fail and you could be injured. Even while passing by one of these pieces of the tire at 70 mph, you can almost always see steel cables and wire jutting out from the pieces of rubber. What most people don't know is that the retreading process does not use steel—the steel is part of the tire when it is first built. Many of the pieces you see on the freeway have actually never been retreaded.

All these tire failures happen in a similar way, whether the tire is retreaded or has original tread: it has to do with heat. A tire builds up heat as it rolls, and more load equals more heat. Low air pressure also creates more heat. This is why you see more of those rubber pieces in warmer southern states than in the northern climates. Heat is almost always the cause of these catastrophic failures, which in some cases cause accidents, serious injuries, and death. Pay attention here because the rest of this story might save you from your own tire failure.

In 1998, the Ford Motor company had a vehicle tire safety crisis with their Ford Explorer. It was a time when Explorer tires had treads flying off, tires exploding, and drivers losing control. There were several injuries as well as deaths as a result of the tire failures. By the time it was brought to national attention, over 46 deaths and 300 incidents had been reported.

So, what happened to cause this?

The tire tread separated from the tire casing, along with the steel belts. The steel belts and the tread on the top simply separated from the sidewalls, and the casing exploded. This can happen in an instant. Low air pressure causes the temperature to increase to a dangerous level, causing the failure. None of those Ford Explorer tires were retreaded tires, but as mentioned already, all tires fail the same way when subjected to high heat levels. But that still doesn't answer our question: what *caused* this heat and why did the tires fail.

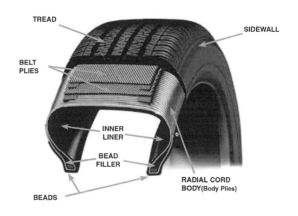

Radial tires are made of a casing with steel belts wrapped around the top just below the tread. The tire and steel start to heat up while driving. Hotter road temperatures and low air pressure cause the heat to increase above what the tire was designed to withstand. The steel is adhered to the casing with rubber, and when that rubber reaches about 212 degrees, it starts to melt, and the adhesion fails. The steel comes off the casing along with whatever tread is above it, regardless of whether the tire was new or retread. But why did the Ford Explorer tires fail so often, when others vehicle tires did not?

In the legal wrangling that followed, there were a combination of factors: The tires had a bit deeper tread (the deeper the tread, the more heat) and many people failed to keep their tires inflated to the vehicle manufacturers recommendations. Hot conditions, maybe a little too much tread, high speeds (speed increases tire heat) and low tire air pressure all combined with a disatrous outcome

If a nail or sharp object gets stuck in your tire, any tire, that lets air out slowly. The low air pressure in the tire will, again, cause it to fail if you drive any distance. Always look at your tires before you drive. Thankfully, most of the new cars and trucks we buy today have air pressure monitors that alert us if the pressure is low, so we know to act in order to avoid this type of situation.

If you are running tires below the recommended pressure for the load and speed, the tire will create more heat. If a deeper tire tread is used, then the risk of failure is increased. Not only did the Ford Explorer have a deep tread, but most people did not regularly check their tire pressures. Add to these factors high speed, hot pavement in states like Arizona, Texas and California, and the steel belt temperature increases high enough to melt the rubber that bonds the steel to the casing. Again, this same scenario applies regardless of whether they were original tires or retreaded tires.

The jet airliners we all fly in, most fighter jets, large trucks, and school buses all depend on retreaded tires, and for a very good reason. They are safe, and they only use about 20% of the materials required to manufacture a new tire. So, using them is a very environmentally friendly option. Retreading also keeps tires out of landfills, and they cost about a third of the price of a new tire.

Now, with your understanding of the cause of tire failure, imagine an 80,000-pound semi-truck, running 10 hours a day with 18 or more tires on it. The driver is required by law to do a safety check before departing, but can they see the whole tire? Can they see a small screw in the tread of a tire? No.

For many years, I testified as an expert witness for accidents related to tire failures, some fatal. I was tasked with solving the cause of the tire failure and explaining what happened. I would also provide an opinion of who or what might be at fault.

One case involved a very well-maintained truck operated by a large company with an exceptional safety program and records. The right front tire failed at highway speed, and the truck driver lost control and crashed. Fortunately, there were no injuries, but the damage was significant, millions of dollars were lost from the cargo damaged in the accident. It was not a retreaded tire that failed. Rarely would any company use a retread on the front. Companies need to keep introducing new tires into the fleet in order to have the fresh tire casings to retread later.

The tread rubber, along with the steel belts, came off in one continuous piece, which is a common occurrence on the freeway. Ironically, this failure was the exact same scenario as what had happened with the Ford Explorers. All the steel belts—as well as all the tread on top of the belts—left the casing and wrapped around the front axle of the truck. Therefore, the driver could not steer, lost control, and swerved off the road, causing significant damage to the vehicle and the load it carried. Attorneys for the insurance company filed suit against the tire manufacturer for the tire failure and loss, and that is where I came in. At this point, the tire manufacturer finds experts to analyze why the tire failed—was there a defect in the tire? Was it driver error, or was it an outside source that caused the failure?

Doing the forensic inspection, an expert will generally suspect heat caused the failure but needs to discover the cause of this excessive heat. While always possible, the failure could be from a manufacturing defect, but it would be very rare. Also, it can be the wrong tire for the application, but this was not the situation here. Nearly all car tires and large truck tires used today are tubeless, but there is a tube built into the inside of the tire casing to hold the air. All tires have some degree of porosity (porous) where the air molecules can very slowly escape the casing; therefore, tires do need to be checked regularly, especially on large trucks. In this case, it took some time to carefully inspect the remains of the casing that still contained the inner liner or tube. Additionally, close inspection of the tread was necessary to determine if any object penetrated through the tread and pierced that inner liner.

All in all, it can be a painstakingly slow forensic analysis, and it helps to have all the pieces available from the scene. In this case, shortly after starting the inspection of the tread—which was still all one piece but horribly mangled—a very small, sharp screw was found. Upon further investigation inside the casing liner, when the two parts were matched up, a very small perforation was found through the tubeless liner. It is possible that this tire would only lose a couple of pounds of pressure a day, as most of these front tires run close to maximum load at 6,000 pounds each, and have a recommended pressure of 100psi.

One of the reasons this particular failure was interesting was that one of the mechanics remembered seeing the screw head when he was walking past the truck a few days earlier. He had meant to tell the driver and check the tire, as most often, the screws do not make it through the steel belts to the inner liner and can easily be removed with no further damage to the tire. But in this situation, that was not the case. Even so, there was no fatality or serious injury to the driver or other vehicles, which was miraculous. It could have been so much worse. It is likely that the driver missed the screw when doing his pre-trip inspection. Although he performed the required inspection, the screw in the tire was likely on the bottom, where it could not have easily been seen.

That big rig you pass running down the freeway has 18 or more tires. The trucks run more often loaded than not, as companies do not get paid to run empty trucks. The driver might have checked the tires but might have been driving up to 10 hours that day. Any tire could have picked up a screw, a nail, a small sharp stone, or a piece of metal debris. I always honk, wave, and point to a low tire on a car or truck when I see it on the road. Or I leave a note on a windshield if I notice a low tire in a parking lot. Somebody's life is at stake here, that of the driver or the other car they could collide with when the tire fails. The point of this whole story is to look at something and understand that although you may have seen it, you might not have understood it. You can save a life, yours, your family member's, or someone you do not know by simply knowing this information and acting on it.

In the year 2000, there was a horrific Air France Concord crash in France. Air France Flight 4590 was taking off from the Paris airport. It crashed shortly after leaving the runway killing all 109 people on board. The plane crashed into a hotel near the airport, also killing four people at the hotel. The reason was determined to be a tire failure. A piece of debris had fallen off a Continental Airlines plane that departed ahead of the Air France plane. The Air France plane's tire hit the metal debris, and it pierced the tire all the way through the tread and casing. The tire exploded, puncturing the fuel tank from under the wing. The raw fuel leaked directly into the jet engine air intake, choking the engine and reducing the needed thrust. All this happened just as the plane was lifting off—a very critical point in any flight. The pilot did not have enough power to lift off from the remaining engine. He had no altitude or time to make decisions. The plane crashed shortly after leaving the runway.

All this is to say, tires almost always fail for similar reasons. Very few failures are ever the result of a manufacturing defect. They are more often the result of improper maintenance— whether on new or retread tires. Car tires are not designed to be retreaded and rarely do we ever see a retread car tire today.

I remember when I was about 27, shortly after we had started the tire company. I was visiting my parents and my Dad said, "Hey, I saw some of your 'calling cards' lying beside the road today." Though it might sound cute to you, it reminded me that so many people see these pieces of rubber on the freeway and have the same thought: "Blame the tire company." However, as you learned here, often that piece of rubber you see was never retreaded. The reason it is on the side of the road is a failure due to heat.

So, now I always look at tires on vehicles whether they're running down the road or parked. Anyone looking at tires for more than a few seconds can spot one that's running low on air, and it is most likely a small puncture causing it. Drivers, however, do not see this unless they are looking for it as the tire is not flat yet but low on air pressure. If that driver drives down the freeway for some distance, that tire is going to fail, and they could be killed. You can avoid serious damage or even a life by leaving that note on the window or honking if you notice it while driving and point to the problem. Let's all help others see what they may not recognize as a danger.

CHAPTER 25

DRIVEN TO SUCCEED

IN SOME WAY, everyone has a connection with tires. Whether you drive a car or truck, ride a bicycle, ride on a bus, or are even in a wheelchair, tires are involved. Also when you make a purchase at a store, the items in that store were delivered by truck. The trucking and transportation industry has a saying, "If you got it, a truck brought it." Tires are a huge part of our lives, whether we realize it or not. Everything we buy from Amazon or any online retailer depends on United Parcel Service, FedEx or the U.S. Postal Service who all use tires on delivery vehicles.

Tires, at their core, are simply a product that is required to allow us to be mobile. Flying across the world in a plane? That plane would not be able to take off or land without tires. Your life depends on tires in many ways. This next story involves innovation and improvements, inventions and the technological manufacturing advancements that have led the entire tire industry for more than 130 years. This story goes back to the 1800s. There is a lesson here about never settling for where we are, but always seeking innovation and to think outside the box, even with something as mundane as tires.

Every day, we entrust our lives and the safety of our families to tires with little knowledge of how tires have evolved over the years. The economic impact of tire development, and environmental improvements in fuel savings and less waste, while improving performance and safety never stop at one particular company.

Well over 100 years ago, in 1888, two brothers with the last name of Michelin, started a tire company. At the time, bicycle and carriage tires were made of solid rubber. The Michelin brothers invented the pneumatic tire (an air-filled tire) and would eventually change the face of transportation as we know it. In 1895, they mounted these tires on a race car. It was the first time a pneumatic tire was used on an automobile. But the real story that continues today, relates to the incredible forward-thinking innovations that seem non-stop by this company. Similar to the lessons about Boeing, The Michelin Company has a focus on what can be, what the world needs but does not yet have, and then to shape and develop the technology to make it so.

Jumping back to my introduction to this industry and why this story has meaning. I landed in the tire business more by chance than intention. The tire industry is not glamorous, not considered high-tech, or prestigious in any way. I remember being in school, thinking, and daydreaming about what career path I would take. While in college I had been interviewed by large, international companies. I worked at a gas station all through high school and college, mostly nights and weekends, so there was a little knowledge learned about tires, enough to make me think it was an industry I was not interested in.

At that time, a gas station attendant pumped the gas, washed the windshields, and checked the engine oil for every car. Relationships and interactions with all the customers was a regular daily occurrence, much different from today. We had a lot of regular customers from many backgrounds. Several pilots lived nearby, sales reps would talk about their careers, Boeing management people, and doctors came through. The customers were mostly professional people. The gas station was in a higher-end residential area near Seattle, in Bellevue, Washington. The customers often asked me how school was going and what I thought my future interests might be. I often pondered their careers and wondered if I would ever be as successful as they were. My parents did not talk about college. They had grown up through the depression and had not continued their educations after high school.

As I mentioned earlier, one of these customers called and invited me to interview for a professional sales position. I was still in college but ended up taking that job and, well, you know the rest. Many years later, because of our success, I would often be asked to speak at university campuses to business school seniors about their future career opportunities. So many students are just like I was—putting in the time and hard work to get an education, but not quite sure where they might use it. During these events, I share the story about the many thousands of small or regional companies that provide excellent career potential, advancement, and opportunities. Many of these companies do not have succession plans in place, providing an additional future ownership opportunity.

If you can learn to see an opportunity, and if you are one who can innovate, and look past the obvious, you can achieve almost anything. There are thousands of future prospects out there, often in what might look like boring industries such as the tire business. My path to success took a different route than most of my friends. Few of us started our own businesses. Few of them achieved success to the degree our company did. I lecture on looking into *every* opportunity, listening to people's stories, and thinking outside the box because doing so made all the difference in my life as it did with so many others we read about.

Michelin, one of the world's largest tire manufacturers, the ones who invented the pneumatic tire in 1888, continued to have a family member involved in running the company for over 100 years. Edouard Michelin, great-grandson to the company founders, became the CEO in 1999. One day, I was informed he wanted to meet with me at my office near Seattle. My schedule had conflicts; I was scheduled out of the area that week, so I asked to re-schedule. I was told by our regional representative, who was the same person responsible for our becoming a Michelin dealer; "You will be in your office on this day. He will walk through your door at exactly 9:00 AM, not a second before or after. He will meet with you for one hour. There is no publicity allowed and absolutely no pictures. Do not even ask. You *must* change your plans. Rarely does any dealer ever have a chance to speak face-to-face with Mr. Michelin." He went on to explain, "We do not even know what airline he arrives on, nor the time of his flight. We are told where to stand at the airport, and he will show up with security and be escorted to your office. Kim, this is a huge deal here. You are the only dealer I know of who he asked see."

Needless to say, with that explanation, I did change my plans. Edouard Michelin did walk in at precisely 9:00 AM. We met for an hour. Note that we did take pictures together after agreeing they were only for personal use. He and I hit it off right from the start: me with my little innovative growing company, and him with one of the world's largest and most innovative companies. We shared many of the same passions for fishing and family. We met a few times after that at Michelin's U.S. offices, and later when he invited Jill and me to spend a week in Lyon, France.

Sound Tire gained the largest market share in the Northwest and Alaska. We were a very large dealership for Michelin. We took advantage of the trip to France along with a few other couples who owned large Michelin dealerships in the United States. Michelin scheduled meetings in Lyon, France, considered the gastronomical capital of the world and conveniently near the Michelin global headquarters. Our small group was traveling with a personal handler assigned to take care of all details. She met us in Lyon as soon as we arrived. She began prepping us for what was to come, going over our itinerary. I'll never forget how I felt when she reminded us of the privilege of traveling with Michelin.

"Every restaurant we will be dining at knows you are here with the Michelin family. While the family does not personally take part in any of the famous 'Michelin Star' ratings, you should expect some of the most incredible service and food you've ever experienced." Many reading this might know the Michelin restaurant ratings are some of the most prestigious in the world. The Michelin Company, in addition to making tires, also produces global travel guides, maps, and restaurant guides.

The trip was incredible! Every place we went to had top-notch service and heavenly food and drink; not to mention the VIP treatment we received on the entire trip.

While traveling, we had left our small children back home. Jill's parents were taking care of them. On one of the last evenings with Mr. Michelin and the group, I called home to check on the children; sharing with Jill's mom about the incredible dinner we had just enjoyed and how special the restaurant was. She asked me the name of the restaurant. "It was something like Paul Bocuse?" Her response was immediate "Kim, Paul Bocuse is the most famous chef in the world!" To this day, it was one of the best trips I have ever taken, and I will cherish those memories for a lifetime. It was a very sad day in 2006 when we learned Edouard Michelin drowned near Normandy, France while fishing. He left behind five children and a lovely wife.

Mr. Michelin respected and supported our business philosophy along with the innovative ways we had been growing. The Michelin Company had also devised several ways to help us in that growth with financial support to buy the expensive equipment required to service the products, and many other out of the box support systems.

At that time, we operated 75 trucks to service fleets like Boeing and thousands of other accounts. Some of the tires we sold were to mining companies and cost well over $280,000 each for the massive mining trucks. Those tires weighed 20,000 pounds a piece! A Toyota Camry weighs about 3,200 pounds in comparison. These large tires weigh six times more than a family car. It takes very specialized trucks and operators to handle these large, heavy tires successfully. Just think of what is involved when they go flat. These large mining machines run 24 hours a day. We would change the tire, mounting a spare to keep the machine running. Then the tire repair itself would take about three days with the technician standing inside this 12-foot-tall tire.

In so many ways, the Michelin company was a partner with our company, just as we were partners with Boeing, Paccar, and hundreds of large companies that led to our commanding market domination. In 1888, the founding Michelin brothers were in many ways in the same situation I had been in. They were fixing bicycles in a small shop. Here were two men, living in a town in central France, wondering where life might take them. One day, they started wondering if they could do something to improve the ride of a bicycle, as the tires then were all made of solid rubber. Bicycles and carriages were the main sources of local transportation. For anyone who rides bicycles today, you might cringe at the thought of hitting a bump with a solid tire on your bike. The wheels would break easily; the harsh ride would jar the spine, where you sit, and negatively impact your overall comfort. Just imagine if your car tire was solid with no air, no flex. The ride would be teeth jarring. The Michelin brothers' invention opened the door to greater innovation as we would learn in the ensuing 132 years, with still more innovations on the horizon.

The brothers could never have known then that 130 years later, Michelin sales would exceed $22 billion. The short version story of the Michelin company's rise to be the world's largest tire manufacturing company is how they created a dynamic organization that had a clear mission and a forward-looking focus that continuously seeks to understand the customer needs before the customer even understands it. Today, they have combined these advances with technology, improving our lives through tires.

This knowledge of Michelin products combined with the choices I made in life, would translate to great opportunity in our business as we were granted a dealership with Michelin at the very beginning. In terms of profits, a Michelin truck tire could be retreaded more successfully than other brands. The more a tire could be retreaded, the more the customers saved. And a retread makes less of a negative impact on the environment. Retreading was also more profitable for our company than the profit on new tires, so there was a win-win there.

Michelin was leading the way in innovation, always ahead of any competition. In our business, we were able to show customers "sea change" advances in productivity and cost reductions through their operations using Michelin products. Our company shared a similar philosophy with Michelin, striving to provide the customer with innovative products that improved operations and saved money. We developed partnerships with customers, together creating operational savings by looking at the bigger pictures, not just the tires used. It was our rapid rise to becoming the largest Michelin dealer in the Northwestern United States and Alaska, along with some other innovative ways we were operating, that prompted Mr. Michelin to visit us.

But what is it that made this little company in 1888 grow to become the largest tire company in the world?

It might not surprise you, but everything we see today in relation to tire manufacturing and wheels was invented by Michelin. What is amazing is that innovation and new product creation could be repeated over the next 130 years! Our minds sometimes hold us back from realizing there is much we do not know, and so much opportunity we do not see. Michelin did not simply invent trendy products, fashion, or style; they developed industry-changing manufacturing and technological innovations. After inventing tires filled with air (pneumatic), the brothers were hard at work developing tires for the burgeoning auto industry. They came up with new sizes, solutions, and better products. They invented the radial tire. At the time, in the 1940s, this was a radical change in construction. Today roughly 99% of all tires used are of radial construction. Michelin developed the tubeless tire and the tubeless wheel. Tubes, while still in use on many bicycles, had been used in all tires, even our cars, until Michelin created tubeless versions. Low profile tires we see on cars all over the world were another invention. The list goes on and on. The company was practicing what W. Edwards Deming taught well before Deming, and a focus on quality were textbook lessons.

Here is a short list of the Michelin company history and inventions:

- Founded in 1888 by two brothers: Andre and Edouard Michelin

- Made the first pneumatic tire (air-filled) for bicycles in 1890

- Invented and manufactured the first pneumatic tire (tubeless) for cars in 1895

- Invented and manufactured de-mountable rims
- Invented the first radial tire in 1948; first introduced to U.S. on the Pinto in 1971
- Invented the tubeless tire and the tubeless wheel
- Invented the low-profile radial

In our business, we were often presented with tires for "adjustment," tires that failed or could not be balanced properly, or that had manufacturing defects of some sort. But we never had the occasion to actually see a defective Michelin tire… ever. We were dealers for many brands, and all of them had defects from time to time, but never a Michelin tire.

After some 30 years in the business, I was attending a technical seminar at a U.S. Michelin factory in South Carolina. As a real-life case study of sorts, we were presented with 20 failed tires, and the class was asked to identify the cause of failure on all 20. In the group of 20 tires, there was one tire in which I was the only person to correctly determine the cause of the failure. That failure was due to a dynamometer test on a large truck. A dynamometer is a large roller that a truck is strapped to and run at full power in order to measure engine horsepower. If run too long, it can damage a tire, which was the case in the failed tire we examined. I had been involved analyzing such a failure in the past, very odd damage to the tire. It is not often discovered until the tire has been in use for many miles.

The instructor in our training, who had been with Michelin for over 35 years, told me something extraordinary. I had asked him if he had ever seen a defective Michelin tire in his career. The answer? "Yes, once we had a tire leave a plant with a glove between the steel belts. When the tire failed, we were able to trace the tire to the plant, the shift, and the worker." Other than that failure, he had never seen a defective Michelin tire!

To put this in perspective, I have seen thousands of tire failures from other companies due to manufacturing defects, while Michelin had never had a failure apart from a mishap which was the fault of one of their employees. Our company handled adjustments for tire problems over the years on many Michelin tires, but all failures and issues were due to either an improperly mounted tire, or a defective vehicle that caused a failure or wear problem, but never due to a tire defect.

As we see the unbeatable safety of Michelin tires as compared to the other manufacturers, I often found it humorous the number of times I've had someone buying tires on behalf of their spouse. The conversation was something like this:

"You want Michelin, right?"

"No, it is just my wife's car. Go ahead with something less expensive."

"Of course, it's just your wife and children. They aren't very important, after all."

Needless to say, the customer usually changed his mind after that comment.

When we started the business, Michelin tires (and radial tires in general) were still new to the construction and trucking industries. I had the vision of the dramatic reductions in costs, coupled with the increases in productivity these tires could bring to construction companies. The mining, logging, road building companies needed these tires; they simply did not know it then. Michelin understands what the customer needs and is constantly looking for ways to improve their products and operations for companies that use these products. Our competition was trying to sell tires alone. We were selling innovation, improvements in productivity, significant reductions in costs, and downtime caused by flat tires on a commercial vehicle.

As an example, in Alaska, when a large off-road log truck had a flat, the customer estimated it cost upwards of $2,000 in lost productivity. They averaged 1.5 flat tires per truck per month. When we mounted Michelin tires, the average was less than one flat per year! The trucks do not run all year, but the savings per truck was tremendous.

Do the simple math here. Operating a log truck half of the year (6 months) and averaging 1.5 flat tires a month equals nine flat or $18,000 per truck. By changing to Michelin steel-belted radials, they could save that amount. A complete set of Michelin tires would cost less than $14,000 per truck, and they lasted three years. The operator would save over $40,000 per truck over that time. At the time, there was close to 1,000 of these trucks operating in Southeast Alaska alone, a huge market.

There are many more firsts and inventions by Michelin that we won't go into detail about, but just consider this: one single company, through continued innovation and focused leadership had vision and invented everything we use today on our cars, bicycles, and off-road vehicles. All cars now have tubeless, radial, low-profile tires that run on tubeless demountable rims.

The point here is that while other global manufacturers kept trying to market and sell the tires they made, Michelin had the foresight to see what the public and industry needed to improve performance, reduce costs and waste, increase safety and satisfy something the customers did not even know they needed. I would guess that over the next 130 years, Michelin will remain at the forefront of innovation. Interestingly enough, they are now creating tires that have no air (but with still the needed cushion and ride qualities) and are the safest yet! This is just another example of being on the leading edge, just as we would expect.

Remember the General Motors story about Dr. Deming covered in chapter 17? Deming realized that without buy-in and commitment from the CEO, initiatives could easily fail. It would be difficult to find any other global company that has been at the forefront of change, innovation, quality, and success as long as the Michelin Corporation. Michelin was practicing Deming's methods of operation as a complete system, eliminating stovepipe departments and implementing a continuous improvement philosophy before any of us knew of Dr. Deming. I enjoy reading about companies who succeed, dominate the markets, and continue to excel. I hope you do also.

CHAPTER 26

GIVING BACK

A HEALTHY, WELL-ROUNDED person is one who looks beyond themselves and is willing to help others. In our business operations, this was reflected in how we helped employees grow. Early on I joined a local Rotary Club. Rotary Club members are community and business leaders who have a desire to improve their communities, both locally and internationally. The clubs also serve as a great networking medium. Other members can be sounding boards and provide advice on related business topics. You can really get to know people in your circle of interest as well as many outside that circle. Being part of a service organization adds balance to your personal and professional development. A Rotary meeting lasts about 90 minutes. You attend once a week or less. I learned many lifelong lessons from joining, being active, and serving others.

All of us live in communities; they can be local, regional, or international. Aside from the businesses we work in, I believe time should be set aside for giving back, helping your community, on a local or international basis. You will be exposed to different beliefs, cultures, and lifestyles through your involvement, and be associated with the others who share a desire to make a difference in our world. Rotary Clubs provide endless ways for professionals to associate with others, raise funds, do projects, and get involved.

There are multiple other opportunities to give back, whether it's in the workplace, at home, the community you live, or even globally. It might seem overwhelming at first to be hands-on or serving others in some way as opposed to simply writing a check and donating but give it a try. Start with baby steps. Look into being involved with an organization or a professional peer group, anything that can enliven your mind and keep you learning. Through that process, you also better yourself, often learning more than you ever would had you stayed in your own bubble.

Rotary Clubs began in the early 1900s. Four men started meeting for lunch once a week in Chicago. They all had a desire to find ways to give back—to do something to improve their community and/or vocations. They 'rotated' the meeting place each week between their offices in town. Eventually, this became known as the Rotary Club. Rotary is the world's largest service organization. There are many other service organizations, but I decided to join a local Rotary Club. It was one of the best decisions I ever made.

Rotary was started with the vision of one man named Paul Harris, who was an attorney. He sought to expand on an opportunity he envisioned. It was the same scenario you've read all through this book: an individual sees an opportunity, envisions how it could unfold and then acts on it. Though the original founder of Rotary had a vision locally and not globally at first, it makes me wonder if they dreamed or imagined that the impact would be far-reaching. Today there are 34,000 Rotary Clubs in 170 countries. There is likely a club in or near your community.

These four men who started Rotary were all successful at some level, had professional careers, and their incomes were average for their vocations. In a short time, they had their first project planned. They planned to add public toilets for commuters in Chicago who used the L Train. The possibilities for these types of projects are endless: picking up trash, painting, construction, collecting clothing for the needy. It didn't matter what the project was at the end of the day; they were looking for a need they could fill, and doing something to help others. As they embarked on these projects together, they learned more about each other's personal and business lives, created friendships, and paved the way for others to join their club. Eventually, they had an idea to create an organization for professionals from different backgrounds and vocations to meet together once a week. They would exchange ideas, add meaning to their lives, and give back to their communities. Of course, in the process, life-long friendships were forged. The Rotary mission statement is as follows:

"We connect people. Together, we see a world where people unite and take action to create lasting change—across the globe, in our communities, and in ourselves."

Rotary has a stated purpose of bringing together business and professional leaders in order to provide humanitarian service and to advance goodwill and peace around the world. It is non-political and non-sectarian; open to all people, regardless of race, color, creed, religion, gender, or political preference.

Similar to many of the other examples in this book, one person had an idea, took action, had self-discipline, followed through and changed the world. Can you see the difference this one man has made in the world?

The club I joined had about 100 members, vibrant business and community leaders. It seemed a natural fit, as I had always had a heart for helping others. The club consisted of bankers, other business owners, local government officials, and school district leaders. About ten years after joining and getting involved, I became the club president. I think I served on every club committee in some capacity over the 38 years I have been a Rotarian.

Every week, Rotary Clubs invited speakers that range from state governors to university presidents, business owners, and authors. The speaker could be anyone the club feels can add value to the group, keep the members informed of current events, and invest in life-long learning. During election years, the club would have the candidates face-off, answer questions, and debate. Rotary Clubs, like any organization, strive to keep themselves current and have people involved who are exemplary leaders and exhibit their leadership skills in both their vocation and in the club.

The club I belong to today donated five million dollars to a huge city park enhancement, offering a playground for disabled and challenged children. The same club does support work all over the world. Our club has sponsored several large projects in Ethiopia, Nepal, India, and Honduras; the list goes on and on. I personally am involved in many of these, travel to these countries, and have made many close friends from around the world who are also in Rotary and help us facilitate the projects.

Of the 34,000 plus Rotary Clubs around the world, many raise funds for joint international projects, sometimes receiving matching funds from The Rotary Foundation for these projects. Just as we find in all of life, work, and play, there are certain people who just seem to make things happen. These types of people are those who have huge ideas and visions for their areas and don't stop until they see them come to pass. It is likely that Rotary clubs around the world donate around three billion dollars annually for various projects, though it is hard to know the real number since each club can raise and spend their money as they choose. Many even have their own club foundations for this purpose.

A single Rotarian in the Philippines came up with what was then considered an impossible idea; that his club could start a project to eliminate polio in his country. He succeeded, and as a result, in 1985, The Rotary Foundation adopted a goal to eradicate polio from the world! The Bill and Melinda Gates Foundation stepped in with an initial $500 million dollars, which was then matched by the Rotarians. The World Health Organization then stepped up, helping to coordinate the global efforts.

Polio was a crippling, horrid disease, and while it was eradicated in most developed countries, it was still devastating millions in other countries around the world. It was thought to be an impossible task to eradicate polio from India, but it has since been done. Throughout 30 years of focus, unrelenting passion, and determination, The Rotary Foundation never stopped chasing the goal, and have made it a point to keep it in the mind of all Rotarians. In the last few years, only a handful of cases are being reported in Pakistan and a few other remote areas. Today still, Rotary maintains the focus on polio eradication—*100% eradication*. Many who have been involved with the process so far understand that if the goal is not completed, the disease will slowly return. At the time of this writing, the goal is almost complete.

Again, he was one person who made a huge difference—a single individual in the Philippines who started a global sea change. But we also see thousands of Rotarians making real, lasting changes in both their own countries and others around the world.

Rotary International adopted what is called "The Four-Way Test" of the things we think, say or do. It is an excellent moral code for personal and business relationships. The test can be applied to almost any aspect of life. You do not have to be a member of Rotary to apply this simple example to your life. The four questions go like this;

1. Is it the TRUTH?

2. Is it FAIR to all concerned?

3. Will it build GOODWILL and BETTER FRIENDSHIPS?

4. Will it be BENEFICIAL to all concerned?

In addition to Rotary involvement, I am also a donor to a large Non-Government Organization (NGO) called World Vision that works globally to empower people out of poverty. World Vision, in just one of their areas of focus, is providing clean water to over five million people every year, more than any private or public organization in the world! I was donating money and raising funds for Micro Finance and Economic Development through World Vision when I started getting more involved. You can start to see the trend here; it seems I cannot sit idle when there is so much that can be done. World Vision works in 100 countries and raises close to $2.7 billion annually for their work. They employ roughly 47,000 local staff carrying out significant projects and humanitarian aid to millions. Today, as mentioned, the organization has a huge focus on water, sanitation, and hygiene (acronym: WASH).

I was starting to see where World Vision could work alongside remote Rotary Clubs in these developing countries. There is a logical synergy combining the local professional World Vision staff with the local Rotary Club members where both organizations are working and completing significant projects. I had been traveling with World Vision to areas we had been supporting with donations. Every country had local Rotary clubs, often trying, with volunteers, to do similar work to what World Vision was doing with professional, paid staff.

World Vision is a faith-based organization and boasts the title of the largest privately-funded humanitarian organization in the world. The U.S. government (and 19 other large governments) through the United States Aid for International Development (USAID) uses World Vision to facilitate projects around the world. The world's largest foundations, such as the Hilton Foundation and the Bill and Melinda Gates Foundation, Coca Cola, Chevron and hundreds more fund World Vision to do humanitarian work in remote areas of the world. When Rotarians travel to countries to help with polio vaccinations, many of the health workers in these countries who give the vaccinations and do the record keeping are hired, managed, and paid by World Vision through international grants.

At a recent Global Health International Forum, Bill Gates stated, "Most people do not realize that about 95% of this humanitarian work is completed by a faith-based organization." Sitting on the stage with him at that forum was the President of the Islamic Relief Organization, the President of World Vision, and the CEO of UNICEF, who happened to be Jewish.

All these organizations work together for global health and peace. However, from day one, as I strived to begin sensible collaborations between World Vision and Rotary Clubs, I was faced with Rotarians who worked hard to block anything I tried to do connecting Rotary Clubs and a Faith-Based organization. Most of those causing issues were based in the U.S., had never visited one of these collaborated projects and were very poorly informed of how these can work.

Much of the work is in Muslim countries. By various government laws, these Faith-Based organizations cannot proselytize. Regarding the Rotary projects, no religious activities are allowed ever. My tireless efforts succeeded, and in a very big way. The logic was so clear, combine the 47,000 professional World Vision Staff with local Rotarians in developing countries who were volunteers. The Rotarians had varying degrees of expertise in the work they were facilitating, but it was extremely difficult for any of them to donate the time required to do a large project and do it sustainably. To combine the best of both organizations would create a gain for both. It is almost like saying "1 plus 1 equals 5" as the impact was so much greater than either working on their own.

There were the local Rotary Clubs in these countries who, through strictly volunteer efforts, were also trying to do water, sanitation, and hygiene (or WASH) projects. I could see, while easy for a Rotarian to hire a drilling contractor to drill a well, that was just a small part of what it took for a sustainable, successful WASH project. Those wells would fail in a few years unless there was community involvement, and management such as having a water board established to collect small funds, repair, maintain and buy the needed parts.

Another critical part of the job was putting together the sanitation and hygiene components, such as training all the local residents. The training alone takes thousands of hours by professionals. The local Rotarians simply could not ever spend the time required to do this training and set up the water management committees to ensure the project lasts many years, and is viable and effective. In our projects, we train the whole community to stop outdoor defecation. Every person has access to ventilated pit latrines in each project, and 100% of every community goes through several hours of training on hygiene, very detailed instruction on handling food, dishes, water, garbage, and so much more.

I could see that having World Vision and Rotary work together was a perfect match. So, I called a meeting with the head of The Rotary Foundation (TRF) and a senior vice president of World Vision International (WVI). John Osterlund from TRF started off the conversation strong by stating, "We do not make good partners."

"We don't either, so this should be a great relationship," the World Vision International vice-president replied.

As written earlier in the book, and how it relates to commitment and Dr. Deming, if the leadership at the top cannot see the value in an endeavor and have the vision of how the outcomes can be improved, no matter who gets the credit, then any efforts would have a higher risk of failure. In this scenario, I had to illustrate the advantages of collaboration to both entities, an endeavor that I would find needed to be repeated often as both organizations change leadership, board members, and have complicated reporting and chains of responsibility. There are not enough words to explain the complexity, the roadblocks, the technical challenges that I believe would have stopped any normal person from attempting this endeavor.

I knew this partnership wouldn't be a walk in the park, and I resolved not to give up until I saw the fruits of our labors. We worked through sometimes frustrating obstacles, differences in cultures, and the variations of leadership in each country for both local Rotary and local World Vision staff.

In every case, the local Rotary club was thrilled to have the help and relationship and they could be as involved as they desired. The local World Vision staff were also very positive, meeting and working with local community leaders that were members of the Rotary club in that country. On the ground in the countries, these projects worked exceptionally well. But then add the layers of leadership above who never visited the collaborations from either World Vision or The Rotary Foundation, and we continued to hear negativity and doubt.

I do not give up on anything easily, my self-talk often tried to tell me I was wasting time but once you see the faces on those thousands of people we served, and the huge increase of the number of girls able to attend school, you cannot stop.

Anyone who does this work is rewarded by those changed lives forever. Personally, you receive a hundred times more than you invest. It is worth it.

The funding we devised would be half from Rotary Clubs and the Rotary Foundation in the U.S., with the other half from World Vision donors who would agree to match the Rotary funding. My work was tough. I had to show the U.S. Rotary Clubs how to broaden their fundraising skills, and how to work with their own Foundation effectively. Then I had to work with World Vision staff in the U.S. to find the matching funds from their donors. After a few missteps, a large Water, Sanitation, and Hygiene (WASH) project was started and completed with collaborations from Ethiopian Rotary Clubs and World Vision Ethiopia. The cost was about $1 million and brought clean water, sanitation, and hygiene to about 50,000 people in Ethiopia.

After the success in Ethiopia, another project was started in Gulu, Uganda. It was near the heart of the Child Soldier kidnappings perpetrated by The Lord's Resistance Army, or LRA. Their leader Joseph Kony abducted 30,000 child soldiers over a horrific 25-year span. Over three million people had been displaced and were living in displacement camps, many run by World Vision, as their villages had been raided, burned, their children taken, and atrocities too grotesque to ever describe! I visited these camps, heard the horror stories, saw unimaginable grief, pain, and suffering.

While Gulu Rotary, World Vision Uganda, and the Gulu World Vision Children of War Center staff completed a $940,000 WASH project, it also became a pivotal mark in the collaborations between the two behemoth entities. I had developed a model where Rotary Clubs, mostly in the U.S., would raise a minimum of $400,000 in funding. This came from many clubs or their Rotary Districts and matched funds from The Rotary Foundation (TRF). World Vision U.S. staff became exceptional at finding the matching funds needed. World Vision is not a foundation that grants funds, although the matching of the funds made logical sense as each entity would leverage the other. We found several World Vision major donors who understood the value of these collaborations and committed funds we could apply as a match to the Rotary projects.

Every Rotarian who has visited one of these collaboration projects says they are the very best they've ever seen. And every year our large, collaborated projects are the largest funded through the Rotary Foundation.

On my first trip to meet the Gulu Uganda Rotarians prior to starting our large project there, I had a memorable experience. The club president at the time was a Ph.D. professor at Gulu University named Gerald Obai. When I asked him what he knew about World Vision, he stared at me with a stoic face. Looking me straight in the eye, he said, "They drive dirty vehicles." Now, let me just say that most Rotarians possess a good sense of humor, and Gerald was no exception. He was describing his impressive view of the work done by World Vision, in his tongue and cheek sort of way. You see, there are very few paved roads in the Gulu, Northern Uganda region, and the roads are a red mud/clay mixture. As you can imagine, vehicles get dirty quickly but only if they are out in the bush working.

Dr. Obai went on to explain, "All you need to do is drive around the region to see what World Vision has done, what they are currently doing, and what they plan to do. You see their project signs all over. They work hard every day, and you can often find them building schools and clinics, teaching health, educating communities how to grow crops, and especially working with women and girls regarding maternal health and nutrition." Gerald went on to say, "Kim, there are 72 NGO's operating just in Gulu, most of them simply drive to each other's offices for lunch, and their vehicles do not get dirty."

The next day, I was planning on introducing the local Rotarians and Gerald to the World Vision staff. We planned this meeting at the Children of War facility in Gulu. As they entered the office, I realized they already knew each other, as most of them had gone to school and grown up together. A few of them mentioned they had lost dear friends to the LRA during the conflicts. Together, we developed a Memorandum of Understanding, clearly defining the roles each entity would play to facilitate a large project. When I left them the following day, they were tasked with developing the collaborated project proposal, all the details, and a budget.

After that was finished, I would work with the Rotary Club in Edina, Minneapolis to help the club raise the needed funds, while also finding donors or other funds that World Vision could provide as a match. I cannot express how impressed I was with one particular member of the Edina Rotary Club who has become a close friend. Tim Murphy has taught me more about this international work than any individual. We arc still working closely today, and clubs in his Rotary District just funded their 4ᵗʰ large collaboration project between World Vision and Rotary Clubs. I mention Tim again a little later, along with other heroes of mine who change the world.

Thankfully, the Gulu WASH project all came together beautifully, and the project was started and completed in just two years. The Gulu Rotary Club was excellent and received a multi-country award from their Rotary District.

Another project followed in Northern Uganda, near Lira, which was still in LRA devastated areas. The displaced people were now moving back to their villages that had been destroyed by the LRA 20 years earlier. There was no infrastructure or water—everything was gone. The Rotary Club of Bainbridge Island, Washington raised $570,000 to do this WASH project, and a large donor to World Vision agreed to match the amount. When all was said and done, it was a $1,140,000 project. That local collaborating team brought clean water to 71 villages on that project alone.

To this day, I am still doing the same kind of work between Rotary Clubs and World Vision. The projects that have both been completed and are still underway exceed $20 million. I am incredibly proud to be part of these Rotary-World Vision collaborations that have brought water and economic development to **over one million people**. In 2018, World Vision brought water to over five million people!

All our projects include new latrines for the girls to use at school. Prior to these projects, there was no privacy or security for the girls. Because of our fifth project in Ethiopia, 36,000 people received water. The women had been spending an average of six hours a day fetching bad water that we would never consider drinking. That water gave them illnesses! Now, they spend minutes a day to get clean water, and the girls of the communities can continue to go to school. There are brand new latrines at every school with privacy for the girls. You see, prior to this, the girls had to stay with their mothers when they fetched water or be subject to abuse. When you can educate the women in these communities, the whole world changes for the better!

Give credit where credit it is due. While it might have been my vision to bring Rotary and World Vision together collaborating on these large projects, it was the individual Rotarians who did the bulk of the work, invested their time, and raised the funds. They traveled with me to the projects beforehand, during the work, and to the celebrations after completion. These groups included exceptional Rotarians like Tim Murphy from Edina, Minneapolis who has traveled, coached, supported, and encouraged me for 16 years. Whenever I thought of giving up, Tim would make miracles happen.

One day a woman named Nina Clancy called me from Visalia Rotary, California. She said, "I am the incoming Governor in my Rotary District. Visalia is the breadbasket of the U.S. I have a dream to do a $1 million food project with World Vision wherever it is needed most in the world." It became "The Million Dollar Dream" endeavor. We found Angola had once been the breadbasket of Africa but was decimated after 30 years of civil war. This could be compared to bombing the California Central valley for 30 years. There was simply no infrastructure left. Seventy-year-old women were eking out a living on small co-op farms because most of the men had been killed in the wars.

Nina raised $250,000. World Vision committed $250,000. The World Vision office in Angola met with the government there and received another match of $500,000. We completed Nina's dream project a few years later bringing in many tons of hybrid potato seeds from Holland, importing fertilizer, installing proper irrigation, and training 2,000 women in small farm co-ops how to successfully grow these potatoes. But the real success was opening the markets in the capital, developing the transportation to take the products to market, and bringing in cash to these farmers. These are complex, well planned, and executed large endeavors with incredible results and sustainable, long term impacts.

There are so many others to thank: Blaine Kelly of Atlanta Rotary spearheaded the largest of our collaborated projects, $3.4 million in Kenya. He raised funds from his Club, Coca Cola, United Parcel Service, USAID, and another nonprofit organization called ADRA. World Vision donors contributed $1.4 million, and collaboratively managed the large project. Without Blaine, the project would never have happened. Hundreds of thousands of people received water, micro-finance, water purification, and more because of Blaine. Blaine's story also adds another compelling aspect as to why these collaborations and partnerships work.

The Atlanta Rotary Club attempted to do this on their own, and with a local Kenyan Rotary Club. They were both struggling, and then the drilling contractor told them all, "We are not allowed in most of these communities unless it is through an NGO, like World Vision. We just cannot go and do the work on our own." Blaine sought the help of World Vision, not even realizing the opportunity to add additional matched funds. Blaine, retired now, was an extremely successful developer in Atlanta. His Rotary Club is one of the world's finest as I came to know.

DJ Sun and Larry Johnson from Rotary Clubs in the Los Angeles area raised $500,000 matched by a single World Vision donor, and we did a $1 million WASH project in Niger, one of the world's poorest countries. They are now planning another project there. Every project has a hero, that one individual who stepped up and changed the world through their efforts. It is humbling to be a partner with these great Rotarians. The Rotary Club in Niger surprised me as they became one of the most responsive, and dedicated Rotary Clubs I have had the pleasure to work with. Tim Arnold from Redmond, Washington Rotary has traveled many times to Ethiopia and asked to collaborate on the recent WASH project there. Today, Tim is again heading up another Ethiopian project to bring water, latrines, and hygiene to 35 schools and communities.

Many said this Rotary-World Vision collaboration could not be done. Roadblocks were thrown in front of me, but I had witnessed the children suffering and would not give up. When you visit a community where children die from drinking contaminated water, you cannot help but think of the anguish the parents experience. When the women spend six hours on average each day fetching water and the young girls cannot get an education, how can you not at least try to help? **When a village gets clean water, the children stop dying, and the girls can go to school. Their futures change for the good in a dramatic way. Once the girls get educated, birthrates drop, child mortality drops, the communities begin to lift themselves up. They receive a hand *up*, not a handout.**

One Rotarian who was visiting a collaborated project we were doing that was funded by her club in the U.S. stated, "I have been in Rotary for 16 years, but today, I feel like I am really a Rotarian."

A woman in a small village where we were working in Kenya reported, "Since Rotary came, the children stopped dying."

In Honduras, as we completed a $1.4 million WASH project, a woman stated "My name is Maria Lopez. I am 70 years old. Our well dried up when I was 16." Now Maria has a water spigot at her home. She had been walking down a rocky, steep, and dangerous route to get dirty water to drink, and of course, lug that heavy jug of water back up that steep hill. Maria looked me in the face and said, "I know you were sent here by God as an answer to my prayers, you are the only person who ever came back, and you did what you said you would do." On my Facebook page, I share a picture of Maria and I together.

Still today, according to UNICEF, some 3,000 children die every day from drinking contaminated water. However, ten years ago, the numbers were over 6,000 a day. Huge steps are being taken to get water to all those in remote areas, especially in Africa. The World Health Organization and World Vision feel that at the rates they are progressing today, they might have water to 99% of these people by 2030. Rotary Clubs and thousands of Rotarians are doing their part as is World Vision and thousands of NGOs. Still today, there are millions of women, spending six hours a day hauling dirty water and need your help.

You can do your part. Make a difference in the world, or in your community. There are so many ways to be involved and contribute. Make the decision to look around you to find something you can do for others. Have the self-discipline to follow through and do it. You do not have to have wealth in order to give back.

Anyone who can get up early in the morning, have a plan, and tirelessly attack the day, can succeed. I have been so fortunate to have worked side by side with others who never stop. They never give up whether it is in business, in their family, and private lives, or in other relationships. There is so much more to this life than just us, what we make, and where we work. Give something back. There are so many ways to do this, again, most often it is right in front of you. However, if you are not looking, if you are not focused on seeing those ways, and managing your self-talk, they can be missed. My work today, in these humanitarian efforts, is without any compensation. The gratitude on the faces of those we have served as Rotarians is more than any money could equal.

In all my life, after founding two corporations, running them successfully for many years, selling them to Fortune 500 companies, those accomplishments seem to pale in comparison to the over one million lives that have been changed because of the collaborations between Rotary Clubs and World Vision. You can make the world a better place, just try. The rewards will exceed your investment in time and money.

CHAPTER 27

THE REST OF THE STORY

I HAVE CONSTANTLY referred to "opportunity in front of us all yet often unseen." There are several lessons here on leadership, self-discipline, and reaching levels of success both personally and professionally. We all have subconscious activity in our minds and self-talk. Anyone can practice, and master positive self-talk and seek to see the opportunities. Learn to ask why things are the way they are, even simple things.

Another concept covered here are the Wonder-Blunder-Thunder-Plunder stages in life. I encourage you to understand what stage you are in, and how to reach the next level. Remember, you can go through this cycle more than once! It does not matter if you are a college student wondering what to do, a young employee starting their first job, a seasoned executive or CEO, you can improve, learn, and change. Re-read the stories of famous people with huge companies as well as people nobody would know like myself, an ordinary person, who made it to the thunder stage before starting a business from scratch and re-entering the blunder stage. Then remember how we almost blundered into failure. Through perseverance, I was able to thunder into two successful enterprises, then sell them after 20 years to Fortune 500 firms.

Being only 26 when starting the first company, then founding JIT Inc. a few years later, my partner and I built both companies through difficult financial periods and adversity. It was not until after selling them we realized much of the "why" in how well they had worked. Much of that success was not taught in any school or learned from any case study from my MBA. In saying this, there is exceptional education available through schools and case studies that apply to so much we do in business: analytical skills, decision-making tools, critical thinking, problem-solving, and so much more. The stories in this book required several additional skills illustrated through true life lessons that can be applied to everyone at any level of life or career.

You, and only you, can decide to be successful, develop better habits, practice self-discipline, and learn to see the opportunities that are in front of you, yet not discovered. Every day, people like you are learning, growing, thinking outside the box, and succeeding in life and work. You can also choose and learn to channel your self-talk towards positive, enlightening words and avoid letting negative thoughts enter those conversations.

Our first company was sold to Bandag, a Fortune 500 firm at that time. Bandag was sold a few years later to Bridgestone. The sale of our company happened after 20 years of operation, and today, the business remains the largest regional commercial tire company in the Northwestern U.S. and Alaska. JIT Inc., our Paccar truck assembly and logistics company, the second company we founded, was still growing and very successful when there was an opportunity to be acquired by Alcoa, another Fortune 500 company. The plans were in place to take the company global: to Australia, The Netherlands, Canada, and Mexico to service other factories. Alcoa assumed operations of that very profitable, innovative company that combined efficiencies for Paccar and several of their valued suppliers.

I was 46 at the time we sold the tire company, a couple years older when we sold JIT Inc. Even though employment income was not needed by that time, I was still motivated to learn, grow, be productive, and do it again. By that time, John and I owned several commercial properties personally that provided an excellent income. I was free to discover new opportunities. Having completed the University of Washington MBA program at the time we were ready to launch JIT Inc. globally, I wanted to do more, to satisfy my desire to improve and learn.

After selling both companies, I was hired by a Paul Allen Company as a CEO and started another career in high-tech. At that time, Paul Allen, through his entity, Vulcan, owned 139 companies, including the Seattle Seahawks football team. Most of the Vulcan entities were high-tech, leading-edge, sometimes 'bleeding' edge companies. Paul was always way out there, pioneering development. Think how Paul Allen and Bill Gates changed the world! Few of us go through a day without doing something on a personal computer and cannot imagine life without one. Today, there are similar opportunities just waiting to be discovered by the next Bill Gates and Paul Allen, two incredible individuals indeed.

There continue to be opportunities for tire innovations. Who will be the individual or company that creates an alternative to eliminate those failures evidenced by the rubber we see on our roads? Many lives are changed every day and people lose their lives as a result of tire failures; how can we solve this? My bet is that Michelin will come up with another invention where air is not needed in a tire.

We are at the forefront of driverless transportation with autonomous cars and trucks. I am driving an all-electric vehicle. When others do the same, gas stations and auto parts stores will be in decline. What is next? It is not hard to imagine not even owning a car. This is easier to do if you live near a city; difficult if you live in a rural area but think this through. The thought of flying around the world was only a dream 120 years ago. Boeing is only about 100 years old. What is next? Who will lead the way? Not that many years ago, building wagons pulled by horses was a huge industry. Like thousands of other businesses, it is gone. Our brains have a difficult time imagining things we cannot see or do not know, but somebody will be creating new products and services, exploring deeper into space, and continuing to understand our brains more than we understand today.

Management and leadership skills apply across every industry, especially in high-tech where social and leadership skills are not necessarily developed as fast as software applications. (Think that comment through again). Every industry has people who want to succeed and grow. I found many in the high-tech arena lacked some self-discipline and hard work habits I had developed. However, I did find many who were very driven to create, could visualize what could be, and strived hard to find methods or develop technology to get there.

I remember when I first interviewed with the Vulcan Board members interested in hiring me. I explained I really had no high-tech experience. They replied something to the effect, "We have the high-tech people; we lack people with management and leadership skills."

At that time, the learning curve (blundering stage, again) was like drinking water from a fire hose. Fortunately, I saw that solid, sincere management and leadership skills can help transform any company and improve the employees and business. It does not matter if it is a tire business or high-tech, the principles are the same. I remember one of the staff engineers kept pushing this new technology called "Bluetooth." The more they learned, the more opportunities and future business could be developed around this technology. Of course, Bluetooth became a common technology.

After leaving my high-tech career, my involvement increased with Rotary and World Vision and I am still adding projects and doing humanitarian work in developing countries. Every day I apply my thunder skills. I am still learning but am also doing a bit more plunder-related activities. Through the work in developing countries, our collaborations have brought water, health, and economic development, through several large projects, to over one million people, most of course who I will never see. Those that I have seen bring a huge amount of satisfaction as we help them help themselves and create self-sustaining communities that continue to grow.

In the book *Factfullness*, the author, Hans Rosling, demonstrates how the world has improved and continues to improve globally. He points out that you do not hear these stories of success in the news. You only see the negative on TV, the sensational reporting that makes the news. This is a great book. It makes me even more proud of the small part our collaborations have contributed to global improvements, especially the huge increases of girls able to attend school.

Throughout this book there are references and stories regarding starting your own business. Anyone can start a business in a day. The ability is not the issue. It is the "why" that matters. What are your goals? Do you have skills to see what others need and do you have the vision of what it will take to succeed where others might have failed? The statistics hold true that most who try starting businesses fail. Some 95% of new business start-ups have failed in the first five years, while people who stay working for good companies, have a far greater chance at success along with the added security.

Do you know someone with a complimentary skill set that you might lack? When we started our first business, my partner had all the skills to build and operate tire retreading manufacturing equipment. We both had business skills. I was more adept at understanding and solving what the customers needed and working with customers as well as training. Together we were successful; much more so than if I had tried to do it alone. I believe this is also very true for my partner. Like Bill Gates and Paul Allen, we had very different skill sets and different strengths. A common theme found in any successful business is the tireless work required to make it happen.

Although our first company was a corporation, there were still only two of us, we were still partners and partnering takes on a whole different skillset as discussed in Chapter 4. The skills to a successful partnership transcend any corporate environment. If you are not a person who can work well with others, and many are not, then you would likely fail at partnerships. However, these are skills you can learn and a paradigm shift can happen as you gain the knowledge. Think about what that means, either for yourself, or how you might help a co-worker or company with your knowledge that creates a change within or for them.

Do not forget the story about "What Is John Doing" (from Chapter 4) and the effect of telling somebody else your concerns or issues, when that person cannot hear everyone else's point of view or know what the whole scenario might be. When you gain knowledge, understanding the full story, you can have a paradigm shift in your point of view, change your focus and direction or energy into something positive, and stop dwelling on negative issues.

Steven Covey, in one of his books, wrote about an experience he had heading to his office one quiet Sunday morning. He was on the train, almost by himself. It was peaceful. He was reading the paper. At a stop, a man boarded with three wild children. The children were loud, jumping, running around, very disruptive. Steven was getting annoyed. The man just sat there and did nothing. He just stared at the floor. Finally, Steven blurted out to the man, something like, "Sir, your children are very noisy and out of control. Can't you do something?" The man looked at him, almost in a daze, and said, "Oh, I am sorry. We just left the hospital. Their mother just died. I guess they do not know what to do." The paradigm shift here is obvious. Steven went from being upset to compassionate in a second. Instead of being angry, he wished he could help this person and the children.

Only you control how you react, what you say in your self-talk, and whether you make the effort to train yourself to stay focused on positive thoughts while working to avoid the negative. You can consciously decide to look for the good traits in others, or you can concentrate on the negative. If you can accept that there are thousands of opportunities you do not see, you can learn how to see some of them. If you stop spending time on negative thoughts, you have more time to look for the productive opportunity in front of you.

Inherently most people do want to improve and succeed. Smart people realize that **we do not know what we do not know** and take steps to learn. Changing your attitude is the first step, convincing yourself to look beyond the obvious. A leader recognizes what needs to be done and organizes people to do it together. Leadership examples are plentiful and you can learn the how and why if you develop the habits of learning and observing. It is, in a simple way, the transition from the wonder-blunder years to the thunder years.

You can read this book, do nothing, and nothing will change. You can choose to learn more. Many books are available on most of what is covered here and can be studied in much more detail. You can apply some self-discipline and grow yourself. You can do as well as, or much better than the ordinary people like myself who started a business, and almost failed twice while doing it.

Most new businesses fail, and business schools, even the best, cannot possibly expose you to all the pitfalls waiting to snag you. Somebody made up a little comment about running your own business; "Running a business is easy, just buy stuff, sell it for more that you paid for it, **and a million other things in-between.**" If you have the tolerance for risk, and courage to take the plunge and start your own business, great. But know that there are many small-to-medium-sized companies that offer great opportunities as well. You just need to find them. You may even be working at one now and not realize the potential in front of you.

In recent statistics for U.S. business, the following was reported:

Percent of employment	Percent
Very Large enterprises	51.6
Very small enterprises	17.6
Small enterprises	16.7
Medium Enterprises	14

There are so many opportunities to succeed in every size company and every career. All companies need leadership. Not all of them have effective leadership, as I mentioned earlier regarding one of the very biggest corporations, General Electric, and the disastrous results as leadership changed, and then changed again, and how those changes resulted in severe reductions in the value of GE stock.

Remember the Paccar story and the start of JIT Inc.? There were very bright people at Paccar, and at their suppliers' companies, yet not one of them could see more efficient time and labor-saving solutions. They simply failed to think outside the box, to ask suppliers for their input, and collaborate to find better, more efficient ways to achieve what they wanted. Stories abound regarding decisions made where the decision-maker failed to engage key stakeholders.

At the Dr. Deming in-person seminar I attended, one of the most memorable stories shared was about one of the largest U.S. automobile manufacturers who built a huge, state-of-the-art robotic facility to deliver car interiors in sequence with the cars on the production conveyors. Many millions of dollars were spent on the robotics. It was all designed to reduce labor costs and be fully automated. It did work, but then somebody brought up a wild idea: "Why not just have the suppliers deliver the interiors to the plant in the same sequence as we manufacture and eliminate the warehouse completely? Instead of unloading the trucks and putting the seats in this massive, automated warehouse, just move them directly from the delivery truck to the car on the assembly line and install them?" That person was correct, of course, but received some resistance from those who ran the robotic warehouse.

They eventually stopped the robotics, and multiple handling of the seats and stopped using the automated warehouse. The $100 million or so invested was a complete write off, a blunder. This simplification is what a "Just in Time" (JIT) simplified process consists of. It is the same scenario that our own little JIT Inc. had done with Paccar. The opportunity was in front of so many, but some highly-educated people failed to question the "why" and other possible alternatives by thinking outside the box.

Another example taught at the Deming seminar goes like this:

This story, while in a corporate setting, can be applied to any decision situation, including decisions within a family, between a couple, or in a small business. In a simple way, it illustrates thinking outside the box. Discovering all the information that could be valuable in making any decision, especially one that involves significant funds, is important. I remember using this story the first day of MBA class as we went around the room introducing ourselves and being asked to provide an enlightening short story.

A large resort hotel with a global operation (think of companies like Hilton or Marriott) had a property with a large spa. Management was in a monthly meeting going over results, discussing future planning, looking at budgets, profit, and loss to date. On the agenda, was a discussion about spending thousands of dollars in the spa to install some sort of integrated, shampoo dispensing system. Apparently, patrons/guests regularly took the expensive shampoo bottles out of the spa.

In the room was a management consultant, hired to help them address other management issues. He was not there regarding this shampoo issue. The consultant asked, "Has anyone spoken to the attendants working in the spa for their ideas on this problem?"

"Why would we ask the attendant? It is normally a college student or low paid part-time person." The consultant explained, "If you do not talk to all stakeholders about an issue they are also aware of, then you really have not done your job properly."

Another management staff person in the room suggested they all go down to the spa right then and ask the attendant on duty that evening. Off they went. You might imagine the look of surprise on that attendant's face as a dozen or so management people entered the spa. One of the management team there explained the issue; that they were spending thousands of dollars each month on shampoo and asked the attendant if he had any thoughts on a solution to the problem. The reply was something like this: "Oh, you want to stop the guests from taking the shampoo bottles? I can fix that tonight; we can simply discard the bottle lids when we put them in the spa!"

While a great story, the application is so basic. In management, people often think "they" are smarter than others, or they simply do not think engaging all stakeholders might change the outcome. Asking a spouse, your children, other company employees, friends, or a consultant for suggestions, can change the decisions you make.

In our businesses, I can remember several decisions we made as "management" that when implemented, resulted in outcomes we had not considered! Not all were negative, but most failed to achieve what we had thought the outcome would be. It is amazing how an employee, a child, or even a division of a large company, can "work around" a management (or parental) decision and change the intended outcomes or results.

So, while we are all making thousands of decisions every day, those that are thought through (those that are not just subconscious decisions) can be improved by seeking input from others, especially those involved with the day-to-day work that the decision affects.

Develop the skills to ask what a company does, why they do it, and if it can be improved. Think outside the box. Strive to get input from others, especially those with different skills than you have before you decide on something. And then be willing to listen. Learn something that might change your direction and thought. Learn to think outside the box. Go back to the end of Chapter 10 and look at the box example.

Remember, there is almost always another way to think about everything. People who focus, even focus hard on something, can often fail to see the other opportunities or solutions that might have been in front of them all the time. You can see in the previous stories; Paccar has brilliant, highly educated, exceptionally well-trained people working in their factories. The same applies to the Detroit auto manufacturers. Yet millions of dollars were spent creating something that had no place being created. Much simpler cost-saving methods could have been implemented but were never considered. Possibly (we do not have all the facts) had the employees met with the suppliers, clearly explained what they wanted to develop to increase efficiency, and worked as partners together they could have implemented what worked best for both as we did at JIT Inc. with Paccar.

In everything you do, every decision you make, strive to get more information and ask others who might know something you do not. Be willing in your company to meet with the people who do the work every day. They can be significant, valuable stakeholders and help craft better decisions. There are thousands of poor decisions made in companies where management decides to implement a solution that only makes the issue worse. Government leaders often do the same, creating laws that have opposite consequences to what they were trying to do.

We read about companies that are now hugely successful, making their founders overnight billionaires and creating many more multi-millionaires along the way. While our simple business excelled over a 20-year period, what is not often understood is the tireless efforts and magnitude of dedication, work, time away from family, and stress that can accompany a new business from the time it is founded until it is built into a success. There are many multi-millionaires who did not start their own businesses but realized the success and financial opportunity in the vocations and companies they chose to work for; thousands of companies, both big and small.

Today we see a newer breed of employee who moves from company to company frequently. Many of them have the development skills that work across several technology platforms. Technology is in constant change creating endless new opportunities. Many companies offer high signing bonuses with stipulations that the employee work for the company for five years. The backlash of this practice is that these talented people quit their jobs as soon as they complete the required five-year period. Then, they sign on with another company and do it again. Five years later they get the bonus promised and jump again. Smarter companies discover a better way to reduce that expensive turnover. They address why so many employees leave after five years (or at the expiration of the bonus period) and implement pro-active ways to incentivize those employees to stay. Those companies that lose that employee, pay another person another bonus and start the cycle all over again. It is generally better for both the employee and the company, to retain the employee. The company can create a win-win for both employee and company as well as decrease the turnover that has become so prevalent in high-tech.

Here is one last story as we consider looking at a problem or opportunity from a different angle. Again, the *Wall Street Journal* contained an obituary about another incredibly successful person whose book I had read shortly after he wrote it. In the obituary it states, "Tom was no stranger to Dreaming Big."

Here was another ordinary person, probably much like yourself. This person was an accountant, lived in a suburban community, had a mortgage, and was building a career. He was comfortable. At the same time, he was always looking for something more. He had dreams of success.

This man was at a community meeting where the neighborhood was struggling to resolve issues they were having with poor service from their garbage collection company. The man's name was Tom Fatjo and as he complained to the board that evening, one of them replied back, "Why don't you do it yourself!" Tom went home and started playing with the numbers: how many homes there were, what a truck would cost to buy and operate, how much time was needed. This was in 1966 when Tom was working in an accounting job every day.

Tom took a big first step. He bought a used garbage truck and started that first day very early before his regular job but found out he really needed two trucks to do the work. He found another used truck and daily was picking up the garbage in his development then also working his "day job." He discovered there was "gold in garbage." It was not simply that you could make a nice profit hauling garbage. He saw another opportunity other people missed. Tom realized there were many small garbage companies, mostly family owned. Several of these small operators were struggling with business succession planning, finding people that might take them over so they could retire. Who would want to own a garbage company? Tom started buying these companies, consolidating, organizing, and implementing better practices, standardization and professional, dependable service.

He started with one truck, then founded what became Browning-Ferris Industries Inc., or BFI. He bought hundreds of local operators to create an international trash-hauling giant that was listed on the New York Stock Exchange. Another trait Tom had was that he gave back. He supported Rice University where he had played football. He started a physical fitness/heath center. His expertise in health and fitness resulted in his appointment to the President's Council on Physical Fitness and Sports under Presidents Jimmy Carter, Ronald Reagan, and George H. W. Bush. During this time, Tom ran over 30 marathons, including 13 Boston Marathons. He wrote a great book titled *With No Fear of Failure*, a good read.

Tom was another ordinary big dreamer; he was always looking for better ways to do things. He saw an opportunity that most of us, even if we saw it, might cringe at as we thought of garbage collection. When Tom began his venture in garbage, they did not have the big containers, clean plastic bins and plastic bags that we have today. Garbage was a very tough business, tougher than the tire business. But consider this, garbage trucks just grind the rubber off the tires on the trucks as they turn so often and start and stop all day long. They were great customers for our tough business. Tom made some great choices while thinking outside the box.

You make your choices, only you. You use thousands of words a day in self-talk. Develop that talk to be positive and consider out-of-box solutions while constantly seeking more information. Focus on keeping your mind open to the fact that your solution, or conclusion, might not be the best. This thinking works in your career, personal life, family situations, and more. As you change your focus toward looking at every issue as an opportunity, you will be amazed how your life, your self-talk, your self-discipline, and your results will start to improve. Never allow doubt and negative thoughts to creep in. You are better than that.

ABOUT THE AUTHOR

KIM LORENZ is an author, entrepreneur and visionary who founded two companies starting at age 26 with no backing or funding, built and ran them successfully and sold them to Fortune 500 companies before he was 47. Through his years as a business owner, partner and CEO, Kim has developed a key understanding of what it takes to succeed in business. Kim's mission is to teach vital tools essential for business success beyond what is taught in business schools. He earned his MBA from the University of Washington, Foster School of Business.

Kim is the former Commodore of the Seattle Yacht Cluband a 39-year Rotarian. Serving as Rotary Liaison with World Vision, the collaborative teams he initiated have completed over $20 million in clean water projects with over 1 million beneficiaries in developing countries worldwide. He is a business consultant, public speaker, a pilot for 40 years, and holds a USCG Captains license. Kim lives with his wife in Bellevue WA.